Next Steps Toward
Teaching the Reggio Way
Accepting the Challenge to Change

Second Edition

JOANNE HENDRICK,
Editor

University of Oklahoma, Emerita

Upper Saddle River, New Jersey
Columbus, Ohio

Library of Congress Cataloging in Publication Data
Next steps toward teaching the Reggio way : accepting the challenge to change / Joanne
    Hendrick, editor.
        p. cm.
    Rev. ed. of: First steps toward teaching the Reggio way. c1997.
    Includes bibliographical references and index.
    ISBN 0-13-049657-X (paper)
        1. Education, Preschool—Philosophy. 2. Education, Preschool—Italy—Reggio Emilia
    (Province) 3. Public schools—Italy—Reggio Emilia (Province) 4. Education,
    Preschool—United States. I. Hendrick, Joanne, 1928-II. Hendrick, Joanne—First
    steps toward teaching the Reggio way.

LB1140.3.F57 2004
372.21—dc21   2003041239

Vice President and Executive Publisher: Jeffery W. Johnston
Assistant Vice President and Publisher: Kevin M. Davis
Editorial Assistant: Autumn Crisp
Production Editor: Sheryl Glicker Langner
Design Coordinator: Diane C. Lorenzo
Photo Coordinator: Valerie Schultz
Cover Designer: Ali Mohrman
Cover art: Special thanks to the children of the University of Vermont Campus Children's
Center for their delightful animal drawings.
Production Manager: Laura Messerly
Director of Marketing: Ann Castel Davis
Marketing Manager: Amy June
Marketing Coordinator: Tyra Poole

This book was set in Zapf Calligraphic by Carlisle Communications, Ltd. It was printed and
bound by R. R. Donnelley & Sons Company. The cover was printed by Phoenix Color Corp.

Photo Credits: All photos provided by chapter authors.

Pearson Education Ltd.   Pearson Education Australia Pty. Limited
Pearson Education Singapore Pte. Ltd.   Pearson Education North Asia Ltd.
Pearson Education Canada, Ltd.   Pearson Educación de Mexico, S.A. de C.V.
Pearson Education—Japan   Pearson Education Malaysia Pte. Ltd.

10 9 8 7 6 5 4 3 2
ISBN: 0-13-049657-X

Preface

Next Steps Toward Teaching the Reggio Way is, in part, a progress report documenting *new* steps toward teaching the Reggio way that American and Canadian teachers have taken in the 6 years since *First Steps Toward Teaching the Reggio Way* was published.

For the first time, it is possible to include chapters on relationships that range from recognizing the rights of infants and toddlers while using the Reggio Approach to creating respectful adult relationships in a multicultural community and enfolding parents into the learning environment. There are several down-to-earth chapters demonstrating how teachers actually construct curriculum as a joint enterprise between them and the children, and also chapters on documenting the results of that curriculum as well as suggestions for creating appropriate settings for learning. There are even chapters describing an experimental attempt to apply the Reggio principles in a number of elementary schools, and one on detailing ways to advocate for the philosophy.

All this new material is supported by a solid explanation of the Reggio Emilia philosophy by Lella Gandini, a leading authority on that subject, and stimulated by a series of challenging questions proposed by the inimitable Lilian Katz. Finally, there is a chapter particularly dear to my heart that recounts a first time visit to Reggio by a group of students majoring in early childhood education.

A note of caution: *Next Steps Toward Teaching the Reggio Way* is a practical book filled with inspiring, yet practical descriptions of ways various teachers have incorporated different aspects of the Reggio Emilia Approach into their early childhood classrooms. But it is NOT a handbook intended to meet the demands of the person in an audience who recently said to me, "Don't tell me all that stuff about philosophy—just get to the bottom line—tell me how to do Reggio and I'll do it!"

The truth is there *is* no way "to do Reggio." Nor is there any author in this book who would maintain that *their* way is *the* way, or the ideal way, or perhaps the only way "to do Reggio." Instead, the following chapters recount individual stories not about "how-to-do-it," but more about "how-we-do-it." It is up to the readers to garner for themselves whatever thoughts and ideas resonate within their own hearts and then begin the long and exciting adventure of incorporating these ideas into their own milieus.

Acknowledgments

There are three contributors in particular whose participation was absolutely crucial to the success of this book. They are Lella Gandini for her incomparable descriptions of the municipal preschools in Reggio Emilia and for her tactful guidance and suggestions related to the content of particular chapters, Lilian Katz for her perspicacious provocations, and Judith Allen Kaminsky for suggesting some additional authors who added immeasurably to the scope of *Next Steps*.

In addition, every author who contributed to *Next Steps* also deserves to be recognized for their practical, readable presentations and for their steadfast devotion to implementing the Reggio Approach in its various aspects. We are indebted to them, in particular, for taking time from their busy lives to share what they are learning while talking and walking the Reggio way.

My thanks, also to Audrey W. Beard, Albany State University; Debra G. Murphy, Cape Cod Community College; Stacey Neuharth-Pritchett, The University of Georgia; Patricia Weaver, Fayette Technical Community College; and Audrey E. Wright, Central Missouri State University. Their reviews of *First Steps Toward Teaching the Reggio Way* provided many helpful suggestions for this sequel.

As always, the staff at Merrill/Prentice Hall have been both helpful and encouraging. Thanks go to Ann Davis, now Director of Marketing, for having the vision to support publication of *First Steps* at a time when Reggio was largely an unknown quantity. And my thanks also go to Kevin Davis, Publisher; Christina Tawney, Associate Editor; and Sheryl Langner, Senior Production Editor—my current co-conspirators—for taking the next step by supporting the current volume. Their encouragement is much appreciated.

Joanne Hendrick

Discover the Companion Website Accompanying This Book

The Prentice Hall Companion Website: A Virtual Learning Environment

Technology is a constantly growing and changing aspect of our field that is creating a need for content and resources. To address this emerging need, Prentice Hall has developed an online learning environment for students and professors alike—Companion Websites—to support our textbooks.

In creating a Companion Website, our goal is to build on and enhance what the textbook already offers. For this reason, the content for each user-friendly website is organized by topic and provides the professor and student with a variety of meaningful resources. Common features of a Companion Website include:

For the Professor—

Every Companion Website integrates **Syllabus Manager**™, an online syllabus creation and management utility.

- **Syllabus Manager**™ provides you, the instructor, with an easy, step-by-step process to create and revise syllabi, with direct links into Companion Website and other online content without having to learn HTML.

- Students may logon to your syllabus during any study session. All they need to know is the web address for the Companion Website and the password you've assigned to your syllabus.

- After you have created a syllabus using **Syllabus Manager**™, students may enter the syllabus for their course section from any point in the Companion Website.

- Clicking on a date, the student is shown the list of activities for the assignment. The activities for each assignment are linked directly to actual content, saving time for students.

- Adding assignments consists of clicking on the desired due date, then filling in the details of the assignment—name of the assignment, instructions, and whether or not it is a one-time or repeating assignment.

- In addition, links to other activities can be created easily. If the activity is online, a URL can be entered in the space provided, and it will be linked automatically in the final syllabus.

- Your completed syllabus is hosted on our servers, allowing convenient updates from any computer on the Internet. Changes you make to your syllabus are immediately available to your students at their next logon.

For the Student—

- **Introduction**—General information about the topic and how it will be covered in the website.

- **Web Links**—A variety of websites related to topic areas.

- **Timely Articles**—Links to online articles that enable you to become more aware of important issues in early childhood.

- **Learn by Doing**—Put concepts into action, participate in activities, examine strategies, and more.

- **Visit a School**—Visit a school's website to see concepts, theories, and strategies in action.

- **For Teachers/Practitioners**—Access information you will need to know as an educator, including information on materials, activities, and lessons.

- **Current Policies and Standards**—Find out the latest early childhood policies from the government and various organizations, and view state, federal, and curriculum standards.

- **Resources and Organizations**—Discover tools to help you plan your classroom or center and organizations to provide current information and standards for each topic.

- **Electronic Bluebook**—Paperless method of completing homework or essays assigned by a professor. Finished work can be sent to the professor via email.

- **Message Board**—Virtual bulletin board to post and respond to questions and comments from a national audience.

To take advantage of these and other resources, please visit the *Next Steps Toward Teaching the Reggio Way: Accepting the Challenge to Change,* Second Edition, Companion Website at

www.prenhall.com/hendrick

Contents

18   *The Atelier Environment: Recognizing the Power of Materials as Languages*   **210**

Charles Schwall

19   *In Our Real World: An Anatomy of Documentation*   **224**

Barbara Burrington & Susan Sortino

I

Introduction to Reggio Emilia

Part I provides an introduction and/or reminder for readers who want to know more about the municipally sponsored early childhood schools in Reggio Emilia. It begins with two classic chapters by Lella Gandini, who was a *pedagogista* there for many years. She explains how the schools came into being, how they operate, and then describes the basic philosophy that forms the educational foundation for what children, families, and teachers do there together.

Because Gandini's information is so valuable, excerpts from it are repeated at the beginning of most parts of the book to refresh the reader's memory about various aspects of the Reggio philosophy.

Baji Rankin's chapter follows the introductory ones and introduces us to some of the basic educational tenets of Dewey, Piaget, and Vygotsky as she points out possible links between those ideas and the educational philosophy propounded by Loris Malaguzzi.

1

A Brief Reggio Emilia Story

Lella Gandini

Adjunct Professor, School of Education, University of Massachusetts,
Amherst, and U.S. Liaison for the Dissemination
of the Reggio Emilia Approach

A simple, liberating thought came to our aid, namely that things about children and for children are only learned from children. We knew how this was true and at the same time not true. But we needed that assertion and guiding principle; it gave us strength and turned out to be an essential part of our collective wisdom.

(Malaguzzi, 1993b, p. 44)

BEGINNINGS

What were the initial steps that led toward what we now know in the States as the "Reggio Emilia Approach"? This is a question frequently asked by the many people who visit the schools in Reggio Emilia, or who view the exhibit entitled "The Hundred Languages of Children," or who listen to speakers, or watch a slide or video presentation about the program. As they marvel at either the real thing or the images that show the extraordinary level of work by teachers and the impressive quality of representation by children, set in such beautiful yet diverse environments, they cannot but wonder: How did this come about?

It all started at a particular place and time, namely Reggio Emilia in 1945, just at the end of the Fascist dictatorship and of the Second World War. It was a moment when the desire to bring change and create a new, more just world, free from oppression, was urging women and men to gather their strength and build with their own hands schools for their young children. Some of these preschools continued until 1967 (when they were handed on to the city government), thanks to the strength, initiative, and imagination of workers, farmers, and a famous group of the time, the Union of Italian Women (UDI).

One of these women told me recently how they would go around from home to home with a wheelbarrow to gather dry food for the children at the schools, and how everybody would contribute, knowing full well that the children, like all of them, were hungry. This woman, who has many lively episodes to narrate, is the mother of the current superintendent of education for the City of Reggio Emilia; she proudly showed me a group photograph of the children from the preschool in her neighborhood (actually a village in the plains outside the city), pointing out her daughter as well as one of her daughter's schoolmates who currently serves as the city's mayor (re-elected three times). How proud this woman remains of the schools of those heroic times.

Each of the preschools for young children of Reggio Emilia has poignant histories of these early years that are kept very much alive. For example, the story of one particular preschool in Reggio, la Villetta, goes back to 1970. The women of a working-class neighborhood on the outskirts of town were growing increasingly upset because their forceful protests and requests to obtain a preschool for their young children were being ignored. There was an empty house in their neighborhood. It was still elegant, though it was surrounded by an overgrown garden. One day the women moved into the house, pronounced it *the school* for their children, and stood fast in occupying the building. In the days that followed they organized their resistance, looked for a teacher, and cleaned and repaired the dusty rooms.

One warm, late afternoon while they were working, a large, beautiful butterfly entered the house and flew from room to room. The women were elated by this visit; they took it as a sign, a message of good fortune for themselves, their children, and their new preschool. Since that day the butterfly has become a symbol of the history of la Villetta. The children designed a colorful butterfly canopy for the entryway and the butterfly now turns up time and again in children's paintings, drawings, and collages.

It reminds us all of the strong involvement of the community in that school (Gandini, 1991, p. 8).

Loris Malaguzzi always remembered the legacy of those committed citizens who started the preschools. In one of his interviews, speaking of the first school, Villa Cella, he said:

> [Those] events granted us something . . . to which we have always tried to remain faithful. This something came out of requests made by mothers and fathers, whose lives and concerns were focused upon their children. They asked for nothing less than that these schools which they had built with their own hands, be different kinds of schools, preschools that could educate their children in a way different from before. . . These were parents' thoughts, expressing a universal aspiration, a declaration against the betrayal of children's potentials, and a warning that children first of all had to be taken seriously and believed in. (Malaguzzi, 1993b, p. 51)

In the region of Emilia Romagna, where the city of Reggio Emilia is located, there is a long history and tradition of cooperative work done in all areas of the economy and organization: agriculture, food processing, unions, entrepreneurship, solutions of crises, etc. Therefore, for people to get together and start the schools, and for teachers and parents to work together to run the preschools now, is in line with established tradition, with a traditional and successful way of life, which, although occasionally disrupted under adverse conditions, such as the Fascist regime, is then revived as soon as feasible.

In the 1950s and early 1960s, a teachers' movement was active in Italy around the goal of innovation in education. With strong motivation and commitment, these teachers hoped to develop new ways of teaching in tune with the new democratic society, with the new realities of the modern world, and with greater relevance to the life of children. In this way they hoped also that the public preschools would become nonselective and nondiscriminatory. Some of their ideas found inspiration and encouragement in the works of John Dewey, and were also influenced by theory and practice coming from France. Furthermore, the work of Jean Piaget and others, and, still later, Lev Vygotsky, proved stimulating and supported the observations and discoveries about children and their development done by teachers. These and several other important foreign works and experiences in psychology and educational philosophy had a particularly powerful impact after the Liberation because they had just not been available during the Fascist era.

In this time of ferment, Loris Malaguzzi took time off from teaching to specialize in psychology at the Center for National Research in Rome. He was aware of the tremendous potential value of all these sources of energy and of combining these with his own energy and ideas. He soon became a leader, first along with others better known in Italy and then by becoming a point of reference for teachers wanting to bring innovation to schools for young children. It was Malaguzzi who was ready and able to support the schools started by common people in Reggio in 1945, and who carried the battle to get the city government to take upon itself the running of the people's schools and open the first municipal preschool in 1963.

With Villa Cella I made a sort of solidarity pact and then another pact with the six other small schools, invented and run by the women and by the popular movement, in the poor neighborhood at the outskirts of the city. I never abandoned them. (Malaguzzi, 1998)

BECOMING A TEACHER

But what were the experiences that contributed to Loris Malaguzzi's philosophy and leadership? We can listen to his own words:[1]

My taking the road toward teaching and becoming an elementary school teacher was written up in advance inside my father's head. Rather than a philosophical choice or a vocation, it pointed to a rapid way to get a salary and eventually make it possible for me to support myself while studying at the university. It also was a choice based on the modest salary of my father, stationmaster of the Reggiane railways, and on my mother's endlessly careful parsimony. I was then—as all others of my age—a passenger ready to board any ship.

When, at the end of the first year of teaching, I said goodbye to my first grade students, there were already drums of war, and my exams at the university. From then on, school, university and war ran for me, at age nineteen, on parallel courses.

My next job was to teach in a village in the mountains. It was an extraordinary experience up there at 2500 feet; for two years I learned many things. I learned to form a deep friendship with fifteen boys wrapped in enormous hand-me-down men's jackets, wearing wooden clogs, speaking only in dialect, who were curious and clever and had determined looks in their eyes. They were like sharecroppers dividing time between school and tending sheep, between homework and the coal pile or the fields.

I learned to make a school function in a stable just vacated, to light the stove every morning and light it again and again because the firewood was green, to fight the tardiness of the children, to help them dry their wet socks, and secure for them free notebooks and more free notebooks from the school system. I had to work with my brain divided in five parts for a classroom that welcomed children from first, second, third, fourth and fifth grade.

My three years of teaching had been decisive for me. I felt I had grown also as a teacher. Certainly I could say that I had become familiar with the ways of teaching, with the quirks and surprises of reasoning and engagement on the part of children, and with the changeable ways of their sense of time. But still far from my mind was the thought that the head and intelligence of young people could contribute something of its own to the hard process of learning.

---

[1] *Note:* I have chosen and translated these sentences from within the 13 pages of posthumously discovered papers, carefully edited and annotated by Laura Artioli in the journal, *Historical Research (Ricerche Storiche)* May, 1998. These papers were among the ones that he prepared for a series of interviews I did with him in 1988–1999 and that were later published in *The Hundred Languages of Children* (Edwards, Gandini, & Forman, 1993b).

I was made aware more than once that I knew how to work with young people and that I liked the job. I had learned that if it were not possible to have the patience of Job, it was useless and stupid to lose self-control. And I had discovered that it was a good idea to stipulate a pact of tolerance and of playful humor and to detach myself from my professional role if I wanted everything to be lighter and more productive. That was the only way to remove school work from a haughty and retrograde formality and to maintain a dialogue with those boys whom I tended to distinguish less by their particular traits and achievements than by their ungenerous and cruel personal stories.

This intuition of seeing a story, a personal and collective history looming behind and inside every boy—without losing the traces of the individual—was a new lesson for me; it was an awareness that surprised and at the same time worried me. It was a lesson that I was to keep in my memory.

THE ESTABLISHMENT OF THE MUNICIPALLY SUPPORTED PRESCHOOLS

The sixties in Italy were marked by the tremendous economic development known as "the boom." This consisted principally of a basic transformation from a mostly agricultural economy (with limited industrial development in the north) to a well-developed and diversified economy with modern industries. Along with this there took place notable development in the area of social services and of workers' benefits, in part due to the bargaining power of a strong union system. Women entered into the work force and demanded support from the government for child care. The same period indeed saw the emergence of the women's movement, which in a way transcended the age-old party division between the right and centrist conservative Catholic forces (which preferred that women stay at home in their traditional roles) and the more progressive, socialist left. Furthermore, in the late sixties and early seventies, a strong student movement shook up the university system and the traditional values of a still highly stratified society.

Through all those years of upheaval, many different groups kept up the pressure on elected representatives to bring innovation in all spheres of life for Italian citizens. Among the results was a series of national laws passed between 1968 and 1971 that were true landmarks, including those that made possible the development of the comprehensive program we are discussing here. They included the establishment of free preschools for children 3 to 6 years of age, infant-toddler centers for children 3 months to three years, a maternity leave (in part with full pay), a new family law more favorable to women, and equal pay for equal work between men and women.

The new law that was passed about government preschools for children 3 to 6 years of age rewarded citizens and city governments, such as the one in Reggio Emilia, that had been working hard to support the grassroots' demands for establishing public preschools and who had moved more quickly at the local level than the central government had done. By the end of the seventies the schools for young children in Reggio

Emilia had grown to 19 in number, and the building of new infant-toddler centers was in full swing.

By the year 2002 there were 21 municipal preschools and 1 teachers' cooperative; when the state and private preschools are included, the city has a network of 55 providing care for 100 percent of the children 3 to 6 years of age. In addition, there are 13 municipal infant-toddler centers, plus 6 run by cooperatives of teachers and parents, supported by the municipality, and 6 centers operated by private organizations— a total of 25 centers providing care for 38 percent of infants under 3 years of age.

FURTHER DEVELOPMENT AND INFLUENCE OF THE PROGRAM IN OTHER SETTINGS: 1980S AND THE BEGINNING OF THE 1990S

Loris Malaguzzi was able to gather around him a group of devoted and competent educators who, along with parents and other citizens who felt strong ownership of the schools, supported his work toward creating and maintaining very high quality programs, continuously updating the preparation of teachers, and exploring new avenues of innovation in teaching young children. In some of the interviews that Malaguzzi granted late in his life, he presented a long list of names of scientists, philosophers, scholars, artists, and writers who had influenced his thought and therefore the work of educators in the preschools that he did so much to shape. His complex system of education, which takes into account the human desire to "do nothing without joy," and which pays close attention to individual as well as group interests and potentials, is a form of socioconstructivism. George Forman defined socioconstructivism and explained it in the following way:

> The basic premise [of socioconstructivism] is that knowledge is constructed as a system of relations, so that the simple association between two stimuli, or between a stimulus and a response, is insufficient for defining the knowledge-building process. It is only through a process of re-reading, reflection and revisiting that children are able to organize what they have learned from a single experience within a broader system of relations. These processes are individually and socially constructed, and herein lies the image of the child as an active constructor of his or her own knowledge, which is one of the fundamental premises of the philosophy and practice that has come to be known as the "Reggio Approach." (Forman, 1995, p. 6)

During the 1980s, the accomplishments achieved so far in Reggio Emilia became known elsewhere in Italy and on the international scene as well. Upon the initiative of Loris Malaguzzi and of leaders in other city systems of early childhood education, along with some university experts in the field, an association for the support of research and development concerning the education of young children, the National Group for Work and Study on Infant Toddler Centers, took shape and began its work. In 1981, the educators of Reggio Emilia prepared the first exhibit about the work constructed with their children. After creating surprise among early educators in Italy, the exhibit opened in Sweden at the Modern Museet in Stockholm. Presenting these inspiring images marked the beginning of disseminating their extraordinary message of hope about early childhood education throughout the world.

To respond to Loris Malaguzzi's dissemination effort and in appreciation of the great interest developing in the United States about the work done in the preschools of Reggio Emilia, Eli Saltz of the Merrill-Palmer Institute and Wayne State University launched *Innovations in Early Education: The International Reggio Exchange,* a quarterly publication that carries articles by Reggio and United States educators who are reflecting on the translation and re-invention of ideas from Reggio Emilia in different settings in this country.[2] Since that first publication in the fall of 1992, more than three dozen issues containing the voice and thoughts of educators from both sides of the Atlantic have been published.

The interest in the Reggio Emilia schools continues to grow as delegations visit in increasing numbers and a worldwide concern for supporting and protecting these extraordinary programs intensifies. Shortly before his death in 1994, Loris Malaguzzi had proposed the establishment of two organizations for that purpose.

In the spring of 1994, the Reggio Children organization was formed in Reggio Emilia to support the early childhood program. One of the goals of Reggio Children is to disseminate the accumulated knowledge in theory and practice. This is done through publication and distribution of books, articles, videos, and slides that document the Reggio approach. Reggio Children also responds to the increasingly numerous requests for information and cooperative exchanges that arrive from all over the world. Reggio Children is a private, for-profit company governed by a board of directors and supported by shareholders—corporate, private (parents, teachers, and other citizens of Reggio Emilia), and the municipality of Reggio Emilia, which holds the majority of shares. Until now, this organization has not been open to individuals outside of Italy. The funds gathered with this activity serve to open other preschools or infant-toddler spaces.

In the fall of 1994 was also formed Friends of Reggio Children, a non-profit, international organization open to all.[3] Many of the retired teachers and parents volunteer to carry out the goals of the association. One of the goals of Friends of Reggio Children is to create an endowment that would establish a library for collecting documents about the Reggio Approach and providing funds for student research on the Reggio philosophy and principles.

---

[2] To subscribe to *Innovations* write to The Merrill Palmer Institute, Wayne State University, 71-AE. Ferry Ave., Detroit MI 48202, or e-mail to j_a_kaminsky@wayne.edu

[3] A one-time, $40 donation will entitle people to become members of an international group of educators who believe in the educational principles that the Reggio program exemplifies and in the right of children to obtain the best care and education possible. To become a member of Friends of Reggio Children, request a form from Friends of Reggio Children, c/o *Innovations,* The Merrill-Palmer Institute, 71-A E. Ferry Ave., Detroit MI 48202. A membership card will be sent to you.

In 2002, a new organization has been founded called the North America Reggio Emilia Alliance (NAREA).[4] It is intended to facilitate communication between members and to extend the influence of the philosophy more widely.

THE ENCOUNTER OF THE REGGIO EMILIA APPROACH WITH THE UNITED STATES

In the mid-1970s, as I was working on my master's degree in education, I became aware of the difference between theory and practice in the United States. In particular, it became clear to me that while theoretical studies were carried on at an impressively high level, what was being done in terms of public funding and investment in early childhood education and toward building high-quality programs lagged far behind—in particular, far behind Italy. Therefore, I started to do a two-way information job. I would bring to various municipalities in Italy who had invited me to work on teachers' training the information and publications about the latest research on child development and education in the States, while in the reverse direction I would bring back to the States information, documentation, reflections, and pictures about the beautiful environments from choice programs in Italy.

Starting in the early 1980s, a number of educators and academics started to take a strong interest in the program, to visit the schools, and to support enthusiastically the dissemination of knowledge about Reggio. Among them were Carolyn Edwards, George Forman, Becky New, Baji Rankin, and Rosalyn and Eli Saltz.

The first article about the Reggio Emilia schools was published by me in 1984 in the magazine *Beginnings* (now part of *Childcare Education Exchange*). Other articles appeared in the following years, for example, a notably comprehensive and informative one by Becky New published in *Young Children* in 1990. At that time also, Lilian Katz became involved in studying, presenting, and supporting the Reggio schools.

After lengthy negotiations, the exhibit "The Hundred Languages of Children" arrived in the United States in 1987. Its powerful message about the work of educators, children, parents, and citizens of Reggio Emilia has now reached viewers at 38 different sites in this country. Through the use of many beautiful and striking panels and videos showing the children actively engaged in projects from inception to completion, the exhibit offers the possibility of learning about the educational and life experiences taking place in those infant-toddler centers and preschools.

Many conferences, seminars, and visits to the Reggio Emilia schools by Americans have also drawn attention to several aspects of the Reggio Emilia Approach. But there remains a frequently asked question that can only be answered by a teacher from Reggio Emilia, Amelia Gambetti, now often working in the States: Can the Reggio way of working with children be transplanted to a school in the United States?

---

[4] Annual membership fee is $75.00 and should be sent to Vickie Jacobs, Administrative Coordinator, 2040 Wilson Ridge Court, Roswell GA 30075.

A TEACHER FROM REGGIO EMILIA COMES
TO STUDY AND WORK IN THE UNITED STATES

After working for 25 years in the preschools of Reggio Emilia, Amelia Gambetti arrived at the laboratory school of the University of Massachusetts in 1992 at the invitation of George Forman. She immediately found great support in Mary Beth Radke, who became her co-teacher. The situation differed greatly from a classroom in Reggio Emilia. Here the schedule for the children was three mornings a week, on a university calendar, and as many as eight student teachers might be assigned to the classroom for each semester. Amelia and Mary Beth started to work on the environment of the school, involving the student teachers, the children, and, at first a little hesitantly, the parents, who came from many different nationalities and backgrounds. Next they gradually developed work on documentation. This proved to be a powerful means of involving the parents and helping the children to feel a sense of belonging and pleasure from learning and from forming friendships.

At the end of that year, I asked these two teachers with such different cultural backgrounds: What suggestions do you have for educators in the United States who are struggling to use the ideas they are learning from Reggio Emilia?

> Mary Beth said: Start with respect for children. Question what it means to you and how your actions reflect your image of the child. How can you improve consistency about respect for the child through what you do every day? Look at collaboration among all adults in the school in a new and different way—try to learn to question things together, to exchange ideas, and trust each other.
>
> Amelia said: People here want quick results. We should help teachers to understand that they have to look for and find answers in themselves. One has to accept the idea that the way to work with children is something that one discovers observing day by day the process of children and teachers. In Reggio with the long experience we have we continue to ask questions, to have doubts, and to work things out together. I know it is not easy, but working here with Mary Beth we realized that sharing responsibility in a true sense gives a great sense of joy. (Gandini, 1994b, pp. 65–66)

In 1993, Amelia worked at the Model Early Learning Center, directed by Ann Lewin, as master teacher consultant. Amelia's job was to work with the teachers; once again she had to deal with a different cultural situation. The Model Early Learning Center was a preschool and kindergarten for 3- to 6-year-olds. The children were Head Start eligible, and the school is operated with partial funding provided by the District of Columbia public schools. Here the question Amelia had in mind was: Is it possible to adapt ideas from Reggio Emilia to an inner-city school for young children?

The first steps she took were to observe the situation and build a sense of trust with and among the teachers, in order to develop a spirit of cooperation. In an interview in the spring of 1995, the teachers said:

> We believed in the most important elements of the Reggio Emilia approach, and it is important to know that we did not face the many issues one by one but we faced them

at the same time as one element supported the other. However, we proceeded in small steps. Considering the child and the child's potentiality brought us closer to establishing a new style of communication with the families. We began to communicate our projects and experiences through documentation, which became more detailed every day. Documentation was not just seen as a product but always an evolution. Everything that we did needed time and organization. The importance of working in a team became clearer through the evolution of projects and the quality of our observations. Our deeper level of observing contributed to our relationship to children, and a new kind of awareness blossomed that did not exist before our new-found skills.

With regard to parents we realized that before we did not let parents know enough about their children's experiences and what was happening in the program. In order to build a relationship of esteem and collaboration it took us more than 40 different meetings. This means that parents had many different opportunities to be involved and to participate in the life of the school according to their different levels of availability and needs. The quality of participation of parents in the life of the school grew, as well as the number of people at our meetings and the variety of initiatives on their part. Of course we need to continue this process; we do not take anything for granted. Every year children and parents change and we have to be available to meet their problems. The work of the team of teachers has been and continues to be very hard. The school is a remarkable place of learning with pleasure; where the presence and the voice of the children is evident all around in a beautiful way. The teachers realize now that when children give time to listen to each other, to use each other's ideas, to respect different opinions and to work collaboratively on a project, then is when they know that the hard work has paid off. (Sheldon-Harsh & Gandini, 1995a, 1995b)

CONCLUSION

In telling some of the story of the schools for young children in Reggio Emilia, I touched only a few of the many facets of that complex history. One source of this complexity is that the system touches the lives of so many people who have been participants in the construction of its success. Furthermore, this dynamic educational approach, which is constantly questioning itself, changing, and inventing new ways of understanding and supporting high-quality children's learning, teachers development, and parents' participation, cannot easily be captured and presented with only one language.

What has happened since the publication of *First Steps Toward Teaching the Reggio Way* and what will happen next? Many textbooks and publications about early childhood include introductions to the Reggio Emilia Approach, which has become well known and is often cited as an exemplary early childhood education. The bad news is that the Approach is at times misrepresented or misunderstood because of its challenging proposal to build early childhood education from the potentials of children, teachers, and parents, and because of the complexity of work and the depth of engagement that this apparently simple premise implies.

The good news is that several educators in the United States have proceeded to consider and study deeply the philosophy, strategies, and practices of the educators of Reggio Emilia and re-construct or re-invent them. As they work, they are doing their best to always keep in mind the background, context, environment, and cultures of each preschool or center, and the parents, teachers, and children who are involved there. This volume contains the narratives, reflection, and creative thoughts by a number of these educators. What they can relate to other educators, and also to the educators from Reggio Emilia, is the value and force of ideas that are rooted in the conviction that education has to be deeply rooted in the respect of people and their relationships.

2

Foundations of the Reggio Emilia Approach[1]

Lella Gandini

Adjunct Professor, School of Education, University of Massachusetts,
Amherst, and U.S. Liaison for the Dissemination
of the Reggio Emilia Approach

---

[1] Earlier versions of this chapter appeared in L. Gandini (1993), Fundamentals of the Reggio Emilia Approach to Early Childhood Education, *Young Children, 49* (1), 4–8, and L. Gandini (1994a), Not Just Anywhere: Making Child Care Centers into "Particular" Places, *Childcare Information Exchange, 96,* 50.

As we saw in the previous chapter, publicly funded municipal and national programs for young children have been in place in Italy for about 30 years. During that time, women have been especially active and effective advocates of the legislation that established infant-toddler centers for children 3 months to 3 years and preschools for children 3 to 6 years of age. Of special note is that in these programs, both education and care are considered necessary to provide a high quality, full-day program. Therefore, the schools combine the concept of social services with education, an approach that is widely accepted in Italy.

What, then, is so unusual or special about Reggio Emilia, a town of 148,000 inhabitants in northern Italy? It is that in Reggio Emilia, the city-run educational system for young children originated in schools started by parents, literally built with their own hands, at the end of World War II. The first school was built with proceeds from the sale of a tank, some trucks, and a few horses. Moreover, right from the start Loris Malaguzzi, then a young educator, guided and directed the energies of those parents and teachers.

Through many years of strong commitment and cooperation, parents and educators in Reggio Emilia have developed the present excellent program, which, in turn, has become a point of reference and a guide for many educators elsewhere in Italy, in various European countries, in Australia and East Asia, and—in the last fifteen years—especially in the United States. Forty years of successful experience with municipal preschools for about half of the pre-primary age children in a city of 148,000 inhabitants have generated much interest. Such interest is evidenced by the number of international visitors, the number of articles and conference presentations describing the work, and the large number of people viewing the Reggio Emilia exhibits. This exhibit, entitled "The Hundred Languages of Children," has been touring Europe since 1980 and North America since 1987 and, as of 2002, has five similar versions that are exhibited simultaneously in different parts of the world.

In 2002, about 93 percent of the children in Italy 3 to 6 years of age attend some kind of preschool, whether municipal, national, or private; in Reggio, almost 100 percent of preschool-age children are enrolled in a variety of such schools. The number of infants under 3 years who have access to public infant-toddler centers in Italy is low, especially in the cities in the south of that country. However, several leading cities have established exemplary programs for the youngest children through an exchange with researchers which "has contributed to the legitimizing and disseminating of new images of the youngest children, their needs and their potentials" (Bondioli and Mantovani, 1987; Gandini and Edwards, 2001). In Reggio Emilia almost 38 percent of infants under 3 are receiving care in public or private center.

Children from all socioeconomic and educational backgrounds attend the municipal programs in Reggio Emilia and other leading cities, and children with disabilities are given first priority for enrollment in either the infant-toddler centers or the preschools.

THE AIMS OF EARLY CHILDHOOD EDUCATION IN REGGIO EMILIA

The Reggio Emilia Approach, developed by the late Loris Malaguzzi and the group of committed, competent educators around him who now continue to develop theory and practice, is built upon a solid foundation of philosophical principles and extensive experience.

Educators in Reggio Emilia have no intention of suggesting that their program should be looked at as a model to be copied in other countries; rather, their work should be considered as an educational experience that consists of reflection, practice, and further careful reflection in a program that is continuously renewed and re-adjusted. However, the Reggio Emilia approach to early childhood education is not considered "experimental." These preschools and infant-toddler centers are part of a public system that strives to serve both the child's welfare and the social needs of families while supporting the child's fundamental rights to grow and learn in a favorable environment in the company of peers and with caring, professional adults.

Bearing these facts in mind, the educators in Reggio Emilia are pleased to share their experience with other educators in the hope that knowledge of the Reggio Emilia educational experience will stimulate reflections on teaching, helpful exchanges of ideas, and novel initiatives in other schools and in other countries, for the benefit of children, families, and teachers.

BASIC PRINCIPLES OF THE REGGIO EMILIA APPROACH

An examination of some of the principles that have inspired the experience in Reggio Emilia immediately reveals that these concepts are not new to American audiences. Indeed, several of the basic ideas that informed the work of educators in Reggio Emilia originated in the United States and are, in a sense, returning to their point of origin. From the beginning of their work in building their program, the educators in Reggio Emilia have been avid readers of Dewey. Over the years, in addition to studying Piaget, Vygotsky, and other European scientists, they have continued to keep abreast of the latest research in child development and education in the United States and have kept close contact with notable scientists such as Jerome Bruner and Howard Gardner. However, their approach, based on continuous research and analysis of their practice, has caused them also to formulate new theoretical interpretations, new hypotheses, and ideas about learning and teaching that are dynamically reexamined.

The following principles, or fundamental ideas, are presented one by one for the sake of clarity, but *they must be considered as a tightly connected, coherent philosophy in which each point influences and is influenced by all the others.*

The Image of the Child

The educators in Reggio Emilia first and foremost always speak about the image they have of the child. All children, each one in a unique way, have preparedness, potential, curiosity, and interest in engaging in social interaction, in establishing relationships, and in constructing their learning while negotiating with everything the environment brings to them. Teachers are deeply aware of children's potentials and construct all their work and the environment of the children's experience to respond appropriately.

Children's Relationships and Interactions Within a System

Education has to focus on each child, not considered in isolation, but seen in relation with the family, with other children, with the teachers, with the environment of the school, with the community, and with the wider society. Each school is viewed as a system in which all these relationships, which are all interconnected and reciprocal, are activated and supported.

The Three Subjects of Education: Children, Parents, and Teachers

For children to learn, their well-being has to be guaranteed; such well-being is connected with the well-being of parents and of teachers. Children's rights should be recognized, not only their needs. Children have a right to high-quality care and education that supports the development of their potentials. It is by recognizing that children have rights to the best that a society can offer that parents' and teachers' rights can be recognized. For example, it is essential to respect parents' rights to be involved in the life of the school and teachers' rights to grow professionally.

The Role of Parents

Parents are considered an essential component of the program and many among them are part of the advisory committees running each preschool. Parents are a competent and active part of their children's learning experience and, at the same time, help ensure the welfare of all children in the school or in the center. The parents' participation is expected and supported; it takes many forms: day-to-day interaction, work in the schools, discussions of educational and psychological issues, special events, excursions, and celebrations.

The Role of Space: An Amiable School

The infant-toddler centers and preschools are, of course, the most visible aspect of the work done by teachers and parents in Reggio Emilia. They convey many messages, of which the most immediate is: This is a place where adults have thought about the quality and the instructive power of space.

The layout of physical space, in addition to welcoming whoever enters the schools, fosters encounters, communication, and relationships. The arrangement of structures, objects, and activities—often readjusted—encourages choices, problem solving, and discoveries in the process of learning.

It is also true that the centers and schools of Reggio convey a sense of well-being because they are simply beautiful. However, their beauty does not come from expensive furnishings but rather from the message the whole school conveys about children and teachers engaged together in the pleasure of learning. There is attention to detail everywhere: in the color of the walls, the shape of the furniture, and the arrangement of simple objects on shelves and tables. Light from the windows and doors shines through transparent collages and weaving made by children. Healthy, green plants are everywhere. Behind the shelves displaying shells or other found or made objects are mirrors that reflect the patterns that children and teachers have created.

But the environment is not just beautiful—it is highly personal. For example, in one of the halls, a series of small boxes made of white cardboard creates a grid on the wall. On each box the name of a child or a teacher is printed with rubber stamp letters. These boxes are used for leaving little surprises or messages for one another. Communication is valued and favored at all levels, and is regarded not as a small matter. For a child to engage in communication by preparing messages deepens human relations and also helps that child to appreciate and become interested in the value of reading and writing before they are formally presented in the elementary school curriculum.

The space in the centers and schools of Reggio Emilia is personal in still another way: It is full of children's own work. Everywhere there are paintings, drawings, paper sculptures, wire constructions, transparent collages coloring the light, and mobiles moving gently overhead. It turns up even in unexpected spaces like stairways and bathrooms. The reflection of the teachers, the photographs of the children, and the transcriptions of their dialogues are part of the documentation displayed to help the viewer understand the process of children's thought and explorations.

The Value of Relationships and Interaction of Children in Small Groups

In preparing the space, teachers offer the possibility for children to be with the teachers and many of the other children, or with just a few of them, or even alone when they need a little niche to stay in by themselves.

Teachers are always aware, however, that children learn a great deal in exchanges with their peers, especially when they can interact in small groups. Such small groups of two, three, four, or five children provide possibilities for paying attention, for hearing and listening to each other, for developing curiosity and interest, for asking questions, and for responding to them. It provides opportunities for negotiation and dynamic communication. Loris Malaguzzi suggested that it is desirable that adults initiate the setting of such situations because a more homogeneous age group helps the communication among children in planning and decision making. This type of small group also favors the emergence of cognitive conflicts; such conflicts can initiate a process in which, while children find a resolution, they construct together new learning and new skills.

The Role of Time and the Importance of Continuity

Children's own sense of time and their personal rhythm are considered in planning and carrying out experiences and projects. The particular, leisurely pace that an observer notices is enhanced by the full-day schedule. Such a schedule, rather than overwhelming the participant, seems instead to provide sufficient time for being together among friends, in a good environment, and for getting things done with satisfaction.

Teachers get to know the personal time of the children and each child's particular characteristics because children stay with the same teachers and the same peer group for three-year cycles (infancy to 3 and 3 to 6). Each year, the group changes environments because their developmental needs and interests change, but the relationships with teachers and peers remain constant and intact.

Cooperation and Collaboration as the Backbone of the System

Cooperation at all levels in the preschools and infant-toddler centers is the powerful mode of working that makes possible the achievement of the complex goals that Reggio educators have set for themselves. Teachers work in pairs in each classroom, not as head teacher and assistant, but at the same level. They see themselves as researchers gathering information about their work with children by means of continual documentation. The strong collegial relationships that are maintained with all other teachers and staff relies on this information to engage in collaborative discussion and interpretation of both teachers' and children's work. Those exchanges provide ongoing practice and theoretical enrichment. A team of pedagogical coordinators, called *pedagogisti*, who also support the relationships among all teachers, parents, community members, and city administrators, further supports this cooperative system.

The team of *pedagogisti* meets once a week with the director of the whole system to discuss policy and problems related to the whole network of preschools and infant-toddler centers. Each *pedagogista* is assigned to support three or four preschools and infant-toddler centers, helping the teachers to sustain and implement the philosophy of the system. The support of each school includes work with the teachers to identify new themes and experiences for continuous, inservice, professional development. In each particular school the *pedagogista* helps the teachers deal with educational issues concerning children and parents. However, the goal is to support teachers by promoting their autonomy rather than by solving problems for them. The complex task of the *pedagogisti* is to collaborate with the various parts of this complex system and maintain the necessary connections, while at the same time analyzing and interpreting the rights and needs of each child, family, and group of teachers.

Organization and Structure of the Program for Children 0 to 6

In the information booklet published by the Department of Education of the municipality of Reggio Emilia, under the title "In Praise of Organization," we read this remarkable statement: "Organization, discounted or undervalued by educational theories—but not by other components of our social and working life—returns as a necessary, dynamic, and constructive element" (Municipality of Reggio Emilia, 1994). The entire Department of Public Education, under the leadership of the superintendent who is an elected official, consists of one director, one pedagogical coordinator, seven *pedagogisti* (of whom one is an expert in special education), and a four hundred-member staff. All of these people cooperate in such a way that together they constitute a pedagogical-didactic coordinating team.

Next to this system and strictly connected with it is a Community Advisory Council for each of the municipality's 21 preschools and 13 infant-toddler centers, composed of elected parents' representatives, teachers, staff members of the school, and citizens from the community. Representatives from each of the 34 Community Advisory Councils, along with representatives of the pedagogical coordinating team and of the administration of the Department of Education, form an Advisory Council Board that deals directly with the city government about questions concerning the schools. This complex system ensures proper representation of all the people connected with the schools and fosters a shared responsibility in running them.

Schools do not have a director on the premises. They are run by the team of teachers and staff members with the support of one of the *pedagogisti*. The *pedagogisti* are an essential part of the system and have a complex role. Each has a degree in education or psychology and helps to guide and sustain the workings of a mix of three or four preschools and infant centers. It is their responsibility to help teachers with the interpretation of the philosophy, to mediate the connections with parents and administrators, to organize training sessions, to follow the development of projects and activities, and much more.

The parents are also an essential component of the system, besides being part, through their representatives, of the Community Advisory Council. They participate in the life of the school through a variety of meetings at the individual level, at the level of the classroom group, or at all-school meetings. Parents also participate in work done through small committees on specific tasks and projects. These are not assigned by teachers or by the administration, but are instead discussed in advance in meetings where all the components of the system and of each school are represented. In this way, when the task is planned it represents a mutual choice, and it will be carried out with strong engagement and motivation by willing volunteers.

SPECIFIC ORGANIZATION AND SCHEDULES

Infant-toddler centers (for children 4 months to 3 years of age) usually have a total of 69 children divided in four groups by age (the first, up to 9 months; the second, from 10 to 18 months; the third, from 19 to 24 months; and the fourth, over 24 months). There are 11 teachers, 1 cook, and 3 full-time and 3 part-time auxiliary staff—a total of 18 adults in each center.

The preschools, for children 3 to 6 years of age, usually consist of three classrooms, one each for the 3-, 4-, and 5-year-old children, for a total of 75 children. There are, however, a few larger or smaller schools that also have mixed-age groupings. Each classroom has 25 children and two co-teachers. In each of the preschools, besides the six teachers there are: an *atelierista* (or studio teacher), one cook, and two full-time and three part-time auxiliary staff members. Every one of these people belongs to and fully participates in the team that runs the school.

The schedule of the preschools and infant-toddler centers is from 8:00 A.M. to 4:00 P.M., Monday through Friday; in addition, there exist alternatives for an early arrival at 7:30 A.M. and an extended day until 6:20 P.M. for families able to demonstrate that they have this need. Teachers and staff members are paid for 36 hours per week, of which 31 hours are in contact with children and 5 hours are used for planning, meeting with parents, working on documentation, participating in professional development, working on community management, or attending to school matters such as correspondence, archives, and the like. The work schedule is planned with great care in rotating shifts to maximize the efficiency of work and the supportive, flexible presence for the benefit of the children. The personnel calendar runs from about August 22 to July 10 of each year. The preschools and centers are open for children from September 1 to June 30. In the month of July, one preschool and one infant-toddler center remain open for families that make a special request for this service. The teachers' salaries are comparable to those of elementary school teachers in Italy. Such salaries are not high when compared to public school standards in the United States, but the benefits, in terms of job security, health insurance, retirement plans, and paid vacations are equal to all public employment standards in Italy. Although benefit plans are under scrutiny now and have recently been reduced, they are still considerably better than those in the States.

The Interdependence of Cooperation and Organization

The high degree of cooperation requires much support, which is supplied by a careful and well-developed structure or organization. From the details of each teacher's schedule to the planning of meetings with families to the children's diet, *everything* is discussed and organized with precision and care. In fact, the high level of cooperation is made possible precisely because of such thoughtful organization. Likewise, the organization is achieved because of the conviction, by all concerned, that only by working together so closely will they be able to offer the best experience to the children. No fewer than six hours in the weekly schedule are set aside for meetings among teachers, preparations, meetings with parents, and professional development.

Teachers and Children as Partners in Learning

To know how to plan or proceed with their work, teachers observe and listen to the children closely. Teachers use the understanding they gain thereby to act as a resource for them. They ask questions and discover the children's ideas, hypotheses, and theories; they see learning not as a linear process but as a spiral progression. In fact, teachers consider themselves to be partners in this process of learning, which might proceed with pauses and setbacks but is an experience constructed and enjoyed together with the children.

The role of teachers, therefore, is considered to be one of continual research and learning, taking place with the children and embedded in team cooperation. Doing this research, reflecting, listening to children with other colleagues, and documenting this process with the support of the *pedagogista* contributes to continuous professional growth for the individual and the group.

Flexible Planning vs. Curriculum (Progettazione)

It flows naturally that, to be truly respectful of children's and teachers' ideas and processes of learning, the curriculum cannot be set in advance. Teachers express general goals and make hypotheses about what direction experiences and projects might take and, consequently, they make appropriate preparations. These general goals and hypotheses are also based on their experience as teachers, their knowledge of each individual child, and the dynamic of their group of children. Then, after observing the children in action, they compare, discuss, and interpret together their observations. They discuss what they have recorded through their own notes, or through audio or visual recordings, and make flexible plans and preparations. Teachers make choices (sharing them with the children) about what to offer and how to sustain exploration and learning. Often, teachers revisit experiences with the children to assess them. They together reconsider the meaning of what they have done and what they have learned in order to offer new occasions for discovery and reinforce learning.

In fact, *progettazione* (or flexible planning) is constructed in the process of each experience or project and is adjusted accordingly through this continuous dialogue among teachers and with children. This process of documentation is an integral part of the daily experience in the infant-toddler centers and preschools of Reggio Emilia (Rinaldi, 1998).

The Power of Documentation

Transcriptions of children's remarks and dialogues, photographs of their activity, and children's representations of their ideas using different media are traces of observation carefully studied. Often these different traces of observation are reexamined and arranged by the *atelierista* with the other teachers—or by the teachers as a team—to document the work (and the process of learning) done in the school. Documentation is made visible and available not only through displays of panels but through many other important means, including books and notebooks, illustrated daily or weekly diaries, small exhibits of children's artifacts, slide or video documentaries, audiocassettes, messages and letters, and so on.

This documentation has several functions. Among these are: to make it possible for teachers to understand children better, in order to plan their work with them; to evaluate the teachers' own work, thus promoting their professional growth; to make parents aware of their children's experience and maintain their involvement; to facilitate communication and exchange of ideas among educators and visitors; to make children aware that their effort is valued; and, furthermore, to create an archive that traces the history of the school and of the children, teachers, and parents that have been part of the pleasure of learning there.

The school space itself becomes an open documentation for anyone who enters and can detect how the education of young children is viewed. In the infant-toddler centers and preschools of Reggio Emilia, the voice and thoughts of children and their teachers are made visible (Gandini, 2001).

The Many Languages of Children: Atelierista and Atelier

A teacher who is trained in the visual arts works closely with the other teachers and the children in every preschool (and visits the infant-toddler centers). This teacher is called an *atelierista*, and a special workshop or studio, called an *atelier*, is set aside and used by all the children and teachers as well as by the *atelierista*. The *atelier* contains a great variety of tools and resource materials, along with records of past projects and experiences.

The explorations and projects, however, do not take place only in the *atelier*. Through the years the roles of the *atelier* and of the *atelierista* have expanded and become part of the whole school. Smaller spaces called *mini-ateliers* have been set up in each classroom; furthermore, teachers and *atelieristi* have been working more and more together, sharing their reciprocal knowledge and skills. What is done with materials and media is not regarded as art, per se, because in the view of Reggio educators the children's use of many media is not a separate part of the experience. It is an inseparable, integral part of the whole cognitive/symbolic expression involved in the process of learning (Vecchi, 1998).

Projects

Projects provide the backbone of the children's and teachers' learning experiences. They are based on the strong conviction that learning by doing is of great importance and that to discuss in group, as well as to revisit ideas and experiences, is the premier way of gaining better understanding and learning.

Ideas for projects originate in the continuum of the experience of children and teachers as they construct knowledge together following the inquisitive minds of children. Projects can last from a few days to several months. They may start either from a chance event, an idea or a problem posed by one or more children, or an experience initiated directly by teachers. For example, a study of crowds originated when a child told the class about a summer vacation experience. Whereas teachers had expected the children to tell about their discoveries on the beach or in the countryside, a child commented that the crowd was all that she remembered.

Another project on fountains developed when children decided to build an amusement park for birds. This project originated from a request by George Forman and me to observe and document on tape, along with the teachers involved, the process of a project as it developed.[2] The Reggio educators met, discussed, and thought about the fact that during the previous year the 5-year-olds had been very interested in the birds visiting the schoolyard. As a result of this interest they had built a small lake, birdhouses, and an observatory.

The teachers surmised that a good way to probe what might interest the incoming group of 5-year-olds was to ask them what they remembered their classmates had done the previous year. Teachers, including the *atelierista* and *pedagogista,* prepared the questions to ask; made hypotheses about what topics the children would be interested in; discussed the selection of the initial group of 11 children; decided where the first meeting would take place; and how, by whom, and with what tools the documentation would be organized. (First column of flowchart, Figure 2–1.)

Then they had the first meeting with the children. The children's conversation was full of ideas and surprises as, in the course of it, they became more and more involved. First, they explored the idea of repairing what had been constructed the previous year; then they thought of improving the area by adding several amenities for the birds to make them feel welcome in their playground. Finally, they became very enthusiastic about the idea expressed by one child of constructing an amusement park for the birds on the playground of the school. (It should be noted that an amusement park is set up each spring at the outskirts of the town.)

After the initial conversation, eight children were interested in drawing what they thought would be useful and nice to include in the amusement park for birds.

---

[2] The narrative of the whole project and several significant episodes are presented in depth in Forman & Gandini (1994), *An Amusement Park for Birds.* This 90-minute video is available at Perfomanetics, 19 The Hollow, Amherst, MA 01002; tel. (413) 256-8846.

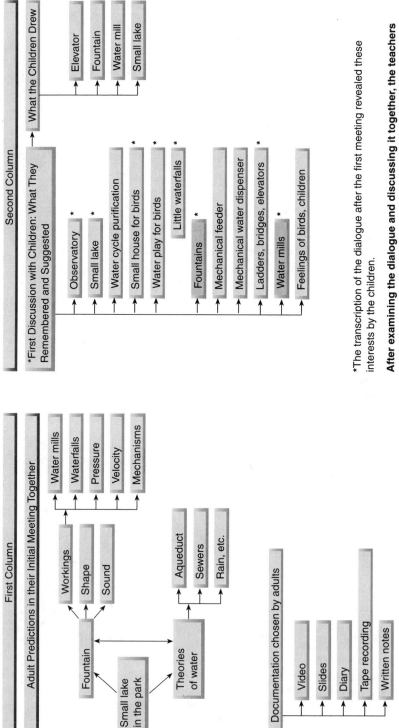

FIGURE 2–1

An illustration of process: An amusement park for birds
Source: Adapted from *An Amusement Park for Birds*, by L. Gandini (1994).

That very evening, the teachers transcribed the first conversation by the children (which they had recorded) and discussed it with the *pedagogista*. (Second column of flowchart, Figure 2–1.)

It became clear to them that two particular topics offered promising opportunities for the next steps in the development of the project. One was the interest in **fountains,** as the city of Reggio Emilia has several that are familiar to the children. The other was **water mills,** as those had been a past source of energy and some still stood in the countryside and could be explored. Both topics presented good possibilities for inquisitive exploration of the way they functioned through conversation and visual representation. All this could be experimented while keeping alive the interest of constructing an amusement park for birds. That was also of great interest to the children and offered as well many promising opportunities for combining learning experiences with pleasure (Piazza, 1995).

Figure 2–1 illustrates the initial steps that transpired as the amusement park idea began to take shape. It presents the hypotheses (possibilities) formed only by the adults before the children's first meeting (first column of flowchart). It also presents the hypotheses suggested by the children, extracted from the transcription of their first conversation and the study of their first drawings (second column of flowchart). Within the children's hypotheses, the two topics chosen by the educators are highlighted.

Furthermore, during the course of the spring and for the inauguration of the amusement park for birds, the children, with teachers and parents, built several versions of the constructions they had suggested in the first conversation along with many other rides and useful objects for the birds. (In the flowchart, those are marked with a star (*).)

Note that this particular flowchart depicts only one of many ways projects may begin. As the rich images and words in "The Hundred Languages of Children" exhibit reveals, there are many additional ways in which such projects may begin (Municipality of Reggio, 1996).

CONCLUSION

In one of his last writings, Loris Malaguzzi (1993c) invited us to reflect on a bill of three rights. He invited us to reflect on the rights of children to realize and expand all their potentials while receiving support by adults who value the children's capacity to socialize, to receive and give affection and trust, and who are ready to help them by sustaining the children's own constructive strategies of thought and action rather than by simply transmitting knowledge and skills.

He invited us to reflect on the rights of parents to participate actively and of free will in the experience of growth, care, and learning of their own children—participation that is so vital to the sense of security for children and parents that it is an essential part of working together, sharing values, modalities, and content of education.

And finally he invited us to reflect on the right of teachers to contribute to the definition of the contents, objectives, and practice of education accomplished through a network of collaboration, supported by the ideas and competencies of everyone, and that always remains open to professional growth and research.

Loris Malaguzzi reminded us that it is respect for these rights that will bring mutual and shared benefits for children, parents, and teachers. It is respect for these rights that will make it possible for them to construct their learning together. And, finally, it is respect for these rights that will render the school an amiable place that is welcoming, alive, and authentic.

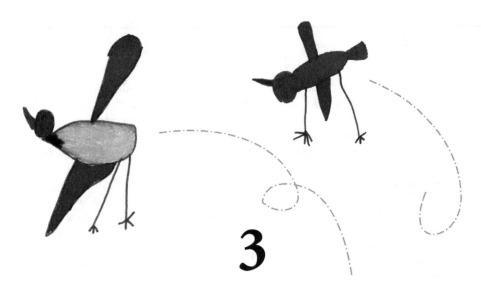

3

Dewey, Piaget, Vygotsky
Connections with Malaguzzi and the Reggio Emilia Approach

Baji Rankin

Professional Development and Training Specialist, La Madrugada Early
Head Start Program, Office of Child Development, Albuquerque,
New Mexico

Dewey, Piaget, and Vygotsky were powerful figures in education and psychology in their lifetimes and all three continue to have strong influences on early childhood education in the United States, in Reggio Emilia, and throughout the world. While these three theorists lived in different eras and worked in very different social contexts, the work of each is *still* a rich source for our thinking and educational systems today.

In this chapter, I present several key points about the lives and theories of these three men. I point out similarities and differences in some of the current debate and reflection about their work today, and I examine the impact of these theorists upon theory and practice in Reggio Emilia. I also look at how Loris Malaguzzi and other Reggio educators, while generating their own ideas and practices, put the principles of these three men into practice in an educational setting more fully, in my view, than any of the three were able to do in their lifetimes.

I will examine only some aspects of the theories and experiences of these men: the role of collaboration and the co-construction of knowledge, the interdependence of individual and social learning, and the role of culture in understanding this interdependence. Dewey, Piaget, and Vygotsky agree that the individual child is active in constructing his or her intellectual and social development; Malaguzzi also emphasizes each child's active role in development.

John Dewey (1859–1952)
Jean Piaget (1896–1980)
Lev Vygotsky (1896–1934)
Loris Malaguzzi (1920–1994)

By looking at the role of culture in the learning process, we can better understand a major difference between Piaget on the one hand, and Dewey, Vygotsky, and Malaguzzi's educational choices, on the other. Piaget kept his focus on the individual child, specifically the child's internal, or endogenous, cognitive development. Vygotsky, Dewey, and Malaguzzi, on the other hand, while recognizing the active role of the child, also gave emphasis to the active role of the environment and culture in influencing and leading this development—a view that has become important in the Reggio Emilia Approach. As Cole and Wertsch (2001) point out in relation to Piaget and Vygotsky, it is not so much that Piaget's ideas conflict with those of the other three; rather, Piaget had a different focus.

JOHN DEWEY (1859–1952)

Dewey was born in Burlington, Vermont, about the time of the U.S. Civil War. His career focused primarily on teaching philosophy and theories of education at the university and college levels. For eight years, from 1896 to 1904, he directed the Dewey Laboratory School at the University of Chicago. Valuable experiences took place there (Mayhew & Edwards, 1936) that we can learn from today.

Dewey viewed learning as "a continuing reconstruction of experience" (1959a, p. 27). Education, for Dewey, was a process of "continual reorganizing, reconstructing, transforming" (1966, p. 50). Distinct from traditional education in which teaching is conceived as a "pouring in" (1966, p. 38) and learning as "passive absorption" (1966, p. 38), Dewey saw education as being active and constructive. This kind of education has a social direction through "a joint activity" (1966, p. 39) within which people consciously refer to each other's use of materials, tools, ideas, capacities, and applications.

Dewey saw children as active, in fact, "intensely active" (1959b, p. 54). The question for educators, Dewey said, is how to take hold of the child's activities and give them direction. "The law for presenting and treating material is the law implicit within the child's own nature" (1959a, p. 28). The content of a school curriculum is best when it grows out of children's social life.

"I believe, therefore, that the true center of correlation on the school subjects is not science, nor literature, nor history, nor geography, but the child's own social activities" (1959a, p. 25).

Dewey pointed out that children's interests and activities are places to begin, but by themselves, children's focus tends to scatter. Teachers have an important role in "leading out" these spontaneous experiences "into an expanding world of subject-matter, a subject matter of facts or information and ideas" (1969, p. 87). Teachers can do this, Dewey said, only when they view teaching and learning as a continuous process of reconstruction of experience.

Reggio educators acknowledge that they have taken ideas and principles from Dewey and interpreted them in particular ways. For example, project work in Reggio resembles the process that Dewey advocated. Reggio teachers start with the interests and questions of the children and then work closely with them to both follow and guide the children to support the investigation. Numerous projects in Reggio— on shoes, shadows, sun, shopping, etc.—demonstrate that when children are supported in a topic of high interest, they are deeply motivated to study a whole variety of subject matter.

JEAN PIAGET (1896–1980)

Jean Piaget was born in Switzerland in 1896 to an intellectual family; his father was a professor of medieval literature. Throughout his career, Piaget worked at several distinguished universities studying a wide variety of subjects, including biology, psychology, sociology, history of science and scientific thinking, and genetic and experimental psychology. His research in developmental psychology and the nature of knowledge had one unique goal: finding out how knowledge grows. His influence on early education in the United States has been profound, inspiring teachers and teacher educators for decades. His work, for example, was a backbone of the first and second editions of *Developmentally Appropriate Practice (DAP)* (Bredekamp, 1987; Bredekamp & Copple, 1997), encouraging teachers to:

□ observe what children are exploring and understanding,

□ find ways for children to be active learners, and

❑ value active education as a way to promote children's cognitive development.

Piaget, like Dewey, believed in education as reconstruction. Two "fundamental
elements of scientific education," Piaget said, were:

❑ the genuine "activity" of the students, who will be required to reconstruct, or in part rediscover, the facts to be learned, and
❑ above all, individual experience in experimentation. . . . (1973, p. 34).

Piaget emphasized the use of "active methods which give broad scope to the
spontaneous research of the child or adolescent" (1973, p. 15), noting that every
child needs to "reconstruct" or "rediscover" his or her own truth using activities of
interest. Reggio educators and Piaget have confidence that children construct ideas
for themselves.

Piaget's attention to an active child and to active methods was similar to Dewey
and Reggio educators. However, Piaget's attention to the development of intellectual
structures was different. Piaget found and focused on internal, invariant, sequential,
and hierarchical stages of intellectual development that all children go through.
Piaget recognized the importance of the social setting in which development and
learning take place and valued the social relations within which an individual child is
able to decenter from an egocentric view and grow. However, Piaget's focus remained
on the internal development of cognition.

Reggio educators disagree with Piaget's view of invariant, sequential stages; they
do not find that all children go through the same stages (Malaguzzi, 1998). Reggio educators, however, do appreciate Piaget's finding that errors, mistakes, and conflicting
points of view—which naturally take place in a social setting—are experiences that
stimulate children's growth.

Piaget did not focus on the social mechanisms of cognitive development or the
role that culture plays in the learning process. Lev Vygotsky, however, did. While the
value of Dewey's and Piaget's work has been widely acknowledged by U.S. educators
for some time, the contributions of Vygotsky are only now coming into prominence.

LEV VYGOTSKY (1896–1934)

Born in a small city in Russia in 1896, Vygotsky was an avid and promising student.
Despite his Jewish background, which limited his chances for a university education,
he won a place at the university and was a very successful student, moving to Moscow
and bringing new ideas to the intellectual conversation there. Vygotsky's dynamic
ideas, in fact, became the center of turbulent debates in the field of Russian psychology and his influence was considerable for a short period of time, despite strong pressure from the behaviorist psychologists.

Vygotsky faced tremendous resistance from the theories of culturally dominant behaviorist psychology and education then championed by Pavlov and others, who maintained that learning depends on positive and negative reinforcement from the environment. Instead, Vygotsky proposed that learning was a dynamic process that involved an exchange between an active individual and an active environment. Vygotsky was a creative thinker, able to understand different, seemingly contradictory points of view and bring to light ways in which these apparently divergent views were unified. Vygotsky did not pay attention only to social or only to individual processes. Rather he viewed them as being dynamic and interdependent, constituting "a unity of the social and the personal" (Vygotsky, 1998, p. 190), a relationship he termed "the social situation of development" (p. 198).

Vygotsky studied how the cultural and historical situation leads and guides the active child. This was in contrast to the behaviorists who gave major importance to the environment alone, and it was also in contrast to Piaget, who focused primarily on the individual's internal development. Vygotsky recognized the active and creative role of individuals. He saw that the child, as a part of the social situation, actively experiences and internalizes the environment, makes meaning of it, and influences the environment, just as the social situation influences the child.

Vygotsky's unified view of the way social and individual growth are intertwined gave rise to his idea of a creative area where learning happens most easily. Vygotsky named this area the Zone of Proximal Development (ZPD) and defined it as the area between the level of independent capabilities and the level of potential development of an individual (1978). When functioning in the ZPD with support from adults or more skilled peers, a child is able to act beyond her/his independent level of functioning. Vygotsky argued and demonstrated that this more advanced functioning can best be strengthened when teachers pay attention to and use the prior knowledge and beliefs of children as the foundation on which to invite more advanced abilities.

Reggio educators value Vygotsky's view, which "legitimates broad interventions by teachers" (Malaguzzi, 1998, p. 84). At the same time, Malaguzzi recognized the ambiguity of this situation when he pointed out that teachers giving "competency to someone who does not have it" (Malaguzzi, p. 83) could easily encourage traditional teaching. Work within the ZPD is effective, Malaguzzi said, when the gap is small between what "the child is about to see and what the adult already sees" (p. 84) and when "the child's expectations and dispositions create an expectation and readiness to make the jump" (p. 84). In this social situation,

> ... the adult can and must loan to the children his judgement and knowledge. But it is a loan with a condition, namely, that the child will repay. (p. 84)

Reggio educators recognize that much of their approach is in tune with Vygotsky's thinking. Malaguzzi expressed his affinity with Vygotsky in this way:

> For our part, Vygotsky's approach is in tune with the way we see the dilemma of teaching and learning and the ecological way one can reach knowledge." (1998, p. 84)

Reggio educators use children's prior knowledge as a place to start projects. They monitor children's thinking throughout a project and use children's ongoing questions and theories to indicate what direction projects should take as they develop.

Following Vygotsky's untimely death at age 38, his work was repudiated and ignored until the political situation shifted in Russia in the 1950s. Now his ideas are generating interest once again throughout many parts of the world. While Vygotsky left his work unfinished regarding implications for teaching (Mahn, in press), interest in analyzing those implications is now increasing.

As word spread (City of Reggio Emilia, 1987; Edwards, Gandini, & Forman, 1993; New, 1990) about the exciting things that were happening in the Reggio Emilia schools of young children, interest in them extended throughout the world. Many people wondered how these remarkable schools had come into being and who could have inspired such a transformation. The answer to these questions begins with one man: Loris Malaguzzi.

LORIS MALAGUZZI (1920–1994) AND THE EVOLUTION OF THE REGGIO EMILIA APPROACH

In spring 1945, immediately after World War II, groups of people in and around Reggio Emilia began to build schools for young children. Citizens of Reggio wanted schools in which they could participate. The schools in Reggio started out as community-run, teacher-directed schools: The teachers decided what children should learn. With one teacher and 30 to 35 children for each classroom of young children, and with teachers having been taught as children and trained as adults in instruction-oriented teaching, the initial approach was traditional.

However, with Malaguzzi's strong leadership, virtually as their director for 25 years starting in 1963, the schools began to change. Malaguzzi worked interdependently with many others and was able to build a strong core of teachers and educational leaders who learned from him and who could engage and argue with him. He worked with other progressive educators in Italy, traveled to other countries to study, and brought new ideas back to Reggio. He challenged teachers to try out these unfamiliar ideas to see what did and did not work with children. He promoted strong dialogue among teachers about these new ideas as he also participated powerfully in this exploration.

Malaguzzi's emphasis was on how theory and new ideas could be generative and useful in the teachers' work with children, as well as how their work with children could influence and shape theory and develop more new ideas. This dynamic, interactive view of theory and practice is similar to Vygotsky's dynamic thinking.

Here are some of the new ideas that Malaguzzi brought to the schools over time:

❑ co-teaching, where two teachers with equal responsibility worked together in one classroom—unheard of in Italy at that time;

- making sure there was time and support for teachers to communicate—and to learn to communicate—with each other;
- ensuring that each school had an *atelierista*, a person trained in the visual arts to work with teachers, children, and parents and to provide a different way of viewing children;
- giving the arts a new meaning and putting them at a central place in the life of the school;
- documenting children's work as a way of communicating to families and the community what was taking place in the schools; and
- viewing the school as a social system, where the whole system must be understood—not just the parts—and where one part affects the whole system.

Malaguzzi provided strong leadership in promoting these ideas, and at the same time he was committed to people talking about and learning from their own experience. Carlina Rinaldi, a leader of the Reggio schools, points out that this is true for children and for adults:

> It is our belief that all knowledge emerges in the process of self and social construction. . . . Children, in turn, do not just passively endure their experience, but also become active agents in their own socialization and knowledge building with peers. Their action can be understood as more than responses to the social environment; they can also be considered as mental constructions developed by the child through social interaction. Obviously, there is a strong cause and effect relationship between social and cognitive development, a sort of spiral which is sustained by cognitive conflict that modifies both the cognitive and social system. (Rinaldi, 1998, p. 115)

Malaguzzi and Reggio educators have built their educational experience on an understanding of the dynamic relationship between individual and social processes for both adults and children. Their term, "self and social constructivism," expresses this idea as well as their practices and their articulated theories.

FOSTERING COLLABORATION AND CO-CONSTRUCTION OF KNOWLEDGE

Documenting children's work to make it visible to the school and community is one example of teachers in Reggio collaborating with children. By observing and documenting children's activities, Reggio teachers have found creative ways to build their sensitivity to children's zones of proximal development. Teachers often video- or audiotape the children's conversations and comments so they can study the thinking and theories of the children with other teachers at a later time. In this way, they are able to stay close to children's thinking and fine-tune their responses to the particular questions and interests of the children. This has proven to be an effective way to extend both teachers' and children's questions and thinking about the project topic.

Time for this collaborative communication is structurally built into the schools of Reggio. For example, as they developed co-teaching in each classroom, they also built time into the paid workday for teachers to reflect with each other. Reggio educators provide strong leadership that encourages teachers and families to express their subjective views. Over the years the adults have developed the capacity for dialogue and reflection among themselves which has enabled both children and adults to grow in their capacity to learn and change.

Malaguzzi provided insight in how this works when he wrote:

> Relationship is the primary connecting dimension of our system, however understood not merely as a warm, protective envelope, but rather as a dynamic conjunction of forces and elements interacting toward a common purpose. The strength of our system lies in the ways we make explicit and then intensify the necessary conditions for relations and interaction. We seek to support those social exchanges that better ensure the flow of expectations, conflicts, cooperation, choices, and the explicit unfolding of programs tied to the cognitive, affective and expressive realms. (Malaguzzi, 1998, p. 68)

This shows up in Reggio practice in how teachers are encouraged to speak with each other about their work. Malaguzzi describes what can happen when teachers talk deeply with each other:

> It is well known how we all proceed as if we had one or more theories. The same happens for teachers. Whether they know it or not they think and act according to personal theories. The point is how those personal theories are connected with the education of children; with relationships within the school and with the organization of work. In general, when colleagues work closely together and share common problems, this facilitates the alignment of behaviors and a modification of personal theories. We have always tried to encourage this. (Malaguzzi, 1998, p. 86)

CONCLUSIONS

There is much in common among Dewey, Piaget, Vygotsky, and Malaguzzi. All consider children to be active, expressive, social, curious, able to grow, and able to learn how to learn. They all believe that education is best when children are active.

Dewey.   Both Dewey and Reggio educators see an intrinsic connection between subject matter and the life experiences of children. They both value children's direct experiences and see that learning is most effective when it grows out of the children's spontaneous activities. Learning takes place best when it is a social process in which educators follow the children's lead, take cues from children's social life, and remain open to new directions. At the same time, both Dewey and Reggio educators believe that teachers have an important role in guiding and channeling children's activities. As Malaguzzi pointed out,

> Once children are helped to perceive themselves as authors or inventors, once they are helped to discover the pleasure and the flavor in inquiry, their motivation and interest explode. (1998, p. 67)

Piaget.   Reggio educators use the elements of Piaget's views that work for them. For example, Reggio educators value Piaget's perspective on the importance of children's cognitive conflict, seeing internal conflict as a way that individual children grow. In small group work, Reggio educators value exchange of different points of view among children. This provides motivation for internal reconstruction that takes place with individual children, pushing children to build higher-order and more coherent understandings, as Piaget demonstrated. Error also plays a central role in the theory and practice of Reggio. Error and conflict are seen as ways of moving forward. This is different from the way they are seen in traditional education.

Vygotsky.   Reggio educators deeply value the interconnections and inseparability of individual and social processes, as did Vygotsky. In an interview with this author in Reggio Emilia in 1990, Malaguzzi pointed out that "it's not so much that we need to think of a child who develops himself by himself but rather of a child who develops himself interacting and developing with others" (Rankin, in press). This view of the child growing within a group context has gained the attention of U.S. educators as well and is now contributing to a growing interest in Vygotsky's work in the United States.

Final Notes.   Learning from Reggio is not about doing something that comes from a distant, foreign world. Rather, learning from Reggio means learning from re-elaborating philosophies that are known and studied in the United States. Those theories, while familiar, have been in part transformed by the experience in Reggio. There, educators have observed children spending their days in rich and supportive educational settings and, with Malaguzzi's leadership, have transformed the theories to become more open to the creative lives of children in classrooms. Learning from Reggio also means U.S. educators learning about ourselves as educators and learning how to go deeper within each person and within each community and each culture in understanding ourselves, young children and families, and how to work together.

Malaguzzi was deeply a theoretician who thought critically and creatively. Theory, in his view, was most useful when it served practice (Malaguzzi, 1992). Malaguzzi dedicated his life to developing dynamic and useful theory and to improving the practice of the schools of young children in Reggio Emilia. His immodest goal of changing the culture of childhood began in Reggio with colleagues in one small city, and this work continues as the Reggio Approach makes an impact on many people and programs throughout the world.

This chapter is necessarily incomplete, a work in progress, as I refer to other people's work and thinking that is also in process. I invite the readers to continue to study and learn about these growing understandings as well. We continue to have much to learn from and about the ideas and principles expressed by these important people.

II

Reggio Emilia as Seen Through American Eyes

 Two ways of seeing Reggio Emilia through American eyes are presented in Part II. In the chapter comparing Reggio Emilia and American schools, Joanne Hendrick looks at Reggio from the perspective of 40 years of teaching about early childhood concepts in American schools. She draws comparisons between that constructivist philosophy and the philosophy of Reggio Emilia, singling out some interesting points of agreement and disagreement between them for discussion.

Next, that more experienced view is balanced by the account of visitors Beth Dall, Nicky DiMario, Sara Lovell, and Kelly Morrison, four students from the University of Vermont, who, with Jeanne Goldhaber's help, share their impressions of the Reggio schools from the point of view of first-time visitors.

4

Reggio Emilia and American Schools

Telling Them Apart and Putting Them Together—Can We Do It?

Joanne Hendrick

Professor Emerita, University of Oklahoma

Having given a number of talks about Reggio Emilia and sensed the frustration in myself and my audience as I attempted to explain Reggio's virtues and glories, I was really helped one day by a plaintive question from a member of the audience who asked, "Well, I can see the schools look beautiful and all that, but what I don't understand is why you think they're so different. Just tell me—what's so different about what they do there from what I'm doing right now in my own classroom?"

This chapter attempts to answer that question by discussing some, but by no means all, of the differences and similarities between the Reggian and American approaches to early childhood education particularly as it relates to intellectual development.

Of course, the risk in drawing such comparisons is that it is so easy to make one approach, in this case the schools in Reggio Emilia, seem like the "good guys" and the other, in this case the American preschools, seem like the "bad guys." Having helped educate several generations of young American teachers, I would certainly hate to think of us as being the bad guys—I believe that American "best practice" is very good—but I also believe that we can make it even better, and one way to improve what we do is to learn as much as we can from other very good approaches. Reggio Emilia is an outstanding example of such an approach.

Another peril in writing this chapter is the possibility that after reading it, everyone, both Reggians and Americans, will be irritated, feeling that I have not fully represented their point of view or what happens in their particular school. Therefore, it is important to emphasize that the following comparisons and generalizations are based on my own American point of view having visited, observed, and studied the municipally supported preschools in Reggio. *It does not necessarily reflect the Reggio philosophy from the Italian perspective.* Also, my comments about preschools in the United States are based on 40 years of teaching, observing, and writing about those schools. The comparisons I draw are based on those schools that would be accepted as representing what is currently defined as good practice while remaining in the mainstream of American preschool education.

SIMILARITIES BETWEEN THE APPROACHES

As Baji Rankin explains in her chapter, Reggians and Americans have many values and philosophical roots in common that stem from Dewey, Piaget, and, more recently, Vygotsky. Among the virtues espoused by these philosophers are the value of inquiry learning and talking together with children as effective ways to foster collaborative learning.

In addition to those roots, both educational cultures believe learning should be based on real, concrete experience; they favor learning by doing; they believe a child-centered curriculum is desirable, that individualizing the curriculum to suit particular children is worthwhile, and that including parents is a significant good. Both approaches support the value of creativity and favor teaching that encourages problem solving and fosters inquiry learning.

With so much in common, why, then, is the Reggio Approach so newly admired by many American preschool teachers? What do the teachers in that Italian city do that is so inspiring and different from Americans' approach?

To answer this question fully would require more space than is available here. However, it is possible to consider three aspects of pedagogy and use them to compare and contrast the Reggian and American approaches to early childhood cognitive education. These are attitudes about children, creativity, and what constitutes effective teaching strategies.

ATTITUDES ABOUT CHILDREN

The teachers from Reggio invariably emphasize that they view children as being rich, strong, and powerful. They see the children as possessing great potential—potential it is the privilege of the teacher to perceive and empower. They see children *not* as having needs but, rather, as having rights—as being entitled to good care and sound teaching because of who they are, not because of what they need.

How does this differ from the American point of view? On the surface, at least, we would certainly agree with it. But underneath, do we really see children this way? It seems to me we view them from a much more protective and possibly restricted vantage. For example, we often discuss "meeting children's needs" and "strengthening their weaknesses."

Many American preschool teachers, while no longer seeing their role as "doing to children," still cast themselves in the role of doing *for* them. They interpret care as being the sort of mothering that actually robs youngsters of their independence—for example, handing them something when they could reach it themselves, buttoning their sweaters, and answering for children instead of giving them time to respond on their own.

Some of us who have gone beyond that and who try mightily to enable children to do things for themselves may still limit our expectations unduly because of our awareness of developmental stages and timetables. Although these standards are of undoubted value as protection against inappropriate academic approaches sometimes favored by administrators, parents, or inexperienced teachers who push children beyond their abilities, we might ask ourselves what is the flip side of honoring those standards? Perhaps we have carried our respect for them too far, and this devotion to the concept has led us actually to underexpect what children can do, thereby, as Eli Saltz maintains, infantalizing our youngsters. Certainly the accomplishments of the young children in Reggio Emilia offer many interesting examples of realizing potentials we have not dreamed possible in the United States.

ATTITUDES ABOUT CREATIVITY

The most obvious differences between the Reggian and American ways of fostering creativity are the multitude and variety of materials the Italians make available for the children to use combined with the special work areas, typically separate rooms they call *ateliers* where children come to construct their ideas. Moreover, a special staff person (an *atelierista*) is provided along with the room to facilitate that process. Although the majority of schools in the United States would not find it difficult to extend the range of creative materials they make available to children, it is a rare school, indeed, that could find the wherewithal to support the salary of an *atelierista* much less provide a permanent space in which that person could hold forth. Nevertheless, as visitors behold the results made possible by this support, it leaves us hungering to provide similar opportunities for our children, and some of us, as the chapters by Karen Haigh demonstrates, are actually finding ways to make this support possible.

But this admiration for the color, beauty, and quality of the Italian children's products often blinds the visitor to another real difference between American and Italian purposes in providing artistic materials. In the United States, a frequently cited benefit of using such self-expressive materials is that they permit children to express their feelings and come to terms with them.

On the other hand, it appears to me that the purpose of providing graphic materials in the Italian schools leans more toward enabling children to express their ideas—to explain, for example, how the water actually gets to the fountain or what causes rain to fall (see Figure 4–1).

Coming from the school of thought that prizes originality and fears stifling it by providing models or, worse yet, urging children to make something just like the teacher has made, I believe I understand the source of our hesitancy about fostering any sort of activity that smacks of copying a model or painting what the teacher suggests. But as Donna Williams found out in her water project (described in Chapter 14), asking children to draw what they have been working on or thinking about certainly does not result in identical products—far from it!

Whereas the teachers in Reggio Emilia *do* foster the children's powers of close observation by providing opportunities for them to "draw from life," this is not intended to be copying, per se. Children are often asked to first draw their ideas—of a poppy, for instance—and then taken to visit real poppies in the field. There they are encouraged to observe the flowers closely, draw them on the spot, and compare the previsit drawings with those results. This process greatly enhances the children's powers of observation and possibly their appreciation of the beauty of the world as well.

FIGURE 4–1

Here some of the children from Reggio illustrate their theories of where rain comes from.

The final difference in approaches to creativity I will discuss here is the kind of support and teaching the Italian and American preschool teachers provide for the children when they are using creative materials. Here, again, Americans are hesitant to intervene in any way lest we cause the bird of creativity to fly out the window. Therefore, children are typically provided with clay or easel paints or carpentry materials and, provided they use them safely, are scrupulously left to discover on their own how to use them effectively.

The Italians, on the other hand, think nothing of showing a child how to wipe the brush on the edge of the cup to avoid dripping or how to wet the edges of clay so it will stick (see Figure 4–2). For me, this was one of the more troubling aspects of watching that staff work until I understood their reasoning.

They maintain that lending adult assistance when needed, whether it be bending a recalcitrant piece of wire or hammering in a reluctant nail, empowers youngsters to move ahead with their creations in a satisfying way. The way I have come to think about this is that there is a vast difference between showing a child how to use a brace and bit to make a hole and telling him where to put the hole or what to do with it once drilled. Although the Reggio teachers unhesitatingly teach skills and lend a helping hand when needed, they would never tell the child where to put the hole (though they well might ask her why she is putting it in a particular place).

FIGURE 4–2
Reggio Emilia teachers do
not hesitate to show children
how to use materials more
effectively.

ATTITUDES ABOUT TEACHING STRATEGIES

One of the clearest ways of telling the teaching strategies of the two approaches apart is to focus on the differing teacher and child roles in the two approaches. (For the purposes of this discussion, we will focus only on some cognitive aspects of curriculum.)

In the American approach, the teacher may use the children's interests as the source for selecting a theme around which to build the curriculum—or she may dredge something out of a box she has saved from last year and the year before that! Having selected a theme, she then plans ahead and thinks up activities and experiences to present to the children that provide some interesting facts and, possibly, opportunities to practice specific mental ability skills such as seeing similarities and differences, practicing elementary classification skills, and so forth. In short, her responsibility is to be the instigator and leader for whatever preplanned learning transpires.

Of course, it would be unfair not to admit that many American preschool teachers also welcome the spontaneous interests of the children and weave these into the curriculum. Even when this occurs, however, it is generally the teacher who takes the lead in determining what will happen as a result of that interest.

The children's role is to participate in the learning activities provided by the teacher, reply to questions, soak up information, use these teacher-planned activities to acquire some mental ability concepts and reasoning skills, and practice them with the materials the teacher has provided.

Rather than seeing the teacher's role as that of leader and developer of curriculum, the Reggio teachers prefer the role of collaborator—working together with children, parents, and other staff members to generate interest, uncover what the children already know and think about that interest, and foster the emergence of projects based on that interest and the children's degrees of knowledge about it. In this approach everyone has ideas and contributes them to a mutual "pot." The result is a fluid, generative, dynamic curriculum that emerges as the interests and concerns of children and adults develop together.

The children's role is to toss the ball of ideas back and forth with the teacher as the project develops. They are provoked into thinking up ways to express their ideas and solutions to problems and expected to try those out and to show other people what they have concluded by means of language, graphics, and child-constructed models. As they say in Reggio, "You don't know it until you can explain it to someone else."

Unfortunately, this mutuality of roles and consequent honoring of the children's ideas as the curriculum emerges has led to a misconception of the teacher's responsibilities that it is important to clear up here. Sometimes students of the Reggio Approach have been left with the impression that teachers always wait for the children's interests and simply follow along with these, but that is a mistaken interpretation of their responsibilities.

In actuality, while it is true that curriculum projects often stem from the children's concerns, once a potential interest has been identified, the next step is for the teachers to brainstorm a number of possible avenues to investigate. As the diagram in Gandini's chapter illustrates, they meticulously analyze these possibilities—examining them for problems and questions they might pose to the children to provoke them into thinking about causes, possible problems and solutions, and/or additional interests to pursue. Then various possibilities are proposed to the children, discussed, discarded, modified or replaced, and then pursued. How different this is from the American approach.

I never discuss how emergent curriculum develops without recalling a member of my American audience who asked, most earnestly and sincerely, "But what if the children don't have any ideas—what then?" This query illustrates to perfection another significant difference between the American and Reggian approaches. It is the amount of genuine attention devoted to what the children have to say. Certainly, we Americans *think* we pay attention and that we will remember how conversations went and what the purport was, but it is a rare school indeed that relies on anything more than the teacher's memory to accomplish this. But when these teacher recollections are compared with actual recordings, these memories turn out to be partial at best.

In the Reggio classroom, the teacher not only listens closely when the children have discussions but also tapes the conversations and transcribes them for later discussion and analysis by the staff and *pedagogista*. Granted, making these transcriptions and taking time to consider them together is a laborious and time-consuming process, but the data it provides about the children's concerns are well worth the effort. As projects eventuate,

FIGURE 4–3
After the children decided which diagram of a maze to use, they next had the challenge of figuring out how to move from one symbolic system to another, thereby translating the diagram into reality.

additional discussions are recorded and their transcriptions are included, along with pictures and other evidence of what is happening, on the documentation boards that are placed about the building for all to appreciate. As we shall see in other chapters, creation of these boards is a highly valued cornerstone of the Reggio Approach because it enables everyone to revisit and reflect on what they are accomplishing or have accomplished. Perhaps if we used this way of remembering what the children have said, we would not have to worry about what to do if the children have no ideas!

I cannot conclude this chapter without singling out one more fascinating intellectual task with which the Reggio teachers challenge the children. We have already witnessed the way children are asked to use any one of a hundred languages to express their ideas. Thus, one child may draw a picture of how the water gets into the fountain, whereas another youngster might make a model of her idea using clay or a series of pipes.

The intriguing challenge is that the children are sometimes expected to translate their ideas from one language (one symbolic system) into another one. They might draw a picture first, for instance, and then use that picture as a reference for transforming that same idea into another language or medium. Thus, having drawn a diagram of a proposed maze, they were then challenged to actually mark that maze out on the school playground, keeping all the proportions in the same relationships as existed in the original diagram (see Figures 4–3 and 4–4).

FIGURE 4–4

FIGURE 4–5
The teacher is pointing out the symbols the 5-year-olds decided to use that they thought the 3's could "read," understand what was intended, and play the same music.

Or they were asked what they could use to represent the sounds of a musical scale so that they could see the differences as well as hear them. Or, to use still another example, having composed a musical accompaniment to go with a story, they had to decide how they could "write it" so the 3-year-old class could understand it and play the same music (see Figure 4–5). In short, the children are often expected to shift from using one symbolic system to using another—this is intellectual functioning of a very high order.

SOME ADDITIONAL COMPARISONS

I have selected only a handful of the most prominent differences between the American and Reggian approaches to early childhood education to discuss here, but so many more insights and possibilities should be discussed if space permitted that I cannot resist singling out a few additional items for comparison. Hopefully, the reader will understand this list cannot do justice to the intricacies and values of either system, but it *does* provide some additional food for thought (see Table 4–1).

TABLE 4–1

A sampling of some additional comparisons of American and Reggian schools

American	Reggian
"Projects" or themes are short-lived, extending a day or a week.	"Projects" may be brief but often continue for weeks or months.
"Topics" are used to provide information and (possibly) practice in midlevel thinking skills.	"Topics" are used to pose problems and provoke thought.
Children acquire a shallow smattering of information on many subjects.	Children acquire in-depth knowledge about fewer subjects (i.e., "know more about less").
Inquiry learning focuses on science tables; some problem solving encouraged.	Pronounced emphasis on "provoking" children to propose reasons why things happen and possible ways to solve problems.
Children may show what they know by talking to teacher about it.	Children show what they know by talking about it but also by using many different media: models, graphics, bent wire, dance, and so forth to explain their ideas: "You don't know it until you can explain it to someone else."

TABLE 4–1, *continued*

American	Reggian
The individual is emphasized; autonomy, self-responsibility, independence are valued.	Existence within the group is emphasized; sense of community and interdependence are valued.
Children select whatever they wish to participate in each day.	Children select what they want to do but are also encouraged to work in consistent small groups based on their continuing interests.
Time is highly regulated and scheduled.	Time flows easily in an unhurried way.
Record keeping is typically limited to results rather than work in progress—shows what children have learned (checklists, portfolios, observations) or do not know.	Record keeping—Documentation boards record what children "know" at beginning and during, as well as end of project; boards used for everyone to *re*-visit and *re*-cognize their work as it progresses.
Teacher changes at least once a year	Teachers remain with children for 3 years.
Staffing is teacher, or teacher plus aide.	Staffing is two teachers of equal rank plus services of a *pedagogista* and *atelierista*.
Hierarchy of staff positions (i.e., director, teacher, aide).	There are no directors; everyone accepts various responsibilities.
Confrontation is avoided.	Debate and "confrontation" with different points of view between adults and with children are favored methods of learning for everyone.
Teachers tend to be isolated; policy about and regularity of staff meetings varies.	Close collaboration between *all* teachers occurs regularly and frequently.

Special Strengths of the American Approach

After such a lengthy review of the sterling qualities of Reggio Emilia schools, it is only fair to balance the discussion by singling out a few of the many strengths where I feel American preschools may have an edge over our Italian counterparts.

For one thing, our devotion to developmentally appropriate practice provides us with a valuable framework of reasonable expectations for young children and of appropriate ways to teach them. In our zeal to help children realize their full potential à la Reggio, we must be careful to retain our hard-won sensitivity to the dangers of overstressing and/or hothousing children right out of their childhood. It would be easy to misinterpret how teachers teach in Reggio and to press the children beyond what is good for them unless we retain that sensitivity.

I also hope we will retain the wealth of fine picture books and the plenitude of block building that I see in American schools and that we will continue to emphasize the excellent large-muscle outdoor equipment prevalent in our play yards. Our emphasis on midlevel cognitive skills and appropriate integration of emergent literacy strategies are additional aspects we should continue to encourage while sustaining our concern for the emotional well-being and stability of the children in our care.

The most valuable strength for us to retain is our ability to persevere despite hardship and adversity. To our credit, we have not allowed low salaries, sometimes inadequate facilities, and an uninformed public to daunt our spirits. Not only do many of us provide good quality care, but we also, as the interest in Reggio schools so amply demonstrates, have kept our insatiable appetite for doing even better.

No matter what differences exist between us, let us agree that the treasure we Americans and Italians hold in common *is* this mutual desire to do the very best we can for the young children in our care. It is this desire, our real concern for young children, and our devotion to fostering their well-being that cause us to so admire our Italian counterparts as we continue to learn from their example.

5

Being There
Reflections on a First-Time Visit
to Reggio Emilia

Jeanne Goldhaber

Associate Professor, Early Childhood Pre-K Teacher Education Program,
University of Vermont

Beth Dall, Nicole DiMario, Sara Lovell, & Kelly Morrison

Students, Early Childhood Pre-K Teacher Education Program,
University of Vermont

Consider all the obstacles to overcome: time, money, anxiety about traveling overseas, and did I mention money? No question about it. Deciding to
participate in a study tour to Reggio Emilia is a huge undertaking. You have
to send in your registration form and deposit many months before the study
tour takes place, often a challenge in itself since you rarely know what you will be doing
so far in advance. You have to get released time from work before anybody is prepared to
deal with the ramifications of your absence. You have to save enough money to pay for
the registration fees and hotel, travel, and meals, or figure out how to raise it in what iron-
ically now feels like a very SHORT amount of time! And, of course, while most Americans have always considered traveling abroad a fairly large undertaking, given it involves
crossing the Atlantic and being separated from loved ones by multiple time zones, the
present-day milieu makes the prospect of traveling to Europe even more unsettling.

And finally, in the back of your mind lingers the question of whether participating in a study tour to Reggio Emilia is worth all of the planning, saving, and fret-
ting. What will you learn that you couldn't otherwise learn by reading the increasing
number of books and articles that have been published about the Reggio Emilia Approach, by attending conferences and workshops in the U.S. that are devoted to exploring the ways in which it can inform American practice, or by visiting the *One
Hundred Languages* exhibit when it comes within driving distance of your home state?

My own experience is that visiting the infant-toddler centers and preschools of
Reggio Emilia is a uniquely informative and inspiring experience. But even after a
good number of visits, I haven't been able to point to what it is about "being there"
that makes it such a powerful experience. So when Joanne and I started exchanging
ideas about a topic for a chapter in this second edition of *First Steps,* we both became
excited by the possibility of including a chapter that could provide both a sense of
what happens during a study tour and how it is experienced by participants who are
familiar with the principles of the Reggio Emilia Approach but who have never been
there. Since four undergraduate students from our early childhood program were
planning to participate in the upcoming study tour, I asked them if they would be interested in joining me in this project. Their response was immediate and enthusiastic.

The rest of this chapter reflects their experiences in Reggio Emilia. Since we also
spent several days visiting early childhood programs in another city in northern Italy
prior to going to Reggio Emilia, this chapter includes references to this visit as well.
Let's begin with short introductions and a brief discussion of the organizational
structure that we agreed to bring to this undertaking.

THROUGH THE EYES OF. . . .
INTRODUCING THE PLAYERS

This story really belongs to Beth, Nicky, Sara, and Kelly, so Joanne asked each of
them to provide the reader with a brief introduction about themselves before rely-
ing on me to filter their experiences through my own perceptions, experiences, and

FIGURE 5–1
Scarfing up *gelati* are students (left to right) Kelly Morrison, Beth Dall, Nicky DiMario, and in back, Sara Lovell.

interpretation as I tell about our visit to Reggio. A brief introduction from them is therefore helpful.

"My name is Beth Dall. I joined the 2002 Reggio Delegation with three other students from the University of Vermont. I recently graduated from the university and received my degree in Early Childhood Education with a liberal arts concentration in psychology.

"My love of children, with a special interest in young children, began early in life through baby-sitting and working in camps."

"My name is Nicole DiMario. I am a senior at the University of Vermont majoring in Early Childhood Education with a concentration in Human Development. When I applied to UVM, it was with the intention of entering the Early Education

Program, knowing only that I loved working with children. I assumed teaching would be the best way to do that. I had no idea that the program I would soon be starting (and am now on the verge of finishing) would change not only how I saw children, especially the very youngest, but also . . . would encourage me to embark on a journey of self discovery. These two things, an ever-changing lens through which I see children and an evolving journey of self discovery, were provoked and encouraged by the Reggio approach. It is an approach that I am drawn to not only for its seemingly complicated simplicity and its respectful attitudes and ideas about how children learn and discover, but also its nearly seamless integration to my life and learning as an adult.

"Just three short months ago the idea of visiting Reggio Emilia was a dream, a wish that I truly never anticipated coming true. But when the opportunity arose to literally make what in my mind had been a mythical place a reality, I made every effort to make it all come to fruition. And I finally got there!"

"My name is Sara Lovell, and I am a senior at the University of Vermont. My major is Early Childhood Development with a concentration in Human Development. I have recently decided to shift from the traditional focus of this university's program (birth through grade three) to explore a smaller age range (birth through age five), learning about some of the other aspects involved in the care of very young children.

"With my new focus in mind, along with my aspirations to one day open my own early learning center, I hoped to gain a clearer understanding of the way the Reggio programs are run and how they came to be."

"My name is Kelly Morrison, and I am a fourth-year student at the University of Vermont. I came to UVM in the fall of 1999 to become a doctor of veterinary medicine. Through financial aid, I had been awarded work-study money; once I arrived on campus, I began searching for a job. I was immediately drawn to jobs that provided me with the opportunity to work with children, not realizing the meaning of my attraction to them. I selected the Campus Children's Center from a list of positions. Over time, I found myself intrigued with the theories and philosophies of the Center. After my first full semester at UVM, I gave some serious thought to my choice of major and decided to switch to early childhood education and development, a degree that I expect to receive in May of 2003."

Obviously we are very different people, with different personalities, and from different backgrounds, but we also have a great deal in common. Most notably, we all love and are intrigued by children and have chosen to pursue a profession that reflects these feelings. As either juniors or seniors in our program, Beth, Nicky, Sara, and Kelly have been attending classes together for the past three or four years. They have read many books and articles about the pedagogy and community of Reggio Emilia. They have also been student teachers in our lab school, the Campus Children's Center, where they collaborated with their mentor teachers during a two-semester sequence in their respective classrooms. And, like so many who have read the books, seen the videos, and listened to the presentations, they have dreamed of going to Reggio.

GETTING READY: ENTERING THE CYCLE OF INQUIRY

After an inordinate number of email exchanges, we finally managed to find a time to meet as a group to discuss the study tour, travel plans, and more general information. I suggested that we look to the cycle of inquiry (Gandini & Goldhaber, 2001) to document this experience and that each of them begin by framing a set of questions to focus their observations and thinking. I reminded them that, like any good qualitative research project, these questions might change and others emerge over the course of the week. These initial questions would be a starting place, perhaps a kind of mental anchor for those moments when they might feel a bit "at sea" during the experience of Reggio Emilia.

We've learned through our work at the Campus Children's Center that after framing our questions, it's helpful to consider what kinds of observation tools we want to use and how to organize our observations while we collect them. In this case, I suggested that keeping journals could serve the same function as the white loose-leaf notebooks at the center that hold the observations, artifacts, and analyses of the children's work in chronological order. Their journals would hold their observations and notes taken during presentations and discussions, as well as their written reflections.

They would also have to make decisions about how to record what they were seeing or hearing. For example, some people bring small tape recorders to the presentations that can be long and theoretical, while others develop a kind of shorthand or forego narrative writing for more efficient lists of bulleted major points. I reminded them that cameras were not permitted during the visits to the schools but that often a simple sketch can capture how the environment has been prepared or laid out, or how information has been organized on a panel.

Finally, I suggested that they not restrict themselves only to writing about the study tour activities, but that they look for opportunities to participate in and reflect on other aspects of community life by visiting neighborhood parks and local museums, or attending community cultural events. However, I was purposefully vague about *what* they should write, hoping that each of them would use her journal in a way that best supported her thinking about this experience.

The students agreed to give their journals to me at the end of the study tour to read and analyze with the hope of learning more about the experience of "being there." I also assured them that I would send each of them the final draft of this chapter to be sure that I had represented their experiences accurately before sending it to Joanne.

In reality, the actual documenting of the experience was not as straightforward as we had planned. In the rush of a very early morning departure to catch their trains at the end of the study tour, two of the students left their journals for me at the hotel desk. While one of the students' journals fit into my room's mailbox, the other one did not. The clerk assured her that he would give me the over-sized journal later in the day, and as you have probably already guessed, the journal was never seen again! When I returned to Vermont, I asked this student to send me a summary of her thoughts and feelings about the experience. I have based the following discussion on this summary and the other three students' journals.

One more caveat: Before I share the meaning I have made of their writing, I must emphasize that like all documentation, this is a very personal and subjective rendering. Beth, Nicky, Sara, and Kelly aren't just any students, they're *my* students. We are a small program and I feel personally connected to each of them. Consequently, I read their reflections with anticipation and some trepidation: Had our program prepared them adequately for this experience? Was the study tour a meaningful experience for them? Had I supported them enough during the stress of travel and the actual study tour? Clearly, I would not be and in fact was not an objective reader!

The students were also engaged in a very personal and subjective process. While keeping their journals, they knew that I—and ultimately you—would be the readers. Surely they considered their audience as they grappled with documenting their thoughts, questions, and doubts. How would their writings affect my view of them as students? Could they really admit to any less-than-positive reactions to the "world's best" early childhood programs? Clearly, the meaning that we five brought to this study tour reflected our individual experiences as well as our relationships with each other and, now, with you, the reader.

Of course, the students' experiences were also framed in large part by the study tour program. The following is a brief summary of the week that will give you a better understanding of the kinds of experiences that influenced the students' reflections.

SETTING THE STAGE

We arrived in Reggio Emilia on a Saturday, having already spent several days visiting some early childhood programs in a small city north of Reggio Emilia. We had recovered from jet lag and were even relatively comfortable reading Italian menus. We had the day to find the famous lions in Piazza San Prospero, eat at least two cones of *gelati* (Italian ice cream), and wander aimlessly through the streets, gazing into one elegant store window display after the other.

The study tour began formally at 5:00 PM the next day, with opening introductions and a pasta dinner for the 165 participants from across the U.S. The following morning, the president of Reggio Children, the group that organizes the study tours, welcomed us and showed a professionally produced film about the early childhood programs of Reggio Emilia. That afternoon, we were invited to attend an interview with Jerome Bruner that was open to the community.

The rest of the week consisted of formal presentations, a film documenting the schools' history, and visits to the infant-toddler centers and preschools. (Visitors are not allowed in the infant-toddler programs when children are present, but they do visit the preschools while children are there.) The last day of the study tour included a presentation from the Municipal Commissioner of Education and Culture, and the week closed with a catered dinner.

This brief description of the program provides a sense of the kinds of activities in which the students participated. It is against this backdrop that Beth, Nicky, Sara, and Kelly addressed their questions and recorded their experiences and reflections.

"CONFUSED, INTRIGUED, AND OUT OF MY LEAGUE. . . . "

The students' journals address many of their initial questions that related to extending children's work and professional development, the relationship between the community and the schools, and the environment. For example, the journals are filled with copious notes taken during presentations and discussions, in particular from Carla Rinaldi's formal presentation on the pedagogy of listening, which probed the relationship between values, theory, and practice.

Their many questions about the relationship between the community and the schools are often addressed during visits to the schools, where they had the opportunity to read the documentation about children's involvement in the community. The film *Not Just Anyplace,* a documentary that describes the history of the municipal system of early education in Reggio Emilia, also generated reflections on the challenges that the citizens of Reggio Emilia faced and overcame to support their young children and families.

Their journals are full of lists that highlight how particular materials were displayed, along with floor plans and drawings. Their interests in the environment are reflected in descriptive and idiosyncratic lists: "intertwined branches hanging from ceiling, metal grater, spoons, spirals as wind chime"; "variety materials separated by color"; "beautiful containers for display"; "little sink studio"; "real wood, silver"; "space under stairs"; "shadow room—light play"; "lots of mats and weaving"; "use of real objects as models for clay work, drawings—adult books." Adjectives like "awesome," "overwhelming," "huge," and "transparent" are scattered throughout their reflections.

However, not all of their reflections about the environments are positive. For example, Beth and Nicky are concerned that two large infant-toddler centers they visited did not include many soft spaces. However, both consider the possibility that their concerns reflect some preconceptions they may have about children. Nicky writes, "I was really craving that (soft spaces). I'm not sure if that was to satisfy my own need or whether it is truly something infants (and toddlers) need." They all agree that some of the schools with long histories are overwhelming in the amount of documentation that is displayed on the walls. Sara concludes that first-timers should not expect to be able to focus on anything else but the environment because, at least for her, "it took over [her] mind" when she was in the schools.

Of special interest to me, however, are the reflections woven throughout their writing that suggest that these experiences led each of the students to move beyond the speakers' subjects and the concrete reality of the physical environments to consider the abstract and complex relationship between culture, community, and identity. This relationship is the thread that I find particularly compelling.

"NOT ONLY ABOUT EDUCATION. . . ."

"Nobody can 'do' Reggio. Your own culture, context, experiences, interactions . . . all play roles in the makeup of the school." Kelly writes these words in her journal after listening to Amelia Gambetti remind her audience that the early childhood programs of Reggio Emilia are constructs of *this* community's particular history, geography, and culture. Kelly admits that she already knew you couldn't "do" Reggio, but that it wasn't until she heard Amelia say it so bluntly that she really understood how interconnected the identity of the school and the culture of the community are. Nicky responds to Amelia's remarks similarly as she writes, "We cannot 'do' Reggio in the States; I think I've known this all along but it is now that I'm truly coming to know my own culture that this concept has such great meaning." It is interesting to note that Nicky writes of knowing her own culture from the vantage point of another.

Beth also considers Amelia's point and applies it immediately and directly to her own context when she writes, "Reggio schools can only happen in Reggio. We have Vermont schools in Vermont. It's important to keep that in mind as we learn more about Reggio."

Sara draws a finer point as she discusses how each classroom develops its own unique culture through the interplay of shared values or philosophy and the specific individuals who "live" in that space.

> If you look at all of the different schools that we saw you see a lot of differences that are conducive to the people who occupy the space. Yes, the same underlying philosophical principals are there, but the subtle differences really create the classroom atmosphere. . . .

They are all rethinking their understanding of the relationship between a school and its cultural context. Kelly also struggles with the relationship between culture and language as she responds to Carla Rinaldi's discussion of documentation and listening as acts of love. She writes, "I don't know if I would have ever phrased it that way and I feel that the gap . . . is (a) clue to the different uses of language between ours and the Italian culture. Having heard this phrase, I absolutely feel the power of it." In a later entry, Kelly returns to this description of listening as an emotion and documentation as an act of love, asking whether she or "anyone else in our culture has ever used such beautiful and meaningful words or phrases to describe such things."

This thread of cultural awareness is woven throughout the students' reflections. Their observations of groups of men gathered in small clusters in the piazzas engaged in extended, animated conversations and of elders chatting together while watching their grandchildren play in their neighborhood parks lead to reflections on how we in the U.S. make use of time and place and what values underlie these uses. Beth marvels at the degree to which the extended family is involved in children's lives, and Sara writes, "Children are thought of very differently in our population as a whole."

Reexamining their own cultural context appears to provoke more personal reflection and self discovery. For example, after learning about the early childhood programs in the first city we visited in northern Italy, Beth confesses how "little I know about services at home." After hearing Carla Rinaldi's presentation on the pedagogy of listening, Nicky reflects on her own identity as a learner when she writes, "I'm curious about how different my questions would be if as a child I was encouraged to ask why. Would I care less about the 'correct' way of thinking? More likely to create my own hypotheses and theories?"

This combination of a deepened sense of cultural awareness and self discovery appears to promote the desire to create change. Nicky articulates this outcome when she writes, "The things happening here in both the schools and the community are quite remarkable as I view them from an outsider's lens, and they do indeed inspire me in both life and in practice." Inspired by the Remida Center in Reggio Emilia that offers workshops to teachers on how to use recycled materials in the classroom, Beth wants to open a recycling center in Burlington. In a final burst of energy, she closes her journal with a 22-item "to-do" list that includes visiting other centers in the U.S., marching in Washington, and learning to sign better. Kelly wonders whether it would be possible to rent space in a museum in downtown Burlington to advocate for children by displaying their accomplishments through documentation. Sara and Beth also write about using documentation to influence the way children are viewed in their communities. Beth summarizes these feelings of empowerment when she writes in one of her last reflections, ". . . I felt inspired to come together as a whole state. The changes need to be made to overcome the views of children we have currently. I want to get home to start changes, slowly but surely."

"... ABOUT MYSELF AND THE PERSON I WANT TO BECOME"

As the following excerpts reveal, Beth, Kelly, Nicky, and Sara returned from Italy changed in various ways. Beth summed it up by saying, "My focus for the study group was to look at the environment and how it guided social interactions within the teacher, peer, and parent relationships. I was able to document a variety of set-ups and materials through journaling, but I needed to spend more time interacting with the staff to gain a greater understanding of how the space was used by the children. I look forward to using the knowledge I obtained through this experience in my career, and to visiting Reggio Emilia again in the future."

Kelly wrote, "Thinking back to my experience in Reggio, I find that I was greatly affected by the voice that children were given within the community. It was moving to see banners full of children's words hanging around the city. Displaying children's words for all to see is such an admirable way in which to honor children."

Nicky concluded that, "While in Reggio I felt overwhelmed, slightly culture shocked, and very impressed. Looking back on it now, nearly three months later, I still feel a lot of those same things. But upon reflection, the trip to Reggio Emilia did so much more than overwhelm me and impress me—it inspired me. While there I was particularly taken by the communities within the schools as well as within the greater context of the city. I have taken this concept away with me. It has both taught me and inspired me to begin to build strong communities in school and out in our own country and, in particular, in our own culture. Strong communities here will look culturally different in remarkable ways than those of the strong communities I witnessed in Reggio Emilia. It is, however, the concept of community that underlies it all. It is just one of the many pieces of a foundation of education that has inspired me."

Sara thought that, "Having looked at the programs and philosophies in Reggio throughout my three years in UVM's program, actually being there has made the discussions and readings a reality to me. Though I could not look solely through the lens I had originally hoped to (due to an overwhelming feeling that I needed to take everything in), it was an experience of a lifetime and leaves me with a strong urge to one day attend again."

Sara and Beth have a richer image of what Lella Gandini refers to as an "amiable" environment (Gandini, 1984, 1991); Kelly and Nicky have a deeper understanding of how to create a sense of community within the school and between the school and the community's citizens.

But they don't just know more. They see themselves differently. Experiencing a different culture, listening to a language rich in metaphor, interacting with educators who see themselves as agents of change seem to invite, perhaps demand, a revisiting of one's own culture, language, and identity. I'm not surprised. I too have experienced the same awakening during my visits to Reggio Emilia.

In his introduction to the documentary film, *Not Just Anyplace,* Ettore Borghi described Italy's liberation after World War II as not "just of the intellect but also of the heart." Perhaps the power of "being there" is the sense of being liberated, being freed to reinvent our identities, and ultimately, to reinvent a world that children deserve.

III

The Challenge to Change

 In this keynote chapter, Lilian Katz identifies issues and poses a series of provocative questions—challenges—that go right to the heart of what it means to espouse the Reggio Approach. Her provocations challenge the reader to consider the potential difficulties as well as the inspiring possibilities that arise when attempting to implement that approach, and draw attention to the fact that change, while possible, is never easy.

As the book progresses, Katz's challenging questions are repeated at appropriate places to encourage readers to ponder them once again as they study ways various authors are answering her challenges to change.

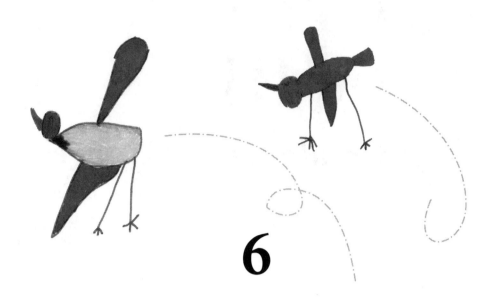

6

The Challenges of the Reggio Emilia Approach[1]

Lilian G. Katz

Professor Emerita & Co-Director, ERIC Clearinghouse on Elementary
and Early Childhood Education, University of Illinois, Urbana, Illinois

[1] An earlier and longer version of this chapter was published in L. G. Katz & B. Cesarone. (1994). (Eds.)
Reflections on the Reggio Emilia Approach. Urbana, IL: ERIC Clearinghouse on Elementary and Early
Childhood Education.

For the last two decades it has been my good fortune to work with early childhood education colleagues in many countries, on every continent, many times over. I have seen impressive and instructive practices in parts of our own country and in many places, including New Zealand, Australia, northern Germany, and in the United Kingdom, especially during the so-called Plowden years. But never have I seen provisions for young children as inspiring as those observed during my 11 visits to Reggio Emilia. Having now visited 12 of their preprimary schools and 2 of their infant-toddler centers, it seems more clear to me than ever that in our own collected literature on early childhood practices, we have been right all along to assume that:

- ☐ young children have active and lively minds from the start;
- ☐ children's dispositions to make sense of experience, to investigate it, to relate to and care about others, and to adapt to their environments are inborn and can flourish under the right conditions.

From our colleagues in Reggio Emilia we can learn a great deal about how such conditions can be achieved. The question is, What steps can we take to bring our own practices closer to those conditions? One of the main goals of this book is to share our ideas about how to help interested readers not only to learn some of the fundamentals of the Reggio Emilia Approach, but also to consider possible ways they might be adopted, adapted, and incorporated in our own early childhood practices. With these goals in mind, I want to take up some of the issues they raise. I will then address some of the principles to consider in bringing about desirable changes.

ISSUES IN ADAPTING AND ADOPTING INNOVATIONS

Doyle and Ponder (1977–78) put forward an interesting analysis of some of the issues of innovation and change under the heading "The Practicality Ethic in Teacher Decision-Making." According to their analysis, the *practicality ethic* has three components. When teachers are faced with pressure to adopt (their term) an innovation, their decisions are based on three criteria, paraphrased here in the form of questions teachers might ask themselves:

1. **Congruence**   Are the innovative practices of Reggio Emilia congruent with my current practices? Do they advance or strengthen what I am now doing? We might note here that another question a teacher might ask in this situation is: Does this innovation suggest that what I have been doing up to now was all wrong? (This reaction is suggested by Sue Bredekamp [1993] in her sensitive account of her reactions to her first visit to Reggio Emilia.)

2. **Resources**   Will those who urge me to change provide me with the necessary resources (e.g., time, space, materials, woman power, etc.) to make implementation possible, feasible, and practical?

3. **Cost-Reward Relationship**   Given the cost in terms of the time and energy required to adopt the proposed innovation, will it provide me with sufficient rewards to make it worthwhile? In particular, will the "psychic" rewards be great enough in terms of children's interest, enthusiasm, and cooperation, parents' support and appreciation, and administrators' approval? The amount of effort is acceptable if the teacher is reasonably certain that the responses of the children and relevant others to the new practices will be clearly positive.

Doyle and Ponder suggest that when the answers to these questions are largely negative, teachers discard the proposed innovation as "impractical." I suggest that we all might consider these three criteria of the practicality ethic before rushing headlong into advocating any change, but especially those implied by the Reggio Emilia Approach. Positive answers to these questions would seem to be essential if we are to adapt our ways of working with young children to be more like those observed in the Reggio Emilia pre-primary schools.

Adoption of the Reggio Emilia Approach in Particular

When thinking about adapting the Reggio Emilia Approach in particular, some additional questions and issues come to mind. First, is the Reggio Emilia Approach adaptable? Can it be made suitable to our context without major or significant distortions? Can it be adjusted to fit our situations, culture, subcultures, and conditions?

Second, there are many elements that contribute to the Reggio Emilia Approach. Our Reggio Emilia colleagues frequently assert that one must have all the elements of their approach to make it work, and to preserve its integrity. This makes the task of adoption so daunting that it may lead to discouragement at the outset. All the elements that constitute the Reggio Emilia Approach took many years to develop and are undergoing continuous refinement. How many years would we need in the United States to get to where they are now? Which elements of the Approach are most and least adoptable and adaptable?

Physical features.   The arrangements and kinds of space available in the infant centers and preprimary schools of Reggio Emilia seem to be central elements of their work. How many of the elements of this feature can we realistically expect to adopt? How long would it take? How would the considerable costs be met? How essential are these physical features? Are they central to the nature of the Reggio Approach?

Parent involvement.   U.S. educators have long had serious concern and commitment to meaningful parent involvement. Can we emulate the success of Reggio Emilia along these lines? And how long might it take to do so? Is their outstanding success with parent involvement due to the extraordinarily high quality of the children's experiences, rather than the reverse? Which comes first? Does parent involvement make high quality experiences for their children possible, or do the quality of the program and the quality of the children's work and involvement they engender entice the parents into enthusiastic, active support and participation?

Collaboration.   We have all been impressed with Reggio Emilia's commitment to collaborative relationships among all the adults involved in their work. I am told that in that part of Italy in particular, there is a long-standing tradition of cooperatives and joint efforts that we in the United States do not share. How can we hope to begin to emulate or adopt such a style of staff relationships? How can sufficient time for such interaction be allocated? The level of collaboration characteristic of the preprimary schools requires a great deal of time and patience during the decision-making process.

Documentation.   The contribution of documentation to the work of our Reggio colleagues is also convincing and very impressive. How much staff time and energy does good documentation require? What kinds of additional resources would be required to yield such a high quality of documentation? How adaptable is this central feature to our situations? How much documentation is enough?

Atelieristi.   How many of us can hope to incorporate an *atelierista* into our programs? How could the cost be met? How much of the Reggio Emilia Approach can be adapted without the constant presence and expertise of the *atelieristi?* Or, for that matter, how important to the whole effort is the availability of an *atelier?*

Pedagogisti.   The pedagogical and other kinds of leadership provided by the team of *pedagogisti* seem to me to be a *sine qua non* of implementing the Reggio Emilia Approach. Indeed, the development of the practices we so much admire seems almost entirely dependent on the quality and frequency of staff development provisioned in their approach. Of special note is that the *pedagogisti* are provided in sufficient numbers to make possible their constant availability, sufficient to enable them to know well every teacher and, indeed, every family. How much of such support do we need and how could the cost of such provision be met?

Three-year grouping.   One of the features of the approach that provides a variety of benefits is that the children stay with the same teachers throughout the three years of pre-primary school enrollment. How adaptable is such a practice in our own programs? I would hope that it might be partially accomplished through mixed-age grouping, a practice that would have potential benefits in addition to just having the same teachers for three years. For example, children in mixed-age groups exhibit significantly more prosocial behavior; show a greater tendency to offer help, instruction, and information; and more frequently facilitate the efforts of others than do children in same-age groups (Katz, 1990). In the United States, interest in mixed-age grouping continues to grow and to be implemented in a number of school districts.

Project work.   Involving young children in extended investigations and in-depth studies of significant topics is not unique to Reggio Emilia. It was first introduced in the United States early in this century (Isaacs, 1930; Rawcliffe, 1924) and was implemented superbly in Britain during the Plowden years (1960s and 1970s). Sylvia Chard and I have been involved in helping teachers incorporate the project approach into their curricula all over North America since the late 1980s (Katz & Chard, 2000). It is my impression that the Reggio Emilia preprimary schools have taken project work with young children further than any other groups of practitioners. In particular, they have succeeded in making the "graphic languages"—as they refer to them—a major aspect of children's project work in fresh and significant ways. Why should we not do more of this as well?

Bringing About Change

The formal and informal literature on educational change continues to grow rapidly. As we contemplate the kinds of changes adapting the Reggio Emilia Approach might involve, it would be useful to keep in mind that real change is fraught with turmoil, uncertainty, and other uncomfortable processes.

Here the work of the Canadian educator Michael Fullan (Fullan & Miles, 1992) and his insights into the complexities of bringing about *lasting* change are useful. The concerns outlined below are based largely on Fullan's work.

Change is learning—loaded with uncertainty.   Fullan reminds us that anxiety, difficulties, and uncertainty are intrinsic to all successful change. All change involves learning and all learning involves coming to understand and to be competent at doing something new and differently (this is well illustrated in other chapters in this book). We have to recognize explicitly that the ability to tolerate the uncertainty involved in unfolding a curriculum a step at a time instead of depending on detailed advanced planning is not easy to tolerate. Note how Donna Williams and Rebecca Kantor (Chapter 14) question themselves concerning whether their water project is truly emergent or just another teacher-generated "water week," and how Cadwell and Fyfe's teachers struggle with growth as they work at adopting practices from Reggio Emilia (Chapter 13).

Change is a journey, not a blueprint.   Fullan's message is not the traditional "plan, then do," but "do, then plan, then do and plan some more, and do some more," and so forth. We can see these processes beautifully exemplified in the Reggio Emilia preprimary schools. As Carlina Rinaldi might put it, a plan is a compass and not a train schedule (1994).

Problems are friends.   Fullan asserts that improvement is a problem-rich process, and as such, the problems should be welcomed. While change threatens existing interests and routines, heightens uncertainty, and increases complexity, Fullan asserts that we cannot develop effective responses to such complex situations unless we actively seek and confront real problems that are difficult to solve. In this sense, he suggests, effective organizations embrace problems rather than avoid them. We might benefit by joint efforts to identify the most likely problems to be expected based on at least a dozen years of experience of the many early childhood educators in the U.S. who have been adapting and adopting Reggio ideas and practices.

Change is resource hungry.   Fullan agrees with Doyle and Ponder (1977–78) that change demands resources. Among the many resources required for the adoption of the Reggio Emilia Approach, time is probably very high on the list. According to Fullan, time is an important, indispensable, and energy-demanding resource. American visitors to Reggio Emilia frequently express envy at the flexible and comparatively relaxed approach to time that seems to characterize their settings. This difference between our two countries with respect to the nature of time may very well be part of the larger cultures, traditions, and histories within them.

Change requires the power to manage it.   Fullan suggests many problems encountered in change can be addressed by openness and interaction among all those concerned with what is to be changed. Openness means that we must all learn a lot about how to respond to complaints, frustrations, disagreements, and conflicts, and see them as part of development. Many Americans who know Reggio Emilia practices well have commented on the striking ability of the adults to argue, disagree, and criticize each other and yet remain close colleagues and good friends. Similarly, the staff takes serious and appreciative note of arguments among the children, and treats them as indications that real growth and learning are in progress. Again, that kind of response to conflict and argument may distinguish our two cultures, and require substantial change in U.S. responses to children's disagreements and conflicts.

Change is systemic.   Here Fullan agrees with our Reggio colleagues that all parts of the system must be involved in the desired changes simultaneously. He points out that change must focus not just on structural features, policies, and regulations, but on the deeper issues of what he calls the culture of the system. Such a stipulation presents overwhelming challenges for U.S. early childhood educators.

All large-scale change is implemented locally.   Change cannot be accomplished from the distance, but must involve all those who will implement the innovative practices, as well as the larger and more distant agencies involved.

WHERE ARE WE NOW AND WHAT DO WE DO NEXT?

Fullan's last point brings me to my final round of questions. Since all real change must be implemented locally, the responsibility for changes is placed right on our own doorsteps. It pushes us to take stock and ask, Where are we now? As potential implementors of the Reggio Approach, what should we be thinking about now? What should or can each of us do now?

Addressing all the elements of the Reggio Approach is a tall order, to say the least! If we cannot do it all, should we do nothing at all? If we decide that we cannot do it all at once, but still want to move ahead, where should we start? Should we, and can we, start at different places? Can some start with inservice training? Others with rearrangement of spaces and materials? Can others start with *ateliers*? Others with long-term projects? Some with documentation? But, of course, there have to be some classroom activities worth documenting! This may become increasingly difficult under the current pressures faced by many early childhood educators in the U.S. (and in the U.K.) to offer preschool children direct instruction in reading. It is interesting to note that Italians, like some other Europeans, do not teach reading: they only teach writing! It is easy to dismiss this comparison by noting that Italian is a much easier language to read than English. However, it seems to me that because English is such a difficult language to read, we should also begin with encouraging children to try to write, and then *introduce the formal aspects of reading later rather than earlier.*

One idea that continues to haunt me is that perhaps we should be especially careful not to call our efforts "The Reggio Approach." Even if our efforts at change are inspired by Reggio Emilia and what we are learning from it, we must take meticulous care how we use the term and what we are implying about the relationships between what we are doing and the practices in Reggio Emilia.

There are several reasons behind this "specter." One is the obvious fact that it would take any of us a very long time to be worthy of that name. Another is that *if we implement the Reggio Emilia Approach insufficiently or inadequately, we might unwittingly and inadvertently give it a bad name, cast doubts about it, and create the impression that it is just a passing fad.*

But if we eschew calling our efforts by the Reggio name—even though inspired by their work—then what should we call them? Why not Developmentally Appropriate Practices? Surely the Reggio Emilia Approach exemplifies developmentally appropriate practices at their best.

Finally, I propose a way of thinking about the challenges we face that is based on "perturbation theory." Imagine, if you will, a cyclist riding along a road without difficulty. Suddenly the front wheel touches a small pebble in the road and is thrown off course. The rider falls, is injured, and her whole life changes forever. In other words, perturbation theory suggests that *even very small items can have huge and lasting consequences.* (If the cyclist is riding very fast, even a very small pebble could create a very large perturbation!)

What we are really asking for in our deliberations together about adopting and implementing the Reggio Emilia Approach are huge and lasting consequences. The question is: *Is there a relatively small pebble that we can put in place now that will ultimately have the large and lasting consequences we hope for?*

My hypothesis is that if we focus our collective and individual energies on the quality of our day-to-day interactions with children so that those interactions become as rich, interesting, engaging, satisfying, and meaningful as those we observe in Reggio Emilia, we will be casting out a pebble that could ultimately have very large consequences. For instance:

- ❑ It could attract greater interest, involvement, and loyalty of parents than all those incantations about parent involvement touted in our commission reports and similar proclamations.
- ❑ We would all be learning about learning and about children's rich and lively minds and their amazing capacities to imagine, hypothesize, investigate, interact, and co-construct fresh understandings of their worlds.
- ❑ It would very likely speak more clearly and loudly than many of the other things we say or do.
- ❑ It would address our children where they are now.
- ❑ *We would be doing what is right.*

That is not to say that we should not be striving to change all the other elements of the system and cultures in which we work. But we have to start somewhere, and our children cannot and should not wait until all the elements are in place. We are all deeply indebted to our colleagues in Reggio Emilia for showing us again and again what is possible when a whole community is deeply committed to its children. Though the work ahead of us is formidable, Carlina Rindaldi (1994) reminds us that the possibility of reaching the vision exists. At the same time, however, she urges us to keep in mind that we see "the Reggio Emilia experience and practices together as a treasure that we have in common, and be careful to look at them with love, respect, and care."

IV

Accepting the Challenge to Change by Changing Relationships

 I confess that I had a problem with arranging the order of the following chapters that all focus on fostering relationships between people. It certainly made sense to put Karen Haigh's chapter first since it provides an overview of the three significant relationships discussed in more detail in the remaining ones. She begins by discussing many practical examples of ways children can enhance friendly relationships among themselves, and then continues with a discussion about building relationships with parents, followed by ways to build sound relationships among members of the staff.

The problem for me was deciding which of the remaining relationship chapters should come next. In a way, relationships with children would be the logical choice since they lie at the heart of the educational process—however, it turned out that the material on relationships with infants and toddlers led so wonderfully well into the chapters on projects that I abandoned that arrangement. Instead, I decided to place the chapter on staff and community relationships next. In it Shareen Abramson and Kabeljit Atwal tackle the potentially thorny challenge of building empathic, respectful relationships among staff members and families who come from a large variety of cultural and ethnic backgrounds. Among a rich array of suggestions they include a noteworthy model for working through the situation when disagreements arise.

Following staff and family/community relationships, I was delighted to have chapters 9 and 10 about relationships with parents because, when *Next Steps*' predecessor *First Steps* was in the making, I couldn't locate any Reggio-inspired programs that emphasized the Reggio cornerstone of parents as part of their programs.

In chapter 9, "Thinking with Parents About Learning," Brenda Fyfe and her colleagues Sally Hovey and Jennifer Strange describe the development of the Parent/Teacher Committee in their school and tell how the staff attitude changed from "collecting and organizing documentation *for* parents—to collecting and ana-lyzing documentation *with* parents."

In chapter 10, "Parents As Partners," the numerous quotations from parents again illustrate ways Mary Hartzell and Becky Zlotoff really do treat the parents at First Presbyterian as partners. They provide a chapter rich with many actual examples of how they implement that part of the Reggio philosophy.

Then, at last, we arrive at the extensive descriptions of building relationships with children. First we have the joy of hearing Carolyn Edwards explain how the staff in Reggio Emilia conduct "the dance of relationships" between themselves and the very young children in their care. Carolyn's discussion of the eight primary compo-nents of relationships sets the stage for Alex Doherty's description of how these com-ponents are recognized and used as the base for developing emotionally worthwhile relationships with the young children at Loyalist College in Belleville, Canada.

Excerpts from Lella's Chapter[1]

The role of teachers.   The role of teachers, therefore, is considered to be one of con-tinual research and learning, taking place with the children and embedded in team co-operation. Doing this research, reflecting, listening to children with other colleagues, and documenting this process with the support of the *pedagogista* contributes to a continuous professional growth for the individual and the group.

The role of parents.   Parents are considered to be an essential component of the pro-gram and many among them are part of the advisory committee running each preschool. Parents are a competent and active part of their children's learning experience and, at the same time, help ensure the welfare of all children in the school or in the center.

The image of the child.   The educators in Reggio Emilia first and foremost always speak about the image they have of the child. All children, each one in a unique way, have preparedness, potential, curiosity, and interest in engaging in social interaction, in establishing relationships, in constructing their learning while negotiating with everything the environment brings to them. Teachers are deeply aware of children's potentials and construct all their work and the environment of the children's experi-ence to respond appropriately.

Some Challenges from Lilian[2]

Collaboration.   We have all been impressed with Reggio Emilia's commitment to collaborative relationships among all the adults involved in their work. I am told that in that part of Italy in particular, there is a long-standing tradition of cooperatives and

---

[1] Readers are encouraged to review the entire portions of Lella Gandini's chapters 1 and 2 that are related to the material in the following chapters.

[2] Readers are encouraged to review the entire portions of Lilian Katz's chapter 6 that are related to the ma-terial in the following chapters.

joint efforts that we in the United States do not share. How can we hope to begin to emulate or adopt such a style of staff relationships? How can sufficient time for such interaction be allocated? The level of collaboration characteristic of the pre-primary schools requires a great deal of time and patience during the decision-making process.

Parent involvement. U.S. educators have long had serious concern and commitment to meaningful parent involvement. Can we emulate the success of Reggio Emilia along these lines? And how long might it take to do so? Is their outstanding success with parent involvement due to the extraordinarily high quality of the children's experiences, rather than the reverse? Which comes first? Does parent involvement make high-quality experiences for their children possible, or do the quality of the program and the quality of the children's work and involvement they engender entice the parents into enthusiastic, active support and participation?

7

Creating, Encouraging, and Supporting Relationships at Chicago Commons Child Development Program

Karen Haigh

Director of Programs, Chicago Commons Association, Chicago, Illinois

We often hear that the Reggio Emilia Approach is based on relationships and that these relationships include all of the interactions among children, families, staff, and the community (Edwards, Gandini, & Forman, 1998). For the past nine years, the Chicago Commons Child Development Program has been exploring and experimenting with various ideas and influences from Reggio Emilia. I would like to share some practical ideas we have experienced and learned from that focus on supporting relationships and making connections with the people whom Commons touches.

The tradition of maintaining meaningful relationships is not new at Commons. Our founder, Graham Taylor, spoke of three main themes when sharing his ideas of the Settlement House approach in the late 19th century. He spoke, in particular, of *neighborship, understanding,* and the importance of *working with* and not for someone (Taylor, 1936). When speaking of *neighborship,* Taylor felt strongly that it was important for people to be able to meet, mingle, and understand others' points of view and feelings as ideas are exchanged. Lastly, he believed that it was vitally important to work *with* people rather than *for* them because working with them creates relationships of cooperation, collaboration, and equality. Working for someone creates a less balanced collaboration and equality, where one may have power over another and inequality results.

Now, more than a century later, the philosophy of Reggio Emilia reminds us, once again, how well Taylor's ideas have stood the test of time as we carefully consider our relationships with other people.

CHILDREN AND RELATIONSHIPS

To foster relationships, we have striven to think of new ways to encourage children to relate to and connect with their world and, in particular, with the people in their world. After our staff began to observe and listen to children's intentions, they developed some challenges for children to pursue. Some of these were short-term activities complete in themselves, while others were embedded into longer, in-depth studies lasting over an extended period of time. Some of the experiences have included the following:

- ❑ After exploring the attributes and qualities of a visual arts material such as paint, paper, drawing media, clay, wire, and so forth, make a gift for a friend with a specific material.
- ❑ Send messages to friends in mailboxes or via a pulley set up in a classroom.
- ❑ Spy on another classmate to see what his or her favorite thing to play with is, and visually represent that favorite item or area.

Reading a story to Butch, the dog.

- ☐ Share your favorite movie or book with a friend and discuss it after the friend has viewed or read it.
- ☐ Draw or otherwise create a portrait of a classmate or friend.
- ☐ Describe what your friend or classmate is like.
- ☐ What could you make or what message could you send to your parents as they attend a parent meeting? In turn, what message can the parents send to their children from a parent meeting?
- ☐ Interview an adult who works in the building about their job and see what you could make for them that would help them to do their job.
- ☐ Interview and observe people working in the neighborhood to see how they use their hands.
- ☐ Observe the dog next door and think about what you could share with him (e.g., read him a story).
- ☐ Explore an in-depth study of friendships, asking questions like, "What is a friend? How do you know someone is a friend or is not? What do friends do for each other? Could you draw a picture of someone doing something for a friend?"
- ☐ After looking at another child's portfolio, share what you think your friend/classmate has learned.

In addition, when children's ideas, experiences, and feelings are displayed throughout the center for others to read and interpret, we are in some ways encouraging relationships as we are creating a dialogue in which children view, interpret, and try to understand one another's work.

Arranging the Environment to Facilitate Positive Relationships

It is important to try to create some opportunities for children to relate and interact in spontaneous, self-directed ways. One example is having two-sided easels next to each other instead of far apart, so children can interact and notice each other while painting. Teachers often want to create a private space for individual children, but how about creating a private space for the individual and a friend? Whenever creating special space for children to sit, try to make it for two children as opposed to an individual child. Although these ideas are not necessarily activities, they are environmental suggestions that encourage interaction.

Many of these activities or environmental suggestions enhance relationships, as they charge children with sharing, knowing, and understanding others, such as: peers from their classrooms, peers from other classrooms, parents, other adults in the center, and people or life within the community.

In many of the previously mentioned activities or experiences, children learn a variety of skills, knowledge, and attitudes. For example, they learn to further develop fine and large motor skills, they learn about the function and value of reading and writing, they learn how to use expressive materials like paint or pencils, they learn about the physical qualities and attributes of objects like pulleys, and so forth. However, what children learn most subtly and powerfully is how they are connected to the world and the people in it.

PARENTS AND RELATIONSHIPS

When thinking about parent partnerships, Chicago Commons staff began to look at parents and families and asked the questions, "Can you separate the child from the family? Can you separate the child from the community?" When a child comes to school or to a center, the child is already in an existing relationship with his or her family and community. So the question becomes, "How can we pay attention to and explore these relationships with parents and the community?"

Revisiting Our Beliefs About Parents

Often teachers in early childhood programs will say they want parents to be involved. I think taking the time for teachers to reflect on why this is so important to them is a very interesting question to pursue. First staff revisited beliefs about parent partnerships, asking, "Why do we want parents involved?" and "Why do parents want to be involved?" Staff also thought about ways they could hear the voice of the parent, as we wanted to change the relationship from one where we tell the parents what to think, know, and how to do, to a relationship where we create an exchange and parents and staff each have knowledge, ideas, and experiences to share with one another.

Asking Parents About Their Hopes and Dreams for Their Children

In Head Start, we are required to have initial home visits with parents of the children at the beginning of the year. Within these introductory home visit meetings, teachers discuss the goals and procedures of the program and also ask questions about the children so they will know them better.

We began to experiment with a different approach in beginning relationships with parents. Instead of giving parents a barrage of information, we began to ask *them* about *their ideas*. This was done by asking them their hopes and dreams for their children. Interestingly enough, parents did not say that they hoped their children would learn their ABCs and 1,2,3s. Some examples of their hopes are:

"I hope he grows up to be a professional person."

"I hope he has a sense of humor."

"I hope my child finishes school before having children."

"I hope my child will do for others."

There were many meaningful, thoughtful remarks by each of the parents who were asked their hopes and dreams for their child. One parent said that she "was sort of thrown by that question, as no one has ever asked me that question before, so I thought of some hopes for my daughter and I thought I better help make them come true!" We have now added other questions to encourage parents to share their ideas. Some of them are:

What kind of adult would you wish your child to be?

What was your favorite family activity as a child and what is your family's favorite activity now?

What was your first day of school like and do you have a picture of yourself as a young child?

The ideas that parents have shared are then displayed within the center or the classroom, so in some way the voice of the parent is included and visible within the program.

Where there's a will, there's a way. In our stairwell, we complied with fire safety regulations by switching from paper documentation to tile pictures of our families.

Sharing Photos of Children and Families

We began to think of new ways to show the presence and the importance of the children and families. One way was to display photos of the families within the entrance. This idea in itself has logistical issues, as we have turnover with our families. Often they have to move or they can sometimes no longer meet the eligibility requirements (which is another chapter concerning advocacy). Therefore we could not keep up with the changes or new families. After visiting the Cyert Center for Early Education of Carnegie Mellon University, we got the idea of purchasing plastic pouches to hold photos. As a result, changes and additions could easily be made.

We saw that photos of children or families displayed within a center can become documentation of the history and life the center itself. A dream was to have photos of all children or families who have attended the program displayed in the center permanently. However, we did not have enough wall space at any of our centers. We had run into an obstacle presented by a fire inspector who stated that we would have to remove all documentation in the stairwells. Then we saw an opportunity within this obstacle and talked to the fire inspector. He approved a display of ceramic tiles to be installed in the stairwells. As a result, we asked each child who attends the center to make a simple self-portrait with black marker on a beige tile. The beige tile matches the wall color and blends in, so one immediately looks at the child's work and not the color of the tile. In this way, we have created a way to respect the children and support the center's history as we portray work from all who have attended the program. In reflecting on this situation, it is important to note that obstacles can lead to opportunities, if you are open to opportunities.

Assets of the Community

Another challenge we created was for family workers (staff who do intake and follow-up with families) and parents to develop a panel showing some of the assets of the community. For some, this led to looking at the history of the neighborhoods. So often proposals or grants request that we describe the many community needs and deficits such as lack of adequate housing and utilities, lack of quality education, lack of preventative health care and quality health care, community violence, poor neighborhood services, and high unemployment or low-paying jobs. Therefore, this opportunity to show the assets of our communities was a welcome change. It allowed us to consider the potential of our communities and, in a way, create a new relationship with them.

Monthly Meetings with Parents and Teachers Together

Parents and staff began to meet together each month to share and think together about ideas related to learning and education. Some of the questions we have asked over the years are:

- ❑ What is your view of the child? What is the public schools' view of the child? What is society's view of the child?
- ❑ What are the goals for children from the child, teacher, parent, and employer's perspectives?
- ❑ What is the role of the teacher and the role of the parent from the child's point of view? Children were videotaped so parents and teachers could review and have discussions about children's thoughts, feelings, and experiences.
- ❑ What is the government's role with child care?

Asking what is the government's role with child care was a particularly difficult question to explore. It was almost too overwhelming, so it was suggested by an education coordinator that we begin by asking, "What has the child's role in society been?" Instead we asked, "What was the child's role in society 200 years ago?" "What was it 100 years ago?" and "What do you think the child's role in society is now?" Then we asked the question about the government's role with children. We realized that sometimes we had to go back and ask other questions in order to lead to the big question.

These monthly parent/teacher meetings are in addition to other required meetings, such as monthly parent policy meetings and monthly site meetings. We developed a new role called *parent liaison* in conjunction with the monthly parent/teacher meetings. A parent from each program within each site volunteers to attend each monthly parent/teacher meeting in order to share a report of it at the monthly site meetings.

Parents Invited to Participate in Studies and Learning Tours

We began to invite parents to be involved with studies in new ways, ways beyond asking parents to collect materials for a study. Some of the activities parents were invited to participate with were: being given an instamatic camera to help the child take a photo of his favorite item or color in the home, taking photos of shadows, exploring a visual arts material at a site meeting, studying hair, studying hands, and so forth.

We have begun to offer two-day Learning Tours where educators from various states visit our sites and hear presentations with a particular focus. The Learning Tours are offered twice per year as a way to share with other professionals what we are learning. Parents were also invited to come and to respond to questions by tour participants. At first we had a panel of parents and teachers seated together to field questions, but it seemed that parents tended to stand back and let teachers respond to questions. So we changed the format to be a panel of parents only, because that allowed their ideas, thoughts, and feelings to be more readily expressed.

As with anything, there continue to be challenges in staff relationships with parents. Commons still struggles with some parents not being able to attend meetings or not being as involved as staff would like because of the parents' busy lives. Staff continue to think about how to be more interested in and open to parents' ideas and not just give parents information. Finally, staff need to continue to think about why they think parents should be involved in the program.

STAFF AND RELATIONSHIPS

When thinking about staff and relationships, I would like to note that the word "staff" and not "teacher" is used. In most cases, and especially in our program, teachers are not working alone. They are working with directors, family workers, administrative assistants, clerk/receptionists, food aides, maintenance workers, central offices coordinators, and administrators. It is a collaborative venture to operate a program that explores and supports learning and human development. So there are many positions and players within the work we do. Therefore when we say "staff," we include everyone—teachers, teacher aides, and assistants—because everyone teaches and their voices and involvement are equally valued.

We have realized how interconnected all these positions and roles have become and how learning and growth for staff is really imbedded in the mutuality of these relationships. Furthermore it is not just one key person exploring Reggio at Commons. It is a group of people who are learning and working together constantly, working together so much that not one person would be able to say he or she alone has been exploring Reggio; rather, he or she has been exploring Reggio as part of a group that depends on each other for reflection, direction, connection, and support in our explorations. No one staff member would be able to explore, discover, and realize without other staff. It is equally important to recognize that the types and number of staff

Automobile mirrors are inexpensive and come in graduated sizes.

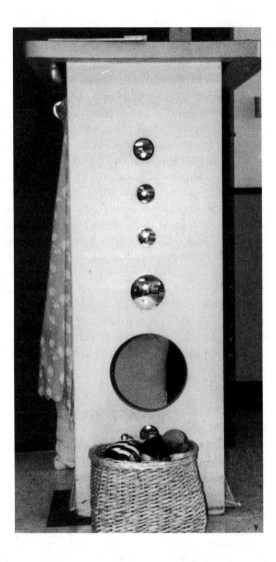

or positions in the program are not significant; what is *done* with the existing staff and positions is the key. It's learning to work with what exists in a program and to see possibilities and potential that matters.

Some reflections on collegiality and collaboration are:

- ❑ There needs to be a common goal or purpose.
- ❑ There needs to be time to meet together and meet regularly.
- ❑ There need to be opportunities to do something together.
- ❑ We need to allow time to reflect or revisit at meetings.

- ❏ We need to think of ways to be inclusive.
- ❏ We need to value and have ongoing dialogues.
- ❏ We have unequal positions, yet equal voices at the same time.
- ❏ Leadership is connected and involved with staff. Leadership and staff give input together.
- ❏ The individual and group develop and are supported simultaneously.
- ❏ There are many ways for people to collaborate.
- ❏ There have to be hopes/dreams for the future.

There has been a remarkable evolution (and in some ways a quiet revolution) of staff development at Chicago Commons. Much of this evolution has occurred within a structure of relationships that encourages opportunities to:

- ❏ create a vision for possibilities
- ❏ have ongoing dialogues and hear others' perspectives
- ❏ create plans
- ❏ have experiences and encounters
- ❏ revisit and reflect

As director, I have realized it is important to try to create an atmosphere or place that is supportive and yet challenging for staff because I believe both are needed in order to grow and develop. Furthermore, it is important to ensure that some kind of action is taken after discussions have taken place. We realized we needed to make sure we actually did something rather than just reflect and talk about something. At times there was a danger of people continuing to talk, talk, talk. Conversation cannot relate just to theory or ideas; it must relate to an action that took place. We need to reflect on the action and talk about what happened and what kind of meaning it could have to us, to the child, to the parent, and to the school. In the end, the relationships among staff and others are about creating opportunities and experiences to dialogue, share, and think together—and then take action.

Some Ways Staff Have Worked Together to Practice Results

1. Learning to share, revisit, and reflect together at weekly meetings, in-services, out-of-town conferences, and seminars by allowing time for dialogue among staff.
2. Viewing videotapes of children together to see and discuss strengths and abilities of children, which has grown into searching for children's interests or areas to pursue.
3. Talking and thinking together about why photos are taken.
4. Reviewing and interpreting children's work (actual words, drawings, videotapes, slides, etc.).

5. Developing environment plans that consider the entire building, such as classrooms, bathrooms, hallways, entrance ways, etc.

6. Viewing slides together as a means to look at the environment or the languages of children.

7. Allowing teams to have their own explorations. Each site developed research questions to explore as they were asked, "What do you wonder about children?"

8. Experiencing staff explorations of materials such as watercolors, wire, charcoal, clay, paper, etc.

9. Learning to think about how and why portfolios are used to collect children's work.

10. Talking and thinking together about how to ask questions.

11. Sharing and discussing documentation among sites.

12. Doing presentations for each other within the agency.

13. Viewing each other's environments.

14. Sharing, documenting, and revisiting our ideas, especially when we go to seminars and conferences.

15. Having an introduction to the Reggio Approach for new staff.

16. Focusing on specific research for each year.

17. Focusing on questions to think about and discuss together during the year.

18. Thinking about the purpose and meaning of journals.

19. Thinking and talking about "what is society's image of the child and what is the public schools' image of the child?"

20. Choosing, designing, executing, and evaluating documentation panels together.

21. Using quality circles to make decisions, policies, and procedures about specific aspects of our program (e.g., choosing agency-wide topics for research).

22. Planning, executing, and evaluating two-day Learning Tours together.

I believe staff at Commons have had the most dramatic changes in terms of relationships, as they have had to reconstruct their relationships with children, with parents, with the community, and with each other. Staff have even been challenged to reconsider their understanding of words and their meaning. For example, we have been challenged to think about meanings behind words like *collaboration, reciprocal,* and *interdependence.* There is a need to think about how different perspectives influence collaboration. Sometimes one can take pride in having a different perspective; yet how different can perspectives be when considering values, ethics, and common goals for the program?

Jane Addams was well known in Chicago for being one of the founders of Hull House and the Settlement House movement, and she was a board member of Chicago Commons for 30 years. When referring to Jane Addams, a working woman once said, "It was that word *with* from Jane Addams, that took the bitterness out of my life. For if she wanted to work with me and I could work with her, it gave me new meaning and hope. The hope of democracy roots in the word *with*." (Taylor, 1936, p. 202)

This quote has become very meaningful to the program as Commons continues to explore elements of the Reggio Approach and the relationships between and among children, parents, and the communities with which we work. It has become more clear to me that staff need to seek out what it means to work *with* and not *for* someone. So our challenge is to think of new ways to work *with* children, parents, and the community.

In thinking about relationships, I would summarize by sharing a poem by Angelica, who says, "Teacher I write a poem,

The sky is blue.
The sun is shining like the light.
Candy canes are good and the markers are loose.
And diamonds are shiny just like your ring.
And a teacher is nice just like my teachers."

Think of all the connections and relationships this child has made to her world!

8

Teachers as Co-Inquirers
Fostering Positive Relationships
in a Multicultural Community

Shareen Abramson
Professor and Director, Joyce M. Huggins Early Education Center,[1]
Kremen School of Education and Human Development,
California State University, Fresno

Kabeljit Atwal,
Teacher, Joyce M. Huggins Early Education Center

[1] We wish to acknowledge and thank the teachers, parents, and children of the Joyce M. Huggins Early Education Center and also the Fansler Foundation and the Kremen School of Education and Human Development at California State University, Fresno, for their contributions to the work described in this chapter.

In the U.S., teachers often struggle with feelings of loneliness and isolation when confronting educational problems. This limited contact with other adults hinders professional growth and the ability of teachers to exchange ideas and learn from each other (Smith & Scott, 1990).

In marked contrast, Reggio educators describe their approach as "based on relationships" among teachers, children, parents, and the community (Malaguzzi, 1993). These relationships are enhanced and sustained by working together to achieve a common goal, an effort referred to as "collaboration." The Italians see collaboration as vital for improving the quality of early care and education, as well as the quality of life for everyone involved.

THE CO-INQUIRY PROCESS

The value of collaboration extends beyond achieving consensus. Even greater benefits are derived when a "learning group" comes together to investigate problems and search for meaningful solutions (Krechevsky & Mardell, 2001, p. 285). By engaging in "collaborative inquiry" (co-inquiry), a process that "consists of repeated episodes of reflection and action" (Bray, Lee, Smith, & Yorks, 2000), the interests and concerns of individual participants coalesce into a group question that can be studied over a period of time.

During co-inquiry, participants learn to bridge differences in life experiences and interpretations, recognize the humanity of one another, share meaning, and find solutions. This ability is described as "intersubjective communicative competence" (Habermas, 1971, 1984, as cited in Bray, Lee, Smith, & Yorks, 2000, p. 23). Similarly, Reggio educators value "subjectivity," understanding one's own individual identity, differences, and perspectives, as well as "intersubjectivity," understanding other's identity and differences, multiple perspectives, and the social and cultural dimensions of experience (Rinaldi, 2001b).

In the Reggio Approach, two critical tools for co-inquiry are "listening" and "dialogue." According to Rinaldi (2002), collaboration requires a commitment to "listening" in a way that is "open and sensitive to the need to listen and be listened to" (p. 2). Genuine listening and dialogue acknowledge a variety of ways to communicate, are not limited by time constraints, accept divergent interpretations, raise new questions, and continually revisit and revise thinking as new ideas are incorporated. Although an individual may have a particular take or perspective on a situation, true collaboration means "letting go of the outcome" in the collaborative search for meaning and a willingness on the part of individuals in the group to contemplate new ideas and never-before-thought-of directions.

USING CO-INQUIRY IN A U.S. CONTEXT: THE HUGGINS EARLY EDUCATION CENTER

The Huggins Center is a training, demonstration, and research center in early childhood education at California State University, Fresno. The university is located in California's Central Valley, an area troubled by a high poverty rate and related problems. The center primarily serves low-income student families. About 150 children, ages 3 months to 12 years, receive subsidized services. Through an innovative arrangement with the local school district, children with special rights (needs) are fully included in the program. Approximately 55 percent of families enrolled and many staff have culturally and ethnically diverse backgrounds.

ESTABLISHING THE STRUCTURE FOR TEACHER INQUIRY MEETINGS

For the Huggins Center, "inquiry meetings" are an important means for professional development.

Physical Space

Meetings are enhanced by having an appropriate, comfortable, and quiet physical space. Such an environment supports reflective thinking and creates an atmosphere of collegiality and trust. The room that is used has couches and chairs that provide adequate seating for 12 people.

Organizing for Co-Inquiry

The center inquiry meeting is held weekly, while another meeting during the week involves staff within the classroom in a similar process. Meetings are held immediately after the children's lunch while children are resting. Each classroom sends at least one staff representative to the meeting that typically lasts two hours. A written agenda and minutes from the meeting are distributed and the classroom representative is responsible for taking back to the other staff what happened in the meeting.

Teachers seek to focus on an area of common interest that provokes questions with the potential for further co-inquiry. During the meeting, which is often videotaped as a record of teacher work and progress, teachers develop a research "plan of possibilities," ideas and hypotheses about potential experiences and activities that might be developed over the next week. The documentation of the actual experiences is brought to the next inquiry meeting.

Sometimes an individual within the group may act as a catalyst, particularly in the initial stages of co-inquiry. This individual may be the director, a teacher who is knowledgeable about the Reggio Approach, or a "deep thinker" on educational and curriculum issues. While care must be taken so that the inquiry belongs to the group and is not dominated, this individual can offer valuable expertise.

During the meetings, teachers ask and refine questions, share observations, listen, analyze, reflect, ask more questions, and plan next steps. They draw on resources of documented events to provide powerful visual images and text to revive memories, tell stories, and relate dialogue to those at the meeting who may not have been present when these events occurred.

FAMILY AND CULTURE: BUILDING RELATIONSHIPS THROUGH CO-INQUIRY

To develop empathetic, respectful relationships, the Huggins Center is committed to recognizing and building on the strengths of the diverse cultures and styles of the staff and families at the center. By becoming more sensitive and responsive to cultural values and family preferences, teachers help to ease children's daily transitions and bring family and culture into the classroom.

Physical Space

The physical space of the classroom supports cultural and family connections. The classroom environments contain objects that represent the rich cultural heritage of the Fresno community. Thoughtfully selected items such as fabric, dolls, craft pieces, and baskets typical of the Latino, Asian, African American, Punjabi, Armenian, and Native American cultures are incorporated as learning materials and classroom decor to create connections between home and school. The classroom entry area includes adult-sized furniture and is an inviting space where a parent and child can browse documentation, read books, and talk with other parents, children, or teachers.

Organizing for Co-Inquiry

The study of family and culture began with the staff exploring their personal histories and generating questions concerning cultural identity and diversity. Some of the questions arising were:

"How do the culture and values of the family come through in the classroom?"

"As teachers, how do we bring our cultural values with us into the classroom?

"What are the cultural artifacts that come into the classroom from home?"

After considering ways to learn more about families and their cultures, the staff decided to study what happens when children enter the center and their parents leave. As one teacher commented, during these transitions:

"We are able to observe the child with the family and without the family."

Another teacher hypothesized:

"When families enter the classroom, they bring their culture with them. By observing arrivals and departures from the classroom, we may be able to learn more about the family."

Initial Observations

The teachers' observations revealed the many variations and issues involved in separations:

"Some families come in and do a whole separation activity. Others are in and out, bam, bam. I observe that some children who don't have a routine seem to have a harder time. Sometimes I have to hold them and make a routine for them. Hug them and walk to the window and see mom go."

"Some of the children like to play games when they come to the door and hide behind the parent so the teacher can't see them. And the teacher says, 'Oh, the child didn't come in today? Is the child home, is he sick?' And the parent will say, 'Oh, he didn't come in today.'"

"Some parents seem to prefer talking to certain adults. Similar race, language, age, or whom they see as in charge. Some of the Moms won't talk to me, but the Dads will because I am a male."

Documentation of Rituals and Routines

For the next meeting, the teachers determined that they would record some specific rituals and routines to learn about the dynamics of parent-child interactions during separation and reunion:

"Mother kisses the daughter on both hands, then in unison, they put their hands across their hearts."

"They read a story before she goes. When mom picks her up at the end of the day, she shows mom what she has been doing in class."

"When Mom picks him up, he doesn't want to go. But if Dad comes to pick him up, he runs up to Dad and jumps into his arms."

"Mom watches him from the door. He comes in by himself."

"Mom gives him a kiss. She talks to him quietly in Spanish."

"He comes in with his grandfather. Grandfather is so lively when he comes in, waving to everybody. He says hello to everybody, both children and adults. His grandson does the same."

"She comes in. She is clinging to her Dad. Dad whispers into her ear in Punjabi, 'You need to behave.'"

"Every morning, he and his Dad come in and his Dad builds a structure on the block platform. He says to his Dad, 'You have five minutes.' So they build this huge, elaborate structure."

The teachers dialogued at length concerning interpretations and implications of these emotionally charged routines.

The Importance of Transitional Objects

A story regarding the importance of a transitional object was the focus of the next inquiry meeting:

"Yesterday a parent came in late. I was already with the group of children and we were singing. She gestured to me that the child was crying because he had with him a puppy plush toy. Mom was trying to get her child to put the puppy in his cubby or give the puppy to her. So there was this tension. I nodded to the parent to bring her child over. He sat on my lap and the song finished. A child put his hand up. He said, 'I have a red puppy at home.' Then all of a sudden every child had an experience they wanted to share about a puppy. Everyone was able to relate. We were able to negotiate the situation. After the stories, the child put his puppy in the cubby. This issue that started as a problem for one child, became a learning experience for the group.

"I realized that children do bring with them from home something of value to them, whether it is a toy or something else. Because everything has meaning. With everything there is a relationship. Why don't we as teachers allow that? Why can't children bring something from home that is valuable to them?"

Another teacher responded:

"I have had problems with children bringing things from home. I am not kidding, there are Power Rangers, big plastic toys. It seems like a problem. I have put a sign up: "Please leave toys at home." Now I feel bad; Am I taking away from an experience that could be happening? I wonder why they are bringing it? Why do parents let them bring it?"

The director added:

> "They all bring them. Could this be a window on culture and what's happening at home? Could the teacher begin to have a small group discussion? The children might verbalize some of the problems; they might begin to come up with some solutions that could be tried out. This could be the kind of issue that allows dialogue with parents. They also may have ideas. The transitional object may become a cultural message, an expression of culture and home in the classroom."

As various transition research projects took shape, communication and relationships with families were enhanced. In one classroom, the teacher asked parents to describe their feelings about separating from their child at school by drawing, painting, and/or writing. One parent wrote:

> "I feel a little sad because I will miss her, but I feel very happy because I know she will have a fun day with her friends and teachers."

The grandfather who brings his grandson to the center drew a symbol of unity, two hands held tightly, and wrote:

> "When I leave R., I feel very proud of him for going to school and learning with his friends."

Through activities like these, parents felt acknowledged and respected by the teachers. The children were pleased about their parents' involvement. They felt more secure because they perceived their parents' feelings as valued. The resulting documentation was assembled as a book and was placed in the entry area of the classroom for parents and children to read together. Several families began to include reading the book as part of the transition routine.

As a result of these experiences, parents felt freer to ask questions and talk about their beliefs and cultural values. At this point, experiences with parents involved "building new relationships, rather than one composed around separation from the mother" (Bove, 2001, p. 114). After one child recited a poem in Spanish to the group, other children also wanted to perform favorite songs and poems from home, some in different languages, often with their parents participating. Photos from home soon followed, including one child's baby pictures taken at his "first tooth" ceremony, an Armenian tradition that was unknown to center staff.

As described by the mother, symbolic objects were presented to the baby at the ceremony. Whatever object the baby touched first was believed to be a sign for the child's future. A family celebration followed. Sharing the photos with the teacher, the mother pointed out that her child had reached for a book. In an intersubjective moment of shared meaning, the parent and teacher looked at one another, both beaming with pride.

HOW TO BEGIN THE CO-INQUIRY PROCESS

To engage in co-inquiry, early childhood educators may need to find creative strategies to overcome program and time constraints. The following suggestions have helped staff at the Huggins Center and other programs to be successful:

    1. Meet at least once a week with at least one other colleague. If there is no planning time in the schedule, eat lunch together or meet before or after school. A breakfast meeting can start the day on an energetic note. If none of these options is possible, "meet" online using e-mail, e-group, or some other communications device.

    2. Set specific goals from one meeting to the next. Come prepared. Review documentation the night before and be ready for dialogue on questions. Help colleagues by providing feedback including positive and specific suggestions. Document the meeting using minutes and/or videotape. Being able to review progress from the beginning may lead to major insights about teaching and learning.

    3. Don't start immediately with a project. Instead, think about particular questions, interests, and issues for children, families, and/or teachers. Study an identified area in more depth using documentation tools—camera, tape recorder, and notebook—to record observations and analyze findings.

    4. Keep in mind that tension can be productive, widening one's perspective and leading to appreciation of different personal histories and viewpoints. A personality inventory or questionnaire may help to improve working relationships and reveal why people have different outlooks on issues and styles of interaction.

OPENING HEARTS AND MINDS
TO PRODUCTIVE CONFLICT

For any group, conflict is a normal consequence of social interaction. According to Reggio educators, a certain degree of "conflict is good." In their view, provocative topics and questions stir interests and emotions that are likely to generate worthwhile projects. By setting aside a predetermined outcome and seeing another point of view, productive conflict can bring about positive change and greater unity. Dialogue, listening, and negotiation are used to explore and accommodate differences without damaging relationships. Often a "third perspective," collaboratively constructed by participants, emerges during the process.

    "HEART" is an acronym that was adopted at a Huggins Center staff retreat to represent some of the elements for building respectful, collaborative relationships and learning more about the Reggio Approach: *Homework, Emotion, Attention, Research,* and *Teamwork* (Figure 8–1).

The procedure below may assist in keeping conflict productive:*

1. *Homework:* Identify the specific issue that is causing concern. Review pertinent parts of this book or other related resources on the Reggio Approach listed in the bibliography. Organize your thoughts as clearly and succinctly as possible. Try to separate the problem from the person.

2. *Emotion:* Identify the feelings you are experiencing as a result. Why are you feeling this way? Are there other factors affecting your feelings right now?

3. *Attention:* Having these insights, contact the individual(s). Propose a time and location for meeting on the issue. This should be a private meeting only for those directly involved. Relax and prepare for the meeting. Visualize yourself and the other(s) dialoguing, listening, and giving mutual attention to the issue.

4. *Research:* At the meeting, present your perspective:

"In my opinion, _____." Or, "I felt _____ when _____."

Then state:

"I'd like to _____." Or, "I'm willing to _____."

Ask for their perspective:

"What do you think?" Or, "How do you feel about this?"

Breathe and listen without interrupting, then paraphrase:

"In your view, _____" or "You feel _____ about _____." Or, "You prefer _____ and you would like me to _____."

Check for understanding:

"Is this right?"

5. *Teamwork:* Look for areas of agreement while acknowledging and respecting differences:

"We have similar ideas about _____ but may need to think more about _____."
"I wonder if _____."
"Might we _____?"

FIGURE 8–1
HEART: Keeping Conflict Productive

6. *Attention:* Be aware of your feelings and be sensitive to the feelings of the other person during the meeting. Be aware of your tone, facial expressions, body language, and the messages being conveyed. Remember, your goal is to have a good relationship by opening your heart and your mind.

7. *Emotion, Homework, and Research:* The next day or soon after, thank the individual(s). Express positive feelings that resulted from the meeting:

"Thanks for our dialogue about _____. I am feeling _____."

As a result of the process, you may also discover that more homework and research are necessary to clarify matters. Do your homework and continue to dialogue! In difficult situations and after three attempts on your own, a neutral, skilled facilitator may be able to assist in the process.

*Procedure adapted with permission of the author: Lane-Garon, P. (1998). *Professional problem-solving process.* Unpublished paper.

Reflections on Co-Inquiry

A Huggins Center teacher reflects on the experience of co-inquiry:

> "As a teacher, I need to be listening more, be more observant. There are many forms of listening. We don't just listen with our ears but with many other senses. We listen by observing. Just by listening to the children and parents, we can find out more about them. And then with their experiences, we can all build together this collective knowledge of culture and individual differences. I feel that as a teacher I need to do more observations of children, of parents, of other staff so that we can work together and be as one community in the classroom."

As co-inquirers, teachers construct their understanding of the fundamental principles of the Reggio Emilia Approach. Teachers feel a sense of optimism as they discover that positive instructional, interpersonal, and socio-cultural changes are possible: "Knowing how to work in a group—appreciating its inherent qualities and value, and understanding the dynamics, the complexity, and benefits involved—constitutes a level of awareness that is indispensable for those who want to participate, at both the personal and professional levels, in effecting change and building the future" (Rinaldi, 2001a, p. 29). The process of co-inquiry brings all those involved closer to the kind of educational community that every person deserves.

9

Thinking with Parents About Learning

Brenda Fyfe
Professor of Education, Webster University, St. Louis, Missouri

Sally Miller Hovey
Teacher/*Atelierista*, The College School, St. Louis, Missouri

Jennifer Strange
Teacher/Preschool Coordinator, The College School, St. Louis, Missouri

Note: Brenda, Sally, and Jennifer are members of the St. Louis–Reggio Collaborative, a network of educators who have been studying the Reggio Emilia Approach to early education for a dozen years. The College School is an independent school serving children from 3 to 14 years of age, with a 40-year history emphasizing experiential and integrated learning. Webster University is an independent, comprehensive international university that has supported the study of the Reggio Approach since 1991 when it hosted the exhibition "The Hundred Languages of Children."

At The College School, family participation is, and always has been, an important aspect of the life of the preschool. We continue to develop and refine ways of sharing questions, observations, and values involving the role of parents. Since the beginning of our study of the Reggio Approach in 1992, we have worked to make children's learning visible. But when we began our study and application of the Reggio concept of documentation, we saw it primarily as a tool for describing experiences and informing parents about learning. Over the past ten years, documentation has become a powerful tool for looking at learning with parents and for thinking with parents about learning. As Carlina Rinaldi states in *Making Learning Visible* (2001), "we place emphasis on documentation as an integral part of the procedures aimed at fostering learning and for modifying the learning-teaching relationship." We have learned that documentation is valued not only for its use in recalling and evaluating experience, but also for its power to support new learning. It enables parents, teachers, and children to reflect and search for meaning together.

At the urging of our mentors from Reggio Emilia, we learned to document and make visible the diverse ways in which parents participate. We have learned from experience that making parent involvement visible through documentation does much more than provide a record to help us recognize and celebrate family contributions. It has the power to influence the effectiveness and depth of future participation in the learning community. We have learned to take the time to study these records with parents in order to generate and design even richer parent participation possibilities.

In this chapter we describe some of the experiences and understandings that currently define our relationships with parents. We describe and illustrate the progression in our thinking about the value of documenting family participation and making visible parents' reflections on learning.

Our stories reveal how we shifted from collecting and organizing documentation *for* parents to collecting and analyzing documentation *with* parents. There are a hundred and one ways, probably a thousand and one ways, in which we can create our lives with parents. We currently use a multitude of strategies to communicate with families, but rather than offer a lengthy list, we have decided to write in more depth about a few key experiences and structural changes that have redefined our relationships with parents.

PARENT/TEACHER COMMITTEE: A SUPPORT SYSTEM FOR BUILDING RELATIONSHIPS

The College School has a lengthy history of family participation. A parent organization has been in place, serving the entire school (ages 3 through 14), since the school opened in 1962. Family involvement has ranged from volunteering in classrooms, to building new playgrounds, to even taking out second mortgages on homes during a time of financial crisis. However, as we learned more about the relationships of families and the early childhood programs in Reggio Emilia, we began to consider what it might mean to strengthen our existing systems of parent involvement in the preschool as well as to invent new systems *with* the parents.

Since the beginning of our study of the Reggio Approach, preschool parents and teachers at The College School have been working diligently in an effort to continuously redefine and/or refine the mission of a preschool parent/teacher committee. Our desire to put such a committee in place was directly inspired by similar committees and groups we had observed in the schools of Reggio Emilia. We were very impressed with the collaborative interaction of these Italian families and schools. Even in our early days of studying this community-based approach to early childhood education, we quickly grasped the idea of the possible benefits from such strong interaction and collaboration.

Early on we made various attempts at establishing parent/teacher collaborative committees. These meetings consisted of organizing family holiday events, examining projects, and/or sharing the learning of this "new" educational approach inspired by the schools of Reggio Emilia. At the close of the 1993–1994 school year, several interested and invested preschool parents and teachers gathered in the living room of one of the families. Amidst this congenial atmosphere, bolstered by food and drink, we reflected honestly on what was or was not working in the development of family/preschool relationships. At that meeting, a stronger and more consistent framework for a preschool parent/teacher committee began to emerge, one that was based on the value of democracy. The parent/teacher committee would be made up of individuals who would represent the larger community of parents.

In the year-end meeting of 1994, strong suggestions for organization were made— not only by the teachers but also by the parents. A parent/teacher committee would form at the beginning of the school year, consisting of three parents from each of the two preschool classrooms. This committee would meet on the first Monday of each month from 3:15 until 5 p.m. or as needed. At least one teacher would attend from each classroom. The *atelierista* would also attend as often as possible. Other administrators and faculty members of the school might be invited, depending on the issue(s) being discussed. At the first parent/teacher evening of the school year, in September, parents would be encouraged to indicate whether they had interest in serving on the Parent/Teacher Committee. At this meeting, a description of the work of the committee would be presented by a parent. It was a new beginning that supported us well in the continuing evolution of family/school relationships in The College School early childhood program.

In a very practical and constructive manner, the Parent/Teacher Committee now functions as an increasingly well-oiled tool of organization, supporting the lives of children, families, and teachers of TCS Preschool in a variety of ways—addressing social, emotional, cognitive, and physical needs as is appropriate. At this time, the Parent/Teacher Committee begins with at least two returning parent representatives. The returning parents are instrumental in launching the work of the committee for the current school year. By midsummer, one of the returning committee members has written a clear and concise description of the TCS Preschool Parent/Teacher Committee. This written piece also includes a form for indicating whether other parents have interest in being a member of the committee or interest in supporting the work

Parents and teachers examining a project.

of the committee in supplementary ways. Attached to this form is a questionnaire concerning parent interests, skills, and hobbies that might be shared with the community of the preschool. The first task of the Parent/Teacher Committee is the preparation of a projections and intentions document for the school year. This document includes:

- ☐ Organization of Preschool Parent/Teacher Exchanges to be held throughout the school year. The first such exchange will be held in September.
- ☐ Continual examination and reflection concerning the ongoing experiences of the preschool community.
- ☐ Continual examination and reflection concerning the relationships of families with the preschool, relationships of the preschool and the larger school, and relationships with the communities of St. Louis.
- ☐ Organization of the Preschool Family Holiday Celebration in early December. Formation of subcommittees will be necessary for this event.
- ☐ Support and participation by committee members during visits by delegations of educators at various times of the school year.
- ☐ Support of ongoing projects of the classrooms.
- ☐ Support of environmental upkeep and renewal as needed, both inside and out.
- ☐ Re-vision of the Preschool Parent/Teacher Committee's Mission.
- ☐ A parent will act as facilitator of the committee meetings.
- ☐ A parent will act as secretary of the committee meetings.

This document may be added to and revised due to emergent needs, issues, and interests as the school year progresses. The committee communicates with all preschool families through written documents that are sent home or are posted in designated areas. The committee may also communicate with families through telephone messages or through e-mail. Through a continuous process of reflection on organization and mission, The College School Preschool Parent/Teacher Committee is instrumental in ensuring the input of *all* members of our early childhood community.

PARENT/TEACHER EXCHANGES: SHIFTING FROM SHARED EXPERIENCES TO SHARED LEARNING

For a few years, members of the committee have been assisting in organizing parent/teacher exchanges with a particular focus on documentation and assessment. The word "exchange" was initiated with intention, as our desire was to promote a dialogue with parents rather than making a presentation to parents. At times, some of these committee parents—or other preschool parents they recruited—have taken an active role within these exchanges as facilitator and/or scribe. During the exchanges we have examined children's emergent knowledge, skills, and dispositions related to intellect and social and emotional development. We do this by studying examples of children's work, transcribed dialogue, documented displays (panels), slide presentations, and video clips.

It was one of these Parent/Teacher Exchange evenings in 1997 that became a turning point in our thinking about parents and documentation. A survey was conducted with all of the parents on possible topics for the next Parent/Teacher Exchange. It revealed a strong interest in children's work with clay. The Parent/Teacher Committee decided to involve parents in an experimental learning activity that might help them gain more insight into the value of clay as a tool and a language for learning. It was a turning point, of sorts, because we wanted to engage parents in reflection on their own learning and we wanted to make special efforts to document their process for future reference.

Prior to the Exchange, parents had been following the ongoing development of clay work by visiting the *atelier* and classroom and reading the experiences and stories of the children on our walls. We revisited this documentation together at the beginning of the exchange, opening with a slide presentation documenting children's explorations of clay. Next followed a hands-on workshop for parents to explore the material of clay for themselves. The environment was organized in much the same way that it was for children. Parents worked in small groupings around several tables. We wanted to encourage conversation and interaction. Soft music was played in the background. Clay, clay tools, and collections of natural materials were provided at each table. Teachers documented with video to capture the exploratory experiences of parents and general atmosphere of the evening. Digital stills were used to capture processes and final works. At the end of the evening, parents were asked to voice or

Teachers and a parent preparing a documentation panel together.

write reflections on their experiences. Here is what Glen and Mary Fox, parents of 4-year-old Nathan, had to say:

> Working with clay is such a tactile experience. It's no wonder Nathan enjoys working with it so much. In 30 minutes we discovered that a shapeless piece of material can take on meaning and depth. Nathan has always loved storytelling and this medium allows one to weave, squeeze, and poke a story out. And it even allows the story to change according to one's mood at the moment. Nathan hates to make mistakes. I can see where clay is much more forgiving when it comes to making mistakes. This suits him.

One parent came into school the day after the parent workshop to show her clay creation to her own child and a small group of 3-year-old friends. They had a lengthy conversation about how the mother made her clay creation and what it represented. At group meeting, the older children in the 4–5-year-old classroom viewed some of the still images of the prior evening's event. They marveled at their parents' involvement with clay and asked many questions of the teachers. Teachers noted that much conversation about the event continued among children as they interacted throughout the day. Parents reported that the conversation continued at home that evening.

The Parent/Teacher Committee met in February to examine the documentation collected on the January Parent/Teacher Exchange. They selected some reflective comments written by parents to be included in a panel of documentation concerning clay as a language of the preschool. The video was edited and made available for parents to revisit. A few who could not attend the Exchange had the opportunity to experience the evening vicariously through this video. The edited video was also shown to the children.

All of these experiences built on each other. From this point forward, we realized the power of documenting parents' reflections on their own learning as well as their reflections on the learning of their children. We learned that documentation of parent participation can be shared, studied, and enjoyed with children as well. Documentation of parent participation can be used as a focus for discourse among parents, teachers, and children, a platform for reflection and intellectual partnership (Forman & Fyfe, 1998).

PARENTS AS DOCUMENTERS: DEVELOPING A NEW ROLE

The success of the clay evening and other experiences inspired us to continue collecting the reflections of parents. In 1999, in an effort to further the understanding of documentation's value, we began to invite parents to become part of the process. A beginning story of this experience concerns the father of a boy in the 4- and 5-year-old classroom.

Steve Walters, energetic and enthusiastic father of Nicholas, was also a member of our Parent/Teacher Committee. Steve has great interest in his son's educational experience and often arranged his work schedule around opportunities to be involved at our school. A project concerning investigation of special places in the outdoors had been in progress since the beginning of the school year. Children, teachers, and parents had organized an early autumn trip to a preschool family's country place so that children could explore this type of outdoor space. Steve said he could join us for the trip. He was asked, along with other participating parents, to carry a pen and notebook to record children's comments and reactions. It was a beautiful day—indeed, the children called it "The Bright Blue Morning of a Perfect Day." Even though it was a kind of perfect day, Steve felt some apprehension. There was a lake; there was a lot of wooded area. He didn't know all of the children. He didn't even know the teachers all that well. He did know that his own child was bouncing with excitement. He couldn't imagine having time to write anything down. He began to wonder how this could be a valuable learning experience. These are Steve's words of reflection concerning this "Bright Blue Morning:"

> *Right away I was pretty nervous. I was thinking, should we all be holding hands? And then I went back into my head to what it was like for me as a kid to have an experience like*

this. I watched the kids and thought that the way they were perceiving climbing a hill was probably way different than the way I was perceiving climbing a hill. And I decided to step back and let them have that moment. I thought about how these kids could dictate how they want to learn—they could show me their own kind of excitement. When I began to give them ownership, the whole day began to change. Now (after this trip), when my own kids bring me a leaf or something else outside, I stop and take time to really look at it carefully. The other thing I've been thinking about is how the supporting of sharing each other's ideas and ways of learning is so essential to this school. I saw it so clearly on this trip. The whole trip was about collaboration, because a lot of the kids are like Nicholas— they could have easily spent the whole day running pell-mell up and down the trails. But, because they've been encouraged to respect others' opinions, they stopped when one child stopped to notice the path of the beavers to their dam. They displayed this calmness, at that point and at other moments of study, that was kind of amazing to me.

Steve's reflections are the result of a teacher interview following this trip. With Steve's agreement, his documented reflection became part of a panel examining the values of the outing. Steve remarked that the process of reflecting was almost as valuable as the experience itself. Not only did he examine the children's learning, but he examined his own learning as well. And, by using a peer's words on a panel, we observed other parents being motivated to consider their own child's and, indeed, all the children's learning in another way.

VIDEO DOCUMENTATION: A TOOL FOR COMMUNICATION AND ASSESSMENT

Steve's reflections were based on an actual experience with children. Video offers parents virtual experience with children, enabling both individual and collective reflection.

Our work in video began in 1997 with a secondhand camcorder donated by a preschool family. With the ability to rewind and play back an experience, we gained new perspective that has influenced our practice of observing children. Video allows us to preserve moments of expression, movement, interaction, and language among children. Revisiting a tape provides an opportunity to examine and make visible the many layers of a child's experience, layers that are impossible to capture otherwise. For us, video has become a valuable documentation tool for communication and assessment, especially in terms of our work with parents.

Early in our experience, we made presentations to parents primarily using video as a peek into the day. Parents seemed to enjoy the opportunity to see their children in action, but perceived these experiences more as entertainment than as opportunities for studying learning. At subsequent meetings we began to ask parents to think along with us about the learning observed. We created structured forums for dialogue and discussion around videos (Fyfe, Geismar-Ryan, & Strange, 2000). Our goal is to develop a culture of "critical visual literacy" as described by Goldman-Segall (1998) in her book, *Points of Viewing Children's Thinking: A Digital Ethnographer's Journey.*

The final episode that we have chosen to include in this chapter focuses on a particular story of how a three-minute video clip of an everyday experience in the life of a 4-year-old can be used with parents to study and uncover significant learning.

In preparation for parent-teacher conferences, we created several edited pieces of video documentation. Anna's story, in particular, highlighted important developmental areas while conveying the true joy of learning. Teachers and parents had already observed and noted her strengths with regard to dramatic play, dance, song, and athletics. Anna's parents, however, had many questions about her emergent understandings of reading and writing. Upon our first viewing of the three-minute clip, we noted the following:

> *The viewer sees Anna at the Message Center table with one other child. A small, folded card has the date, written numerically, on both sides. A large picture dictionary stands on an easel behind Anna. She turns her body and chooses an illustration accompanied by a word. Turning back to the table, she uses a fine, black pen to copy the letters into her spiral notebook. She fills the page with words beginning with the letter P. The word* parade *is printed, though she reads it as "band" as she looks at the illustration. The voice of the teacher is present from behind the camera, supporting and provoking Anna in her work, "What do you think your parents would say if they saw you working here?"*
>
> *Altering her voice to mimic her parents, she replies "Oh my goodness, you did that yourself?"*
>
> *At the end of the session, Anna straightens her workspace, returns her journal to the proper shelf, and claps her hands in a gesture indicating she is finished for the day.*

The video provides us, teachers and parents, with vivid details about Anna's process. Studying the tape together enabled us to notice even more details and make hypotheses about her emergent understandings about reading and writing as well as her social, physical, and cognitive development. The following are a few examples of our interpretations:

- ❑ The movements of her body are subtle yet significant. She faces the table to write, twisting her trunk to refer to the dictionary behind her, then turning back to the table. The continuous physical movement does not disorient her. She is able to keep her place as she copies one letter at a time.

- ❑ Her language, voice, and expression are deeply connected to her work. She plays with words and letter sounds by singing the name of individual letters in each word that she copies. Her tone of voice swoops and dips, following the curving movement of her pen as she draws the letter *S*.

- ❑ Anna taps and twirls her pen through her nimble fingers while she chats or thinks. She has a strong, firm grip on her writing utensil, allowing her to print with ease and confidence.

❑ Anna becomes a mentor for her peer, offering support in writing the date on her journal entry. The date card is written as 2-21-02, and she reads it aloud as "two line two one line zero two."

❑ Anna reads the word "parade" as "band." We consider this an intelligent mistake because she is using visual clues to make sense of the word.

Like most parents of young children, Anna's parents were quite interested to know about Anna's emerging reading and writing skills. The video gave them an opportunity to see just how she uses her journal. Not only does Anna recognize, read, and print many letters and numerals, she completely integrates pretend play, drama, and social activity into her experience. Of course they were quite pleased to see her having fun and exuding charm throughout this vignette. On another level, a video like this can provide parents with a sense of assurance that their child is indeed moving toward the world of literacy.

FINAL REFLECTIONS

Ruth Josselson, in her book, *The Space Between Us: Exploring the Dimensions of Human Relationships* (1996), states

> People create their lives within a web of connection to others. The cast of characters in a life and the nuances of interconnection provide the richness, the intricacy, the abrasion, and much of the interest in living. Life unfolds as a kaleidoscope of relationships, with varying pieces in shifting arrangements.

A web of connections is what we aim to create with families. In many ways it has taken a certain amount of risk for both teachers and parents to enter the "new" relationships that we have described. It is a far simpler task to address children's learning through standardized checklist assessments rather than to invite a dialogue requiring teachers and parents to examine, reflect, question, think, and learn together. Entering into such an exchange can mean opening to the possibilities of disequilibrium, disagreement, and abrasion of emotions. On the other hand, what could be of greater value than examining the many capabilities and potentials of children through several points of view? Through these dialogues we might possibly achieve greater understanding about the issue of invested learning and what it means, not only to children but to adults, as well. The shifting arrangements in our thinking with parents about learning characterize our continuous change over time. The kaleidoscope of relationships that characterize our relationships today has indeed provided richness, intricacy, and interest in living and learning with parents and children.

10

Parents as Partners

Mary Hartzell

Director, First Presbyterian Nursery School, Santa Monica, California

Becky Zlotoff

Teacher, First Presbyterian Nursery School, Santa Monica, California

with contributions from parents Ami Cohen,
Laurie Grotstein, and Tracey Glazer.

CONTEXT OF THE SCHOOL

First Presbyterian Nursery School has been serving families in Santa Monica and adjacent areas for nearly forty years. The school welcomes families from all religious, ethnic, and economic backgrounds. Approximately 100 children attend the morning program with an optional extended day for working families. Children begin school between two-and-a-half and three years of age and continue until they enter kindergarten. There are five classrooms, each with two co-teachers who move together with the children to a different classroom each year. In addition to the classroom teachers, there are part-time science and music teachers, a studio teacher, a teacher assistant, office administrators, and a director. Diversity is a value and the parents raise money to support a strong financial aid program.

The activities of the city all around us support our curriculum. Each Wednesday, the children can shop at a Farmers' Market in front of the school. They can walk to the library, post office, and many local shops as well as ride the city bus to the pet store and fire station. The children sometimes visit parents and other family members who work in the neighboring office buildings. The Pacific Ocean is a block away at the bottom of a high palisade, and the children walk the many steps down to the beach and to an adjacent marine study center.

THE IMAGE OF THE PARENT

"In Reggio, there is an important architectural feature, the piazza, that functions as a public gathering space for the students, the staff, and the parents and symbolically reaffirms their status as a cohesive social unit. Moreover, there is the fact that these families are living and working in a small town, linked by a common culture and true proximity to each other."

"But here in Los Angeles, with our geographic and cultural diversity, the challenge is to create a psychic public space that gives people the same sense of connection. We come from different backgrounds and go home to different neighborhoods. But parents' lives are intricately, intimately entwined here because we're talking about our children, often crying about them and despairing of ourselves, wondering how it can be that we love them when we feel frustrated with them and ultimately celebrate them. The hard, deeply rewarding work of raising a child is a shared endeavor that binds us together. The school is our common ground."   —Laurie Grotstein

Before we, as educators, began our journey with the Reggio philosophy, we saw parents as a support of our work, rather than including them in the work. To change this relationship, we had to change our image of the parent. We had to learn to trust the parents, to involve them in the learning process, and to provide them with a deeper experience of the work we were doing. Several years ago, to help educate the parents about the Reggio Approach, we arranged a day trip for parents to the "Hundred Languages of Children" exhibit at Mills College in northern California. The 10 parents who went, along with the director and several teachers, had many opportunities for discussion throughout the day. Parents and teachers began to experience each other in a new way. This shared experience served as a provocation for deeper parent/teacher collaboration.

"That exhibit changed my way of viewing young children. I was amazed that children could think, reason, and express themselves in such varied and sophisticated ways. It was pivotal for me in realizing that learning happens not in handing your child off to a school, but in the interactive relationship between child, teacher, and parent."   —Ami Cohen

THE FIRST CONTACTS THAT ESTABLISH THE SCHOOL'S PHILOSOPHY AND EXPECTATIONS

Just as the environment upon entering a school creates a first impression of the school, so too the initial contacts with parents create the foundation of the relationship between the parents and the school. We give monthly tours for prospective parents where the director begins with a discussion of the school's philosophy and the possibilities for parent involvement. These discussions take place in our community room, in which there is an entire wall of documentation titled "A Day in the Life of the School" that was conceptualized, photographed, and physically created by a group of parents. This documentation and the visibility of parents in documentation throughout the school communicates the richness of the parent experience to our visitors. After an initial greeting from the director, current parents lead a tour of the school, talking about their own experiences and our philosophy in context. Parents are encouraged to ask questions and return to the community room after the tour for an open dialogue with the director.

In late spring, after families are accepted into the school, the parents attend an orientation where they have the opportunity to learn more about the fundamentals of the Reggio Approach. They visit all the classrooms to read documentation and to get a sense of the development of the work from the youngest to the oldest children. The rest of the evening is spent in a discussion of the practical implementation of the school's philosophy. We show a video with interviews of alumni parents discussing the evolution of their understanding of the value of the Reggio Approach. It was made by parents and shows them participating in the daily life of the school and giving their perspective on their children's experiences. The current and incoming Parent Association presidents share what they have learned about the value of parental involvement for parents, children, and the school community and offer the new parents an opportunity to become involved in the strong organization that provides a structure for parents as partners in the school.

"At First Pres., there are a number of factors that help make our community intimate and cohesive; foremost among these is a guiding belief that every parent, like every child, has a voice here. This is crucial because when parents feel heard, they are much more likely to listen to others, including their children and their children's teachers."   —Laurie Grotstein

FACILITATING THE TRANSITION
FROM HOME TO SCHOOL

A child's first school experience is a significant milestone for each family. The school respects both the child's and the parents' initial experiences. To facilitate the transition to school and to lay the foundation for a collaborative community, the teachers give great attention to these new relationships and begin making connections with the new families during the summer months. We offer a short series of transition classes, during which the children and parents have a chance to spend time at school with their new teachers and explore the classroom. In these classes, the teachers begin to learn about the children's interests, and they use this information to help create a welcoming environment in the fall. For example, in a recent transition class, the teachers observed that all of the boys and several of the girls spent time building with train tracks. After discussing their observations, the teachers made a note to get train books from the school library and to bring engineer hats and other train accessories from the resource room so that the children could extend their experiences when they entered school in the fall.

The teachers also take photographs of the parents and children working together in the classroom. These photographs become part of a panel that welcomes the families to school in the fall. Connections are also made through the "family books." Each child receives a notebook that contains a welcoming letter from the teachers along with their picture. It also has blank pages with questions designed to give children and parents a way to tell their family's story. There are pages to tell about relatives, pets, family activities, and celebrations. These family books begin a strong connection between home and school. The parents understand, from the start, that their voices are valued. It is an acknowledgment that parents are children's primary teachers and that we, as new teachers of these children, can learn a great deal from the parents.

On the first day of school, there is a special place in the room for the family books. The pictures of their family and familiar activities help children to feel more comfortable in their new environment. It gives them something tangible to hold on to when they are thinking about their parents. These books also give the children a way of making connections with each other. For example, one day during the first few weeks of school, Emma, a 3-year-old, was on the rug looking at her family book. Keith, another 3-year-old, walked by and saw a picture of her dogs. He ran to the shelf and got out his family book. He brought it over to Emma and showed her a picture of his dog. They talked about big dogs and little dogs. The next day, building on the connection they had made through their family books, Emma and Keith played in the house together, pretending to be dogs. These interactions served as the foundation of a deeper relationship between these children and made it easier for them to initiate relationships with other children in the class. Through reading the family books, the teachers get ideas about family experiences, traditions, and cultures that can be incorporated into the life of the classroom with the support of the parents. Showing respect for and interest in the families helps everyone—children, parents, and teachers develop trust in each other and in this new experience.

Teachers also make a home visit during the first few weeks of school, during which they talk with the parents and get to know the child in his or her own environment. The documentation of these visits strengthens the home/school connection when they are made visible either on a panel or in a book.

CONTINUING TO BUILD CONNECTIONS BETWEEN HOME AND SCHOOL

Having set an expectation of open communication and collaboration between parents and teachers, each classroom has a designated area to help achieve it. This area is where parents sign in, give information about pick-up times and after school plans, and read about upcoming events and the life of the classroom through the daily journals. There is also a notebook where parents can leave notes for the teachers, sharing home information that might be important to the child's day at school. Projection reports that describe possibilities for experiences and investigations are posted in the parent area. Often, after reading these projections, parents offer materials, resources, ideas, or expertise that can deepen the experiences for the children. At the end of each day the teachers, with input from the children, write a daily journal, sharing some pictures and words from the day's experiences. The daily journals are available for one week in the parent area and then are collected into a book that can be borrowed for the weekend and shared between parent and child together at home. Having insight into their child's daily activities gives parents a way of asking relevant and open-ended questions. These kinds of communications build stronger connections between parents and teachers and between parents and their children.

"Every child is telling a story and it is our job to listen to it. A child who has had the experience of having an adult take the time to get down at her eye level and patiently record her words is a child who is going to feel that she has something valid and interesting to say. Documentation empowers children to feel truly heard by adults. That's why so many kids leave this school with the ability to communicate with grown-ups; it's because they feel the respect of grown-ups. It's a great ideal—to have a school where the kids are really heard—but it takes more than a pencil and paper to be effective. It requires having a community of parents and teachers who want to work together for the benefit of children."   —Laurie Grotstein

We continue to build the connection between home and school during those first months. In the younger classes, the children are given small bags they can use to take home an item borrowed from school or to carry to school an item from home. Sometimes they take the bag home on Friday and bring it back on Monday filled with a memory of their weekend experience, such as a shell from an outing to the beach, a ticket from a museum visit, or a tortilla recipe from Grandma's house.

Children and teachers also might write a note together asking the families to support some aspect of an ongoing classroom investigation. For example, while investigating leaves, the Green Room children sent home a series of notes asking their parents to help them gather edible leaves, write down what edible leaves they ate, find recipes, and collect colorful leaves. After a month, the teachers wrote a note asking parents to share their experiences of this home/school project. Here are two parents' responses: "Leaf study has been a valuable experience in our house. Amanda has recently taken an interest in helping me in our garden. She is now very aware of which plants are herbs and she has become more vigilant of her baby sister putting plants, leaves, or flowers in her mouth." "I have enjoyed working with Zoë on a project that links home and school. We would talk about what kind of leaves the children ate in school and then compare them to what we have at home. When we went to the Farmers' Market, Zoë and I looked at all the produce with an eye toward leaves you can eat. It is sometimes hard to truly engage with Zoë about what she does in school. This investigation provided a context. I'd like more of it!"   —Tracey Glazer

This shared small project inspired several parents. One mother who loved to garden created an herb garden at school with the children. She found a dad who also loved to garden, and together they worked with the children to grow edible leaves in large terra cotta pots donated by other parents. Another parent, a mother with a passion for camping, arranged a hike in the woods during school hours and an optional overnight camping trip that was attended by most of the families and both teachers. Parents and children regularly collect natural materials and other items from home to enhance the work in the classroom mini-studios and in the Studio.

During vacations, families record their experiences by writing memories in a book or collecting items in a bag or small box. These experiences can provoke new directions for curricula or support ongoing curriculum investigations. By making these strong connections between home and school, by placing a high value on family experiences, and by communicating with the parents about what is happening in the classroom through daily journals, documentation panels, and class notes, collaboration develops and teachers', children's, and parents' learning is expanded and deepened.

"Through documentation we are invited in, as parents, to see what our children are doing in daily experiences. It changes the expectation of parents when they see pictures of parents involved around the school. They begin to formulate a new equation: I, as a parent, get to be a part of all this, if I choose to be."   —Ami Cohen

CREATING A LEARNING COMMUNITY FOR THE CHILDREN

"So how, specifically, do you have a deep level of parent involvement that is integrated into the school and that impacts the learning of young children? First, a willingness on the part of the director, the staff, and the teachers to create an open environment, one that is inclusive and collaborative; an environment where listening is vital; a place to belong, a place to find a friend, a place to discover oneself alongside your child. In short, our community is a second home where people have opportunities to offer up their diverse abilities in uniting together for the common good. Projects don't happen here in isolation. Instead, they happen through negotiation and a sharing of information and ideas. In turn, parents also open themselves to letting teachers show them aspects of themselves and their child that may be challenging at times to see. The basic belief is that both teachers and parents are sharing information, building trust, and having honest communication and, because of this, they jointly are able to reflect the child in a multidimensional light."   —Ami Cohen

When we deepen the connection between parents, teachers, and children, we begin to create a community because we are listening and learning from each other. About three times a year, there are classroom meetings where parents and teachers can share an experience, like working with clay, painting with watercolors, or making music, and then discuss the current work in the room and brainstorm together about possibilities for the curriculum.

For example, at a classroom meeting in the Rose Room, a class for 3-year-olds, the parents began by breaking into small groups to a create a short musical composition that expressed a feeling. A basket of instruments was provided and after a great deal of fun sharing their compositions, the parents discussed their creative experience. The teachers shared how the children were investigating musical instruments in the classroom. They explained that one day at Morning Meeting during their greeting song, one child made the sounds and motions of playing a trombone instead of singing. Other children joined him in "playing" the trombone. Each day after that, the children discussed what instrument to "play" during the greeting song. Observing this continued interest, the teachers brought various instruments like triangles, rainsticks, tambourines, and finger cymbals into the mini-studio, where the children began investigating the shapes, materials, and sounds of these instruments. After listening to the teachers' sharing of the children's experiences, the parents had many ideas about how to support this interest. Two fathers who were musicians would bring in large drums and play them with the children. A mother said she would invite her father to come and play the bagpipes. A father knew that the pipe organ at a nearby church was being repaired. He would bring in some of the old pipes and arrange for the children to visit the church and hear the organ. Music continues to be a strong focus of these children as they move into their second year.

Through the collaboration of parents and teachers, the learning opportunities for children are greatly expanded. Many parents become involved in their children's ongoing investigations and others find new ways to contribute to the classroom. After one class meeting, a parent commented: "Thank you so much for these classroom meetings. I learn so much about Lionel and myself. You help me see my child in an elevated way."

CREATING A LEARNING COMMUNITY FOR THE PARENTS

The director facilitates bimonthly discussions where parents can dialogue about the concerns and challenges of raising children. Parents drop in to talk, listen, support each other, and be supported. New parents often find these morning meetings to be a place where lasting friendships are begun. "The morning discussions play a vital role

Parents as Partners   113

in bringing parents together in an informal and nonjudgmental setting where we feel free to admit our parenting challenges." —Laurie Grotstein

Recently we created a parent area with a small couch, two chairs, bookshelves, and a documentation board next to the office where parents can meet on an impromptu basis.

"First Pres. has always been a community—because of its relationship to the church, to the neighborhood of Santa Monica and, primarily, because of the culture of openness that exists here and is cultivated by the director and the staff. So community doesn't have to be invented. But there are always opportunities for growth. Two years ago, I was asked to serve as co-president of the Parent Association. Now, even though the school is committed to the proposition that every parent has a voice, I began to realize that not every parent knows they have a voice. So we tried to remedy that situation by developing some new channels of communication. We started using e-mail, which was new to the school. By the end of the year, more than 60 percent of families were receiving online information such as recaps of Parent Association meetings, and we were getting feedback from them. The immediacy of e-mail makes it an ideal way to keep parents in touch with the daily business of their child's life at school. We're now planning to expand our Internet program to connect parents and teachers by classroom, as a supplement to the documentation process that already exists here." —Laurie Grotstein

The Parent Association, which was started 15 years ago, has an organization and structure that provides the flexibility to grow with each new group of parents. It was the Parent Association that set up classroom mailboxes on the Internet, and the teachers are now exploring new ways to use e-mail to collaborate with the parents. It involves over 100 parents serving on 23 committees. There are committees that organize school-wide events like picnics and parent/teacher workdays that reach out to the community with food drives and support to a local childcare center for homeless families and another center on the outskirts of Mexico City. There is a committee that produces our monthly newsletter, while another supports the documentation process. And of course there are hospitality, parent tours, library, school safety, and fund-raising committees.

The Parent Association organizes a series of parent education evenings each year, choosing topics that parents have requested such as Bringing Reggio into Our Homes, Keeping Children Healthy, and Transitioning to Kindergarten. This vibrant and active Parent Association brings parents throughout the school together, involves them with the entire staff, and strengthens our sense of community. As we have become a school community in which parents, teachers, and children respect each other and are open to learning from each other, we have developed a true partnership with the parents. There is a richness and authenticity to our relationships that is the direct result of our collaboration; this creates the possibilities for deeper learning for all of us.

"As we become more whole as parents, as we are given dignity, listened to, and have a safe and joyous place to learn and express ourselves, we offer this to our children. We do this not only by way of example, but also by empathizing and connecting to our children's developing sense of becoming their full selves—listened to, respected, questioning, discovering, and ultimately empowered." —Ami Cohen

11

Caregiving Through a Relationships Lens

Carolyn Pope Edwards

Professor, Departments of Psychology and Family and Consumer
Sciences, University of Nebraska, Lincoln

From the beginning of life, babies are eager to engage and interact with the people around them. Even at such a young age, they are capable of directing their attention and interest beyond the family toward any adults and children who seem friendly and exciting or loving. Although parents mediate their child's early interactions and relationships, infants actively reach out for relationships and want to manage their pace, content, and degree of closeness. In today's world of childcare and working parents, these babies have new opportunities to become part of social groups beyond their immediate families. They want to be participants in the community (Malaguzzi, 1993; Rinaldi, 2001).

THE DANCE OF RELATIONSHIPS

Thus, nonparental adults such as providers, teachers, and directors of early childhood programs become significant figures in children's lives—implicit or explicit partners in what we have called a "relationship dance" (Edwards & Raikes, 2002).

Sensitive, emotionally available parents create the framework for interaction with the infant by responding to the baby's cues, engaging the baby in mutual gazes, and imitating the baby. The baby, born with a primary ability to share emotions with other human beings and the need to join in and "learn a culture," eagerly joins the relationship dance (Thoman, 1987). The child depends on the nurturance and concern of others in order to survive, so right from the start, relationships are crucial to existence. Attachment, which forms as a result of the first satisfying relationships, organizes further development by providing the child with the foundations and motivations to move forward and get to know, interact with, and trust meaningful people. The intimate family circle soon widens to include peer friends and teachers, thereby extending the dance to include new relationships.

Close relationships, first within and then reaching beyond the family, are believed to be critical to healthy intellectual, emotional, social, and physical development in childhood and adolescence as well. These conclusions have been documented by diverse fields of science, ranging from cognitive science to communication studies and social and personality psychology. They also include many studies showing how relationship dysfunction is linked to child abuse and neglect, aggression, criminality, and other problems involving the lack of significant human connections (Shonkoff & Meisels, 2000). More positively, in recent years developmental scientists have also explored the facets of relationships that contribute to security and trust, promote skill development and understanding, nurture healthy physical growth, infuse developing self-understanding and self-confidence, enable self-control and emotion regulation, and strengthen emotional connections with others that contribute to prosocial motivation (Dunn, 1993; Fogel, 1993; Thompson, 1998).

In extending the dance of primary relationships to new relationships, a childcare teacher can play a primary role. The teacher makes the space ready—creating a beautiful place that causes everyone to feel like dancing (Edwards & Raikes, 2002). For a new baby who is just entering, the teacher must take the initiative to become attuned and get into rhythm with the baby by following his lead. Because the newcomer enters the program "in the arms" of parents, the teacher also enfolds parents into this process.

Gradually, as the dance between them becomes smooth and familiar, the teacher encourages the baby to try out more complex steps and learn how to dance to new compositions, beats, and tempos. The dance partnership can also widen as both infant and adult try out new partners, and as new peers or teachers are added to their group. As the baby alternates dancing sometimes with one or two partners, sometimes with many, the dance itself becomes a story about who the child has been and who the child is becoming, a reciprocal self created through close relationships.

This chapter describes the kinds of benefits these widening relationships can provide for very young children and outlines some specific steps that teachers in Reggio Emilia have taken to ensure the best, most "amiable" environments.

THE PRIMARY COMPONENTS OF RELATIONSHIPS

Given children's requirements for human support, teachers and caregivers need a basic vocabulary for talking about children's emotional health and well-being. Children have a variety of needs and desires that their cultures must respond to in appropriate ways to build satisfying relationships. According to Josselson (1996), there are eight such needs whose satisfaction contributes to fostering relatedness. These are holding (i.e. the need to be held), attachment, recognition and validation, mutuality and companionship, passionate experience, identification, embeddedness, and opportunities to give care and help other people. As each way of building relatedness emerges within the life course, it is at first concrete and elemental, but then becomes more symbolic and complex.

We will describe each need (summarizing Josselson's descriptions), suggest how satisfaction of this need relates to positive outcomes for the child's development, and finally describe how the infant-toddler environment (physical and human) can satisfy this need in an appropriate way.

Certainly, we would not claim there to be only one appropriate solution. Just as there are many styles of dancing, so throughout the world cultural communities embed their children in close, rhythmic relationships with caring people in many ways. The language and customs may vary, but their essence is similar and the primary needs the same (Whiting & Edwards, 1988). It is only necessary for the caregivers and cultural community to "hear" the child and "speak" back.

Holding

Holding is the most primary need but is not easy to describe. It involves our earliest interpersonal experience of being encircled and contained safely by protective, powerful arms. Clinical psychologist Erik Erikson (1985) called the resultant sense of safety and predictability "basic trust," and David Winnicott (1965) described the "good enough" mother who provides an adequate "holding environment." In the absence of such basic caregiving, exemplified by feeding, carrying, calming, and protecting from too intense stimuli, babies are overwhelmed by fear and anxiety. The developmental outcomes of adequate holding are sense of safety, confidence, optimism, and a general expectation of support. Children can open up to the world when they know that someone will be "there" when needed—not smothering them, but also not letting them flail around and become exhausted and desperate. Thus, the caregiving environment must provide safety, protection, nourishment, and comfort.

Well-being, or "being at ease," is promoted in Reggio Emilia through beautiful, orderly, harmonious, "amiable" spaces (Gandini with Bondavalli, 2001; Rinaldi, 2001), as well as through adult readiness to hold and touch children and use endearing terms to soften moments of interaction.

Attachment

Attachment is the second relational need and the one most substantiated through research. Attachment arises from the child's need for proximity, security, comfort, and care. John Bowlby (1969) spoke of the child's "bond" or "tie" to the mother and argued that attachment constitutes a primary biological system. Attachments provide the child with relief when distressed and with security to explore. When attachments are disrupted, children may enter the separation cycle of first, protest; then, sorrow and despair; and finally, indifference. The developmental outcomes of secure attachment are emotional regulation (the capacity to feel, express, and control emotions in culturally appropriate ways) and competence motivation (the desire to learn and move forward in development).

Educational supports for attachment in Reggio Emilia involve devoting attention to delicate beginnings, satisfying celebrations, and careful endings as children and families move through the centers; harmonious separations and reunions each day; and close communication and continuity of care between home and center over time. Skilled, attuned caregivers know how to establish rapport and empathy with children and families and bring children into the life of the center and the new circle of relationships there (Gandini with Bondavalli, 2001; Edwards & Raikes, 2002).

Recognition and Validation

When the child looks into a special adult's eyes and is looked at in return, this creates an emotional meaning between them (Trevarthen, 1995). Each receives the sense of being recognized, or "seen." Eye-to-eye contact with babies is something natural and universal, but all the senses can play a part in the experience of being recognized and appreciated, as when babies are "heard," "touched," and "noticed." Through such moments, the child begins to realize that he or she, and everyone else, is a "self," with a subjective inner life. The developmental outcomes of adequate recognition are self-identity and the beginning of empathic understanding of others.

Educational supports for recognition and validation are a human and physical environment that makes visible each child and family. Instead of feeling impersonal and anonymous, the environment individualizes the experience of coming into the center. The children find their names, faces, personalities, connections, favorite things, and preferences reflected through the ways that teachers speak to them, display photographs about them, and organize routines and activities. Reggio Emilia has embodied the philosophy of "education as relationships" (Malaguzzi, 1993) through particular ways of communication and documentation (Gandini & Goldhaber, 2001). These welcome the child to social life in the group and mirror and interpret each child's and family's place in and contribution to that life. The process is well summed up by Carlina Rinaldi, who said, "You cannot have a school in which the child doesn't feel right, in which the teacher doesn't feel right, in which the family doesn't feel right. It is essential to create a school and infant-toddler center in which all the subjects feel welcomed, a place of relationships" (2001, p. 53).

Mutuality and Companionship

Mutuality, being with others and joining in, is first seen in the infant's joint attention ("looking together") that then evolves into pointing and sharing. The psychologist Colwyn Trevarthen (1995) has written of the child's desire to produce meaning through emotional joining, and the great pleasures the child feels when moving or communicating in synchrony and rhythm with others, thereby creating a "space of we." The developmental outcomes of experiencing adequate mutuality are capacities for cooperation and companionship.

The educational supports for mutuality are easy to provide. Children need time and space for involved, ongoing peer relationships and rituals, such as are portrayed in *The Little Ones of Silent Movies* (Reggio Children, 1996), a story of make-believe with the children and fish at the Rodari infant-toddler center in Reggio Emilia. As children mature, they also develop mutuality by participating in group games and expressive activities involving singing, shouting, clapping, and hand motions. They eagerly join in with dancing, chanting, marching, and chasing. These ancient and joyful forms of play create heightened emotion through the use of synchrony, rhythm, and/or patterned turn-taking and alternation.

Passionate Experience

Passionate connections involve intense feelings and create a drive to be with another person, touch them, and overcome separation. Young children do feel passion—for parents and for peers. They then must learn to express their feelings in socially acceptable ways. It helps them to work through their feelings if they can play out scenarios that attract and fascinate them and talk through their thoughts and feelings. Symbolic and verbal behavior carry them beyond the real world into the realm of imagination and back again. To do this emotional "work," children need spaces that invite complex pretend play, and sometimes enclosed places that provide a sense of seclusion and privacy from the larger group, where imagination often flourishes best. The developmental outcomes of passionate feelings are capacities for intense and tender relationships, heightened imagination, and fantasy, and rich symbolism.

Educational supports include allowing and encouraging children to have intense friendships and attractions to particular "special friends." At the Diana preschool in Reggio Emilia, the 5-year-olds set the table for lunch leaving aside a little table for two, where "sweethearts" could sit together (*Diana Hop*, Reggio Children, 1990, unpublished). The book, *Tenderness* (Reggio Children, 1995), tells the story of two 5-year-olds at the Villetta preschool. Daniele has known Laura since they were little; he feels that he "loves" her and wants to marry her when he grows up. She says he is her "bestest" friend ("it's like my heart almost explodes"). The story presents some of their conversations about heaven, birth, the beginnings of the world, and the future.

Identification

Identification is a process that draws us to observe and imitate those whom we admire and want to be like. Through identification, the child takes the admired other into the self and participates in adult power and competence. Sigmund Freud (1969) was a great theorist of identification, but Albert Bandura (1971) and other social learning theorists have operationalized the concept and validated the theory. Identification provides the child with moral guidance and helps her make choices based on what she thinks the admired adult would do. The developmental outcomes of adequate identification are the establishment of conscience and faith in the goodness of adults.

Educational supports include caring adults who act as moral models and support ethical behavior and discussion in age-appropriate ways. The project narrative, *A Journey into the Rights of Children* (Reggio Children, 1995), portrays children's own concepts of their rights in discussions at the Diana preschool in Reggio Emilia.

Embeddedness

Embeddedness has to do with being part of a social group—a community of place, kinship, values, or memories and shared experience. Children's early experiences of group belonging have to do with group experiences that usually extend beyond the nuclear family. Belonging to a group provides the child with an important part of self-identity, especially in traditional or collectivist societies, but also in individualistic ones, even though people may be less aware of its influence. Rituals, literature, history, myths, and folktales are the cultural expression of embeddedness—as are such negative outcomes as exclusion and ethnocentrism. The cultural psychologist, Barbara Rogoff (1990), believes that "participation" and "apprenticeship in thinking" are the means by which children appropriate the cultural tools and skills of language, communication, and interaction. Children become embedded in a particular cultural community.

In Reggio Emilia, educational supports for group belonging are provided by documentation, project work, and group decision-making. These group activities create a sense of classroom community and bridge children to the wider world around the school. The project narrative, *Theater Curtain: The Ring of Transformations* (Reggio Children, 2002), portrays how children from the Diana Preschool designed and created a glorious new house curtain for the Ariosto Theater. The book, *Reggio Tutta: A Guide to the City by the Children Themselves* (Reggio Children, 2000), begins with a survey of the children in the municipal infant-toddler centers and preschools and presents their collective portrait of the city identity and their advice about visiting and living there. This unique "guidebook" demonstrates that even young children can have a strong sense of place and embeddedness. Other ways that children learn symbols of group life include folktales, drama, and puppetry. Puppetry is especially important in Reggio Emilia, and a professional puppeteer serves all of the schools. An old saying about children and storytelling goes, "Adults listen to stories with their heads, but children with their hearts."

Giving Care

The philosopher, Nell Noddings (1984), has written about the ethics of care and responsiveness as organizers of experience. The roots of care and responsibility lie in the first, simple, socially valued behaviors seen in most toddlers, when they share and show, try to help with household work, try to help someone in distress, and imitate and seek others' attention to prolong pleasure. Being helpful and kind allows the child to feel competent, powerful, and grown-up. Prosocial behavior moves the child from dependence to interdependence, and its developmental outcomes are dispositions toward kindness, helpfulness, responsibility, and leadership.

The educational supports for giving care are opportunities to help, give care, show kindness, and take the lead. The anthropologists, Beatrice and John Whiting, showed how nurturance and prosocial responsibility are fostered in a multitude of cultures where children share in the subsistence work and sibling care in large, multi-age households (Whiting & Edwards, 1988).

In Reggio Emilia centers, children become part of a community where they are inducted into the life and rituals by the oldest children, then gradually grow themselves to become the "big kids" teaching the little newcomers. Children participate in the ordinary routines of daily life, such as setting the table and preparing cots for naptime.

Even small children have occasions to give as well as receive care, as illustrated by Bondavalli's story about Francesca, a girl aged 24 months, who helped another toddler, Mattia, settle in at the Peter Pan Infant-Toddler Center. When Mattia was distressed over being separated from his mother, Francesca watched closely and then came over to him and said, "Come on, Mattia, don't cry! You will see, your mommy will come back." Mattia accepted this and began to really like Francesca and to feel comfortable in the group (Gandini with Bondavalli, 2001).

CONCLUSIONS

Children need more from their childcare program than just the possibility of secure (secondary) attachment. They also need human relationships that provide safety, recognition, friendship, intensity, identification, belonging, and opportunities to be helpful and caring. Educators can look at the quality of their programs and services through a "relationship lens" so that practices support rather than undermine relationships. There are many ways to support and strengthen relations between each child and all of the others—peers and adults—at the center. Through acting on the insight that all children can form multiple connections and enter a group life, teachers can support them in moving out with skill and confidence.

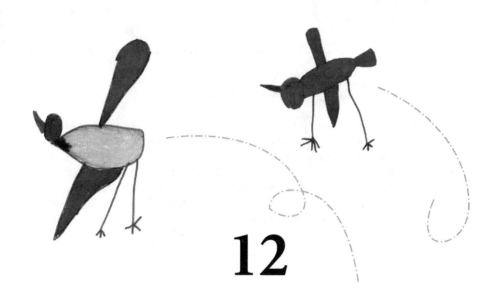

12

The Relational Rights of Children in Our Care

Deborah Alexandrea Doherty

When my colleagues and I first heard Carolyn Edwards' presentation at the National Association for the Education of Young Children (NAEYC) about children's relational needs in infant and toddler care, we became excited about what it could say about our program. Our context in Canada is a laboratory school for infants, toddlers, and preschoolers in a small community college that had been on the path of dialogue with Reggio Emilia educators and their approach for five or six years. We were confident that we were working with children, parents, teachers, pedagogy, and environments from a relationships framework, but we wanted a new way to reevaluate our own values and re-enchant ourselves about children's processes of self-development.

As we began to document the eight relational needs in a presentation for each other, we reflected more deeply on our values and the pedagogy of relationships. The beauty and challenge of this schema had a dynamic effect and (thinking about ways that Reggio Emilia has inspired us) provoked us to look at relational *rights* of the child! In other words, we went from thinking about children's wants and needs to talking about what we *owe* to them and *should do* for them. I want to illustrate this by telling some of the stories the discussions led to in our school.

HOLDING

We first looked at the value of the relational need (right) of holding, and asked what we thought it meant. Holding is a simple value, yet elusive. We searched for its traces in our school. How did this value reveal itself in our interactions? How did our environment mirror this relational right? We nostalgically revisited our documentation to see how we had captured images of holding. Then we discussed the very specific ways we could make the relational right evident in our everyday relationships with the children, parents, pedagogy, environment, rhythms, and rituals of the day.

As a metaphor for holding, I chose the phrase, "embracing the essence," to symbolize to my colleagues how we try to carry out this value. Then I must tell you how surprised I was, when preparing a slide presentation for my colleagues, to discover virtually no photographs portraying teacher-child interactions during which a child was held in anyone's arms! I asked us to examine their hearts and minds and ask the difficult question, "Do we value embracing the children?"

After individual and collective reflection, we emphatically concluded that we do, but perhaps were not making it transparent to others. Did we take this value so much for granted that we did not think it needed recording? We asked ourselves, How did our documentation reflect our practice and what we were communicating to parents and children? Were we thereby giving the impression that our pedagogy was more important than the relationships? Were we working so hard to illustrate teacher efforts and the work of children that we were overlooking the importance of presenting the tenderness of relationships?

Many days we enjoyed the luxury of beak-to-nose encounters, when children and birds beheld each other through the window glass.

We next turned to our environment and asked about its holding qualities. We decided that in order to answer the question, we needed to turn it around and consider it from the children's point of view. How did the children embrace and (be)hold their environment? One example that became important for us involved the children's delight in the warm sunlight coming in the window. They would climb up on a radiator to bask in the sunshine, and then (good caregivers that we were) we would encourage them to keep their feet on the floor. Then one day, we stood back and listened to the silent dialogue between child and window. The question confronted us, "Really, why can't the children sit in the window?" We began to build a structure that would straddle over the radiator and offer a pleasing construction and safe haven for the children to regard the world outside. Our children began to observe the coming and goings of parents, other children, and vehicles.

About that time, the children had begun a relationship with a sea gull that opportunistically visited during their stroller walks. Our babies (and the gull) enjoyed snack during their walks, and sometimes cracker and muffin crumbs would be left behind. What did these trails mean in "relationship language"? Could they be a trail for the children to find their way back to school, a communication for the birds, or both?

It was as if a question was resonating from the environment: What would happen if we placed birdhouses in the window? Would the birds follow the crumbs back to school? Would the birds understand the communication? Putting out birdhouses, we indeed did find that the birds came to meet the children, just as the children had met them on the walks. Many days we enjoyed the luxury of embracing the moments of beak-to-nose encounters, when children and birds beheld each other through the window glass.

We also asked ourselves whether we value tenderness and softening in the children's classroom. How did the environment caress the relationships that were beginning to form? Did the environment embrace, hold, nurture, and regard each child? Our previous experiences with the radiator and the birds allowed us to take the risk of not answering the question immediately. Instead, we attended to the dialogue between children and objects that may not have involved speaking out loud but nevertheless would communicate to us if we would listen. This hypothesis allowed us to trust ourselves, and the faces and responses of the children then told us that they felt we also trusted them and considered their knowledge and feelings to be important.

Finally, we again reflected on our documentation. How did it reflect our values about beholding the children in their environment? Again, we discovered that by concentrating so hard on illustrating the theories and investigations of children and teachers, we inadvertently were making the assumption that the basic relationships did not need to be captured. We were overlooking the importance of presenting the tenderness of relationships, whether person to person or baby to bird.

To make the relationships more visible, we found many things to do. We placed photographs (Polaroid pictures, 3 × 5 inch color reproductions, and 8 × 10 inch black-and-whites) in prominent places in the playroom. We also offered the families plastic bags at registration time to use over the summer to capture their child's summer interests, as a foundation for experiences and pedagogy next fall. Then, when fall came, we shared in the children's bags of treasures and invited our parents to display them on a wreath that dangles from a grapevine on our ceiling. (If you hang the wreath horizontally, its resemblance to a nest is evident.) We placed family albums in all of our rooms to embrace the families throughout the day. We also measured the height of each parent, child, and teacher, intertwined sets of ribbons of these three lengths in a circle, and placed these around each doorway to symbolize our ongoing support of each other. We put images of the children onto their blankets and transitional objects with elastic ribbons, so the children could have cozy moments throughout the day with objects conveying love and warmth. The photos also invited the children to offer these important moments to each other.

ATTACHMENT

The second relational right of attachment suggested the metaphor "to hold most closely and let go," a phrase that returns to the first right and builds a bridge to next steps. As teachers, we pondered how to build good relationships with the other sides of the parents-children-teachers triangle.

We examined the environment in light of the metaphor. How did the environment create a space for the children to feel secure enough to know that they could venture forth connected to the ground but could also take flight? At the time, teachers altered the rooms each week to reflect themes such as a jungle, harvest celebration, or seawater aquarium. We looked at the traces the children left behind in their play (kind of like the crumbs for the birds) to try to find places where they especially liked to play or be together. We hung a large, blue parachute (from a nearby military base) from the ceiling in their cuddly area, and kept available children's blankets and objects of attachment like teddy bears and soft pillows. The parachute streaming down created a translucent space that drew a soft, dreaming energy into a billowy envelope where children offered each other warmth. The good feelings spread throughout the day, and often at nap time children would retrieve each other's blankets and tuck each other in to sleep.

Carla Rinaldi once spoke to the Canadian delegation about how "the other" defines us—how the teachers in Reggio Emilia could offer us a definition of ourselves and our country, and how we from another country could offer the teachers in Reggio insights about themselves and their culture. Thus, knowledge comes through contemplating contrasts, like light and shadow, up and down, and ultimately, like you and me. How could we help the children to experience the idea that through contrasts with things that are different from us, we can see how we are all the same? We made a risky hypothesis, "What if we introduced an overhead projector into the toddler room and shone the images throughout the room?"

One day, with little fanfare and a lot of faith, the overhead projector made the acquaintance of five of our most inquisitive and vivacious toddlers. The children placed their faces close to the lamp, squinted, and smiled. They placed one hand close to the warmth of the glass, jiggling their feet, and then placed their colder hand close to the warm one. Their toes beckoned them to bend down low so they could hear the fan whirring musically, and they pointed to the grate that allowed the air to circulate. They smiled their widest grins and went running off to bring a friend. The exploration continued, and they began to improvise. They brought their teddy bears and favorite toys to say hello to the overhead and to share in the warmth of the experience. Then they sat on the overhead together and noticed the big shadow that appeared on the blue parachute. They looked at each other, pointed at the shadow, and looked at each other again. Were they wondering what could make such a shadow? They hopped off the projector, maybe to tell this new friend (the projector) about the big shadow, and pointed to show the shadow on the big blue parachute. And in trying to introduce the shadow to the light, somehow the shadow disappeared. As teachers we could have solved this mystery for them, but we knew that holding close also means letting go. We supported the children for several hours, encouraging them to capture the light and the shadow meeting together. The source of their embrace eluded the toddlers until two little boys looked at their favorite toy on the glass of the overhead, smiled at each other, turned to look at the parachute, and discovered together the shape of the toy! The children's love affair with light and shadow persisted throughout their toddler and preschool years. The group helped create a large shadow screen, a light table in the studio, and ultimately a light and shadow *atelier* in our school, as measures of their attachment.

Next we looked at the process of acquaintanceship when children joined the program. We regarded every new relationship, with everyone and everything, as making a new acquaintance or friend. Welcoming each child, toy, ritual, and routine as a new friend illuminated the possibilities of attachment. We examined the rhythms of the day, identified the most important appointments to keep (meal and rest), and allowed the other moments to flow around them.

To safeguard the attachments that were forming, we organized ourselves into primary caregiving groups. From the beginning, children became part of a group composed of a teacher and some friends, and together they would move from infancy through preschool. They experienced appointments and experiences together, often separately from other groups. We looked at opportunities to smooth and reduce transitions during the appointments and experiences of the day. The Italian systems offer us the concept of *insertimento* for the settling in process of incorporating a new child (and family) into the group. To help the children feel attachment for their whole classroom, we placed their photographs on items for which they demonstrated affection, including blankets, cots, cubbies, water sippers, and daily journals.

RECOGNITION

The relational right of recognition inspired the metaphorical phrase "eye to eye, ear to ear, hand to hand, and mind to mind." Collectively we teachers strongly identified with this value and its emphasis on the individual child. We had observed other programs that treated the child only as part of a group and did not validate the image of each child. Remembering this together created feelings of isolation, a kind of ironic confirmation of the need for recognition and the value of the self-reflection path we were traveling.

We were inspired to see each other for our strengths, not our differences. Sharing insights and actively listening to one another, we experienced the same comforting sensations of recognition as the children do. But then we were reminded of how we view the children (Are they needy? Do they need us?), unsettling our image of ourselves as strong and venerable. Letting go of that self-image and co-creating curriculum with babies and toddlers was an adventure that shook our egos and minds but nurtured our hearts and souls.

Just as we needed to recognize the vulnerable side of ourselves, we also needed to recognize the capabilities of our children. We often underestimate the symbolic capacities of small children because we assume they are in a sensory-motor stage of development. Yet our infants and toddlers created both two- and three-dimensional representations. We introduced play dough in our infant and toddler rooms many years ago, and the children used the medium as a language of expression and means for communicating ideas to each other. They liked to tell stories as they manipulated the material, often speaking of an unrelated experience as their small hands almost absent-mindedly created characters and creatures to be shown and shared. One child at age 3 began to create a whole cast of dough and plasticine characters that he used

We recognize and reflect each child's ongoing presence by using photos, recorded texts, and panels.

to carry on "Claymation" shows for his friends that he would direct and record and ultimately post on a website.

How did we try to recognize and reflect each child's ongoing presence in the environment? In photos, recorded texts, and panels, we endeavored to ensure that we nurtured everyone's hopes and possibilities. We also used images to make it legible to even the youngest children. For instance, we labeled the children's juice sippers with black-and-white pictures, and placed them in a small refrigerator in the dramatic play area ("symbolic representation"), so they could identify and meet their own needs to drink. The children also could retrieve their friends' sippers by recognizing the image on the side, and then a pair might take their cups and retreat into a quiet area together.

MUTUALITY

I chose the metaphor, "and heart to heart," to signify the relational right of mutuality as a continuation of the "eye to eye" of recognition. Cooperation and companionship begin with seeing oneself reflected in the eyes of another, which extends into joint attention and sharing of objects and builds into heartfelt action together.

In illustration, we return to the parachute and projector, which offered the children many moments of heart-to-heart companionship. They would bring beloved objects to their old friend the overhead projector, who would shine them forth not only on the blue parachute but also on the floor and ceiling and even their own bodies. They would burst into delighted laughter at recognizing a shadowy Barney toy, silhouetted truck, or gray shape of a leaf resting on their tummies. They would choose items together and then make up jokes and little shows for each other, moving to more advanced levels of role-playing and pretending. One particular little boy who was going to be a ring bearer in a wedding liked to retrieve a pillow from underneath the parachute, turn on the overhead, and then perform the "wedding march shadow charade." He would peek around the folds of illuminated material and smile until his teacher and friends cried out, "The wedding!"

This area became a place where children could plan experiences together. We made overhead transparencies of each child's photography, so they could use and share symbolic representation of themselves while they were at school, and more importantly, when they were not! They also could communicate ideas through light-and-shadow puppet shows and charades. One day, a 16-mm film projector was the toddlers' object of play, with the parachute serving as the screen. As before, the children introduced the

The mutual friendship of two babies enjoying togetherness in the translucent space of a parachute, the resonances of their relationship becoming part of their every experience. These children will spend the next five years together and continue through elementary school together.

movie image to the floor, ceiling, and each others' tummies. It became an ongoing ritual of mutuality for these children to go with the teacher to get this film projector, walking down the long halls of the college to the audio/visual area, finding the projector, and bringing it back with movies to enjoy over and over again.

PASSION

The fifth relational right—passion—suggested the question, "Who (and what) do the children love?" "Percolation of joy" was the metaphor I chose to describe how they absorb love and contentment from those who care for them, and carry those feelings through their days and lives.

When reflecting on this, we recognized a conflict between our professional intentions of focusing on children's development and outcomes versus our personal involvement in their daily passions, which gave us so much satisfaction and pleasure. We decided to regard the school as a place of little stories that have a right to be captured and embraced, and we shifted our focus from the obligatory to the passionate. We looked within our spaces for niches of joy.

Imagine 16 children (aged 3 to 30 months) playing in the classroom when a puppet, in a surprise visit, announced his arrival by tapping his nose on the window. Slowly, in waves, the children recognized the sound as an invitation from their beloved friend, Crazy Cow. They pointed to the window and ran toward it with friends, screaming, clapping, and laughing. The teachers provided a next step by asking, "Should we sing the Crazy Cow song?" The children nodded and danced, swirled, hopped, stamped, and sang at the top of their lungs until, at the song's end, Crazy Cow blew kisses and waved goodbye. The children offered kisses and farewells in return, but then, lo and behold, a puppet friend of Crazy Cow made his entrance, and the joyous chorus began again. This continued through all six of Crazy Cow's "friends." The children anticipated and announced each arrival and departure, ascribed characteristics to each puppet, and later created mailboxes and birthday parties for the puppets.

We created slide, video, and panel documentaries. We made overhead transparencies of the characters, laminated stick-puppets, and audiotaped the songs. When preparing our first panel of Crazy Cow and Friends (with their songs below the characters' photographs), we asked our toddlers their opinion of the panel. Its legibility was evident as they pointed to each photograph (beginning of course with the star, Crazy Cow) and serenaded each character's song. When we asked them where to place the panel ("On the wall?"), they adamantly shook their heads. They refused all our suggestions, so we asked them to show us. They took the panel and carefully placed it on the floor in front of the window where Crazy Cow had appeared. Then they danced and sang right on top of the panel, revealing their emerging capacity (developmental milestone!) toward decoding abstract visual symbols that were connected to strong memories and characters they were "crazy" about.

IDEALIZATION AND IDENTIFICATION

This relational right suggested a metaphor of "concentric circles." Gianni Rodari (1996), in *The Grammar of Fantasy*, wrote about how significant words affect the mind like a "stone thrown into a pond," provoking an infinite series of expanding waves and chain reactions (p. 5). In a similar way, relational moments affect children in profound ways that flow out through their work and play. Eventually, the underlying patterns (abstract values about human relationships) are internalized by children as lasting ideals.

We asked ourselves, Do our interactions and environment reflect good values, character, love of learning, and respect for others? We decided to reexamine our *ateliers*, as we thought they might mirror our values most clearly. (We have *ateliers* for infant/toddler sensory experiences, music, two- and three-dimensional episodes, and light and shadows). One story in particular illustrates how a child made visible his idealized image of his teacher as "co-learner."

Suzanne, a teacher, had invited Quinn to paint at the easel and asked him if he would paint a picture of her. He agreed and showed her just how he wanted her to

Self portrait: Quinn with teacher and toys.
Coloured drawing by Quinn Doherty-Prince

stand. When she praised his painting, he asked, "Well, how about you paint me now?" When she said she didn't feel confident about doing it, he reassured her, "That's all right. I think it will be just fine." When she finished, he told her, "Pretty good!"

Later, the portraits of Quinn and Suzanne were displayed side by side in the *atelier*, with supporting documentation. They revealed Quinn's and our values about reciprocity and shared control. Evidence of Quinn's internalized images was seen in his teacher, himself, and his world—a documentation called "Quinn with Teacher and Toys." Yet he would not have been drawn into producing that series of portraits without Suzanne having been ready to step out of her intended role and follow his idea, producing a pair of portraits that made visible the value of mutual respect and equality between adults and children.

EMBEDDEDNESS

Children are rooted by their self-understandings and relationships to others. They take in the culture(s) around them and weave their own autobiographical narrative (a "story of myself") to find a sense of belonging. Because Canada is a bilingual country, I chose the French verb, *rechercher* (to research), as most appropriate to the concept of relocating, remembering, and reviewing experience—turning over rocks in the earth to see what discoveries hide beneath. As we reflected on the right of belonging, we felt our metaphor would be "roots and wings." Caregivers (whether teachers or parents) have the responsibility to give a group of children a rich foundation in which to spread their roots and grow, so that they can later find their own possibilities and fly off toward the sun and stars.

We pondered what kind of *rechercher* infants and toddlers must do to establish firm roots and belonging. We decided that their clear, sometimes primitive demands ("I want that toy and it is mine!"), as well as their pure offerings of hugs and kisses, were bedrock experiences of being part of group life in our school. Their basic explorations in sensory play likewise provided them with the starting point for all their later, culturally shaped concepts and projects. Thus, when the children encountered elemental materials (water, cornmeal, tissue paper, cotton balls, tapioca, rice, paint, or clay), using authentic tools for their research (brushes, spoons, rakes, and scoops), while negotiating their actions in a group of peers, we could see them gaining the chance to reach down into their past and move upward toward new possibilities. Each such encounter led to the next until the resourcefulness of each child and the group became visible, and we asked "What can we now create together? What stories are you reminding us to express?"

We fervently hope that reverberations and re-stimulations of these experiences throughout their lives will allow our children to recapture their early moments of discovering themselves. For us teachers, too, (re)living with the children their moments of embeddedness allowed us to find again (*rechercher*) our basic sense of connectedness.

The foundation of experiences is built upon learning through sensory play, while learning from children and teachers. The sensory pool is filled with tapioca and tools to expand the possibilities of the moment.

GIVING CARE

As we came to the last relational right, we selected the metaphor "a tendency to tenderness." Whether our children choose to be rooted or to spread their wings, should teachers not wish for them the tendency toward tenderness, wherever they are, whomever they meet?

Reflecting on young children as givers of care led us up against two seeming contradictions. In the first place, we adults believed ourselves (not the children) to be the caregivers. Indeed, to be honest, we often felt empowered by the children's need for us and secure in the resources we provided. But remembering how Loris Malaguzzi inspired us to think of the child as strong, competent, and full of resources, we felt a disequilibrium. Thus, we were provoked to alter our perceptions of the neediness of the children. As our thinking shifted, we began to embrace a co-creative image of child and teacher, projecting competency and possibility onto both sides.

In the second place, when we looked at children's exchanges with one another, we did not always see them as giving each other care! The infant and toddler years, as we saw them, were translucent in their intensity and highlighted by vivacious children climbing, biting, dumping, pushing, grabbing, and thrusting. Yet, we had also found that when messages of tenderness surrounded the children and they became a cooperative group, different possibilities became apparent. We knew that our infants had communicated to us their wish to take care of the birds encountered on their daily walks. We revisited the many moments when our toddlers offered blankets and tucked each other in at sleep time, and our babies retrieved bottles and sipper cups and offered milk to one another. We concluded that a "pedagogy of listening" (Carlina Rinaldi) builds trust and security within each child, as well as reciprocity and relationship with the teacher.

A tendency to tenderness, and to helping one another, is where it begins and where it ends, only to begin again.

CONCLUSION

The journey we took in recasting the relational needs (rights) of our children in metaphorical terms helped us teachers reflect on many aspects of our experience and consider many questions that deepened as we understood the issues more fully and in shared language. The first and simplest right of holding ("embracing the essence") ultimately prompted us to ask, How together are we? We pondered the second right of attachment ("to hold most closely and let go") and came to wonder, How do differences bring us together? When we reaffirmed children's and adults' rights to recognition ("eye to eye, ear to ear, hand to hand, mind to mind. . . ") and to mutuality (". . . and heart to heart"), we learned how the environment offers different tools for fostering being together. We came to ask, Why do strength and vulnerability require each other? And likewise, in more stories than I can tell, the rights of intensity (passion), belonging (embeddedness), identification, and opportunities to be helpful and caring gave us our own meanings for Malaguzzi's vision of education as relationships.

Final note: I wish to thank the teachers, *pedagogistes, atelieristes,* children, parents, administrators, and politicians of Reggio Emilia past and present for offering us a relational dialogue that resonates across the miles. I also wish to thank my colleagues at the Centre for Early Childhood Education, administrators, parents, and children from whom I have learned so much. I offer a tender thanks to Carolyn Edwards for her encouragement, support, and collaboration in composing and revising this chapter.

V

Accepting the Challenge to Change by Doing Project Work

 The success of project work rests upon the fundamental ability to talk with and listen to children, so Part V begins with the chapter by Louise Cadwell and Brenda Fyfe demonstrating how to have a genuine conversation with them. The chapter includes practical advice about how to carry on open-ended discussions that uncover what the children know and encourage them to put their ideas into words. It then adds an actual example of such a discussion between a teacher and children, and concludes with a discussion by four teachers analyzing in Reggio style what had been said in the teacher-child discussion and formulating ideas of potential projects that might emerge from it.

Another important component of project work is making certain the project truly emerges from the concerns and interests of the children. In chapter 14, we are invited to sympathize with Donna Williams and Rebecca Kantor as Donna agonizes over her initial attempts to generate such a curriculum by following the children's lead during an investigation of water. At the chapter's close, she offers some helpful conclusions she reached about how to tell whether a project is truly emergent or is just another teacher-generated experience.

Lest readers conclude that project work must wait until children reach the ages of four or five, in chapter 15 Nicole May, Rebecca Kantor, and Michele Sanderson provide delightful evidence to the contrary by explaining how two young children, Gus, aged 18 months, and Meredith, 23 months, participated in a project based on a series of "lost and found" experiences.

Finally, Pam Oken-Wright offers us a description of how the 5-year-olds in her group spent several months investigating the questions of what snow is and where it comes from. The inclusion of pictures illustrating each step of that investigation, together with an "investigation map" showing how one provocation led to another, will be a big help to readers yearning for clarification about how such projects develop.

SOME EXCERPTS FROM LELLA'S CHAPTERS

Projects provide the backbone of the children's and teachers' learning experiences. They are based on the strong conviction that learning by doing is of great importance and that to discuss in group as well as to revisit ideas and experiences is the premier way of gaining better understanding and learning.

Ideas for projects originate in the continuum of the experience of children and teachers as they construct knowledge together following the inquisitive minds of children. . . .

It flows naturally that, to be truly respectful of children's and teachers' ideas and processes of learning, the curriculum cannot be set in advance. Teachers express general goals and make hypotheses about what direction experiences and projects might take and, consequently, they make appropriate preparations. These general goals and hypotheses are also based on their experience as teachers, their knowledge of each child, and the dynamic of their group of children. Then, after observing the children in action, they compare, discuss, and interpret together their observations. They discuss what they have recorded through their own notes or through audio or visual recording and make flexible plans and preparations. Teachers make choices (sharing them with the children) about what to offer and how to sustain exploration and learning.

. . . [F]lexible planning is constructed in the process of each experience or project and is adjusted accordingly through this continuous dialogue among teachers and with children.

A CHALLENGE FROM LILIAN

It is my impression that the Reggio Emilia preprimary schools have taken project work with young children further than any other groups of practitioners. In particular, they have succeeded in making the "graphic languages"—as they refer to them—a major aspect of children's project work in fresh and significant ways. Why should we not do more of this as well?

13

Conversations with Children

Louise Boyd Cadwell

Studio Teacher/Researcher, The St. Louis Reggio Collaborative,
St. Louis, Missouri

Brenda Varel Fyfe

Professor of Education, Webster University, St. Louis, Missouri

A network of teachers from several schools in St. Louis, Missouri, has been working together for 3 years to study the principles and practices of the Reggio Emilia Approach. The content of this chapter is drawn from our work with these teachers and reflections on our individual and collective experiences. We wish to express our thanks to all of the teachers, parents, and administrators with whom we collaborated in this learning process and especially to Jan Phillips, director of the College School, a private and independent school in Webster Groves, Missouri, who took the administrative lead in codirecting this project with us. And, of course, we are indebted to all of the Italian educators who have been and continue to be our friends, teachers, and colleagues.

We have chosen to focus on one particular area of our learning that has been strongly influenced by the Reggio Emilia Approach—dialogue with children. Louise begins by reflecting on what she learned as an intern for 1 year in Reggio Emilia and then practiced and further developed through her work in St. Louis. She identifies potential barriers and conditions that affect teachers' abilities to facilitate and analyze dialogues with children. This discussion is followed by a set of guidelines for facilitating good conversations.

To illustrate the process of analyzing dialogues and using them to inform emergent curriculum, we have chosen to share a synopsis of a meeting among a team of four educators who came together to study the transcripts of dialogues that had been facilitated by Louise. Brenda describes this meeting and the curriculum planning that emerged from the study of children's words. This is followed by her analysis of the process of planning for emergent curriculum and the professional development benefits for teachers who collaborate in this kind of work.

CONVERSATIONS WITH CHILDREN

A key component of the work in the Reggio Emilia preschools is dialogue—serious talk with children about their ideas on something of importance. The group of children can be large (the whole class), medium (around 10 to 15), or small (around 4 to 6). Teachers also have conversations with pairs of children or one child at a time. The idea every time is to explore the children's ideas.

The teacher's role is to ask good, open-ended questions that stimulate children's thinking and provoke discussion—to facilitate, orchestrate, and gently guide so that the conversation does not stray too far from the subject, so that every child has a chance to participate, and so that children consider the matter at hand with all their critical and creative thinking skills. The teacher should not fish for right answers or impart information. Rather, the teacher's role is to extend and deepen the children's thinking. This approach is a departure from the traditional idea of the teacher's role.

The motivation for placing these conversations at the center of the curriculum is to enable children to develop their critical and creative thinking ability to its fullest capacity; to promote cooperation, interaction, and negotiation among children; and to celebrate children's natural curiosity and wonder about the world and how it works (Fyfe & Cadwell, 1993). It is also a way of taking time together, teacher and child, to focus on important aspects of life and living; to examine an experience, object, or idea closely; and to wonder and search together.

Carlina Rinaldi, senior consultant to Reggio Children, said recently:

> Children are searching for the real meaning of life. We believe in their possibilities to grow. That is why we do not hurry to give them answers; instead we invite them to think about where the answers might lie. The challenge is to listen. When your child asks, 'Why is there a moon?' don't reply with a scientific answer. Ask him, 'What do you think?' He will understand that you are telling him, 'You have your own mind and your own interpretation and your ideas are important to me.' Then you and he can look for the answers, sharing the wonder, curiosity, pain—everything. It is not the answers that are important, it is the process—that you and he search together. (McLaughlin, 1995, p. 68)

We have learned from the teachers in Reggio Emilia not only how important it is to listen but also how important it is to schedule time together to carefully read and understand transcribed conversations. When studying the conversations, we need to ask, What knowledge can we say these children have? What examples can we find in this conversation of their use of intuition, conjecture, and logical and creative thinking? When have they made analogies and used metaphors to communicate their ideas? How has listening to the ideas of their classmates challenged them, informed them, or offered them a new way of viewing the problem? What misconceptions do they have? What can we, as adults, learn from them about the way they look at and think about this subject? What might we do next with these children and perhaps a larger group with whom we could share these initial ideas to support further learning?

In the Reggio meetings, they might also analyze the teacher's participation. Were the questions good ones? Did the teacher do a good job facilitating the conversation? What about the timing of the questions? Was she or he supporting the children enough? Did every child participate? Why? Did the teacher intervene too much or too little? In this way, with the critical support of their colleagues, the teachers become better and better facilitators of this kind of inquiry.

The educators in Reggio Emilia prepare for conversations. They devote enough time and full attention to the children and their ideas in a quiet space, giving children and teachers the respect they need. They then study the transcripts with colleagues to use children's ideas as the core of the curriculum. This is a style of working for them.

BARRIERS

It has been difficult for teachers here to move into this process. After 3 years of working together in our network, we all have a better understanding of the difficulties we face. We have identified seven barriers to incorporating quality conversations and discussion with children into our curriculum planning and daily practice.

The first barrier is fairness and equity for teachers and children (Fyfe, 1994). Is it fair to give a small group of children this kind of focused attention? What happens to the other children? Do they feel left out? Is it fair for one teacher to have the luxury of focusing on a small group of children for 45 minutes or more? Isn't she or he supposed to be responsible for all the children? If there is no coteacher, how would this ever be possible? If there is, is it fair to leave the coteacher with the majority of the children?

Teachers must agree to differentiate their work so that one can stay with a small group while the other monitors the rest of the class. When there is no coteacher, parent volunteers or teacher aides might be used to monitor the activity of the larger group while the teacher facilitates a small-group conversation. In some cases, teacher aides or parent volunteers might learn how to facilitate dialogue among children. The fairness issue has come to be reframed. Teachers who have experienced the power of small-group conversations are beginning to ask, Is it fair to deny children the opportunity to participate in small-group conversations? How am I ever going to know what these children are thinking if I do not take the time to really talk with them?

The second barrier is noise. It is impossible to have a quality conversation if children and teachers are distracted by the noise of a busy classroom and constant distractions of other children who interrupt. To think, listen, and discuss, children and teachers need separate, quiet spaces. These are hard to come by in early childhood settings. Some teachers have shared this problem with parents and found that together they were able to develop a fund-raising plan and designs to renovate or build new spaces that support quiet, small-group activity. Others have reorganized rooms or made arrangements to use temporarily unoccupied rooms (e.g., a resource room or lounge) or, in good weather, a secluded place outdoors.

A third barrier is expectation. Traditionally, most teachers do not expect young children to sit in a small group for a reasonable amount of time to discuss ideas and theories about the workings of the world. Teachers might think this is too much to expect of preschool children. Maybe it is even harmful to them to expect them to sit and think when they might rather play with manipulatives, blocks, or dress-ups.

Many of our colleagues have been amazed at what happens when they take the time to listen to children's ideas, seek to understand their points of view, and help children listen to each other. As a result, their former beliefs about the length of a young child's attention span change quickly.

A fourth barrier is rationale. Why do this? What value is there for children? What value for teachers? What do children and teachers learn from this kind of activity? How do you make use of this kind of information? Where do you go with it? How does it fit in with the rest of the curriculum? What happens to the skills and information teachers are supposed to teach if they are spending so much time listening to children's ideas?

Teaching is a complex activity. Emergent curriculum requires teachers to study the ideas expressed in children's conversations and actions. Most conversations are loaded with possibilities for topics or questions for further study. It is often not possible or appropriate to consider following up on every idea. Teachers must make decisions about which of these are most worthy of pursuit. This is a time when the goals and values shared by teachers and parents should be considered. It is a critical juncture for connecting our curriculum goals with children's ideas and interests.

A fifth barrier is lack of skill. It takes skill and practice to be able to lead a productive conversation with young children. It is only human to avoid situations in which one feels inept and prone to failure, but teachers need to risk failures and flops in order to learn. A sympathetic group of coworkers struggling to learn together can provide the support and modeling needed to acquire these skills.

A sixth barrier is recording what the children say. It is possible to take notes, but it is very hard to lead a conversation and take notes at the same time. A tape recorder works well, but that requires time to transcribe the tape. If there are two people, one can record, but that requires two teachers with one small group. Parent volunteers may be willing and able to assist in either taking notes or transcribing tapes.

A seventh barrier relates to the time, energy, and skill necessary for teachers to review and analyze conversations and then plan, based on this study. Finding time for this process of planning for emergent curriculum takes commitment, organization, and skill. Unless it is done, a necessary piece of the curriculum puzzle is not in place. Conversations are left behind without connection or relationship to the life of the children and teachers in the school. They become isolated events rather than critical connectors and resources for children and teachers.

Granted, these seven barriers raise complicated issues, and surmounting them has not been easy or without anxiety. Clearly, what seems a relatively simple, new way to work with young children may turn out to require teachers to rethink and change their assumptions about and expectations of children, their way of organizing their time and style of working, and their way of developing curriculum and planning their days and activities (Fyfe, 1994). It requires them to develop new skills and take risks, give extra time, collaborate, and critique each other. None of these changes is simple. After 3 years, we are still struggling with some aspects of all of them, even though we have made progress together and are committed to finding solutions.

FACILITATING GOOD CONVERSATIONS

What have we learned through our attempts at having conversations with children?

1. Think about appropriate questions beforehand. Try to brainstorm with colleagues first. Think about what kinds of questions would stimulate children's curiosity, provoke and challenge them to wonder and hypothesize, invent, and compare.

2. Arrange to have the conversation in a quiet place where neither you nor the children will be distracted.

3. Choose a group that you feel will benefit from being together and that will work well together for any number of reasons. Combining interested children with not so interested children, verbal with not so verbal, can work. Pay as careful attention to the group composition as the situation allows. Some opportunities will be more spontaneous than others. A group of five seems to be an ideal small-group number when working with 4- and 5-year-olds, but this figure may vary depending on the particular children.

4. Plan in advance how you will record. Some people can write quickly and keep up with the flow of the conversation, though this task is difficult. If you tape-record, be committed to listening and transcribing the important parts of the tape as soon as you can. If another teacher can be with you, one can lead and one can write.

5. Let children know right away that you have no interest in quizzing them and that you do not know all the answers, that instead you want to wonder and search with them, and that you are interested in big ideas and you know they are too.

6. Communicate through your tone of voice your wonder, your belief in the children's capabilities to think creatively and critically, and your excitement at this opportunity to talk together about important ideas.

7. Use the questions you have prepared as possibilities. Remain open to the flow of the conversation. It may go in interesting directions you had not anticipated. On the other hand, guide the conversation back to the main subject if it strays too far off.

8. Be the children's memory. Every once in a while, summarize for them what has been said, using children's names, if possible. This will help them realize you are listening carefully and that their ideas are going on record. It will also help them look backward to what has been said and move forward with new ideas.

9. When the children begin to talk to each other, debate, or ask each other questions, try to stay in the background as much as possible. This way the conversation begins to belong to them, they become more invested, and they begin to learn to discuss among themselves without intervention.

10. Enjoy the conversation! Laugh together. Be amazed at their perspectives. Share some of yours.

11. Use the conversation. Share some of the things that were said that day or the next with the whole group of children. Use it again with the same group or a different group. Ask children to expand on their ideas, critique their ideas, draw their ideas, paint or sculpt their

ideas—translate and transform them into different languages. Analyze the children's ideas with your colleagues to decide what to do next—further questions, further exploration, or work with drawing or sculptural materials.

12. Children and adults need time and experience with this way of being together. Most children need time to understand what this is all about—that you really are serious about wanting them to think and tell you and the other children what they think and that you have high expectations of them.

13. As adults, be brave enough to critique each other's conversations with children. It will help you gain skill and confidence.

ANALYZING CONVERSATIONS IN ORDER TO PLAN FOR EMERGENT CURRICULUM

Planning for emergent curriculum is based on the ongoing observations and study of children. The study of group conversations can reveal children's curiosity; their understanding of the dimensions and relations of complex situations; and their ability to create analogies, metaphors, anthropomorphic meanings, and realistically logical meanings. Our image of the child is built on this understanding of young children's capacity. If we underestimate it, our curriculum plans will fail to engage and challenge them.

Group conversations can provide a great deal of information about questions, concerns, and ideas that could be the focus of further investigation or exploration. When teachers understand these ideas, they are better able to think of ways to provoke children to dig a little deeper or rethink an idea. They are more likely to be able to connect with what Vygotsky (1978) calls children's zones of proximal development, the distance between the level of capacity that children might be able to exhibit on their own and their levels of potential development, attainable with the help of adults or more advanced peers. By understanding children's current schemas and everyday knowledge, teachers are in a better position to know how to offer children the appropriate kinds and amount of scaffolding to support and challenge them toward new levels of learning.

In the next section, we share what we have learned about the process of using conversations as a basis for curriculum planning. We thought this approach could best be communicated with an example. We do not claim that this is an example of how teachers in Reggio Emilia might plan for emergent curriculum. We have studied the Reggio Approach for several years and give credit to their influence on us, but our work is, and always will be, an interpretation of theirs.

A conversation with a small group of children was analyzed by a team of teachers. The conversation, with a little background on the experiences that preceded it, is presented, followed by a description of the curriculum planning meeting based on it.

The children and their teachers had already begun an investigation of the changes in the natural world that were happening all around them. They had taken walks outside to look, listen, and smell. They had collected leaves and examined them on the light table, then used tempera paint, watercolors, oil crayons, markers, and black pens to do observational drawing and painting of the leaves. These experiences ensured that the children had common reference points for a group conversation. The teaching team agreed that it would be a good time for Louise to engage small groups of children in conversation about their observations, ideas, and theories related to this subject, so that we might better understand how to go forward with this project.

A CONVERSATION ON LEAVES

The College School, October 21, 1992

Michael—4 years, 11 months   David—4 years, 9 months
Katie—4 years, 8 months   Dan—4 years, 6 months
Meredith—4 years, 10 months   Elysia—4 years, 9 months
Devyn—5 years, 2 months   Louise Cadwell—teacher

Louise: What do you see?
Michael: This part is white and this is red [turning the leaf over]. I wonder why? That must be the skin [pointing to the underside]. This must be the body [pointing to the top]. The sticks, the little things going out in the leaf, must be bones!
Katie: You can see parts of bones on mine, too. See the things pointing out. The red is the body. Those little stubs must be the bones.
David: I found the spine!
Katie: I found the spine, too.
Meredith: I know that. Everybody has a spine.
David: It's straight. [Feeling his spine] I can feel the bumps of it.
Meredith: It's like little hills. It goes up and down.
David: Don't break it [the spine], then you can't move at all.
Katie: This part is like the leg [pointing to the stem].
Louise: Does the leaf walk?
Michael: No, it flies! I guess its flying is its walking.
Katie: And it jumps and skips.
Louise: Why do you think the leaves fall?
Devyn: Because at the end of fall they kind of curl up to sleep, because they are tired.
David: Because they are dead.

Louise:	When they fall off the branches, are they dead?
Devyn:	They are asleep, when they fall. They curl up so they don't get cold. The leaves fall down because they are asleep. They die. It's too cold for them to live.
David:	But the tree doesn't die. Maybe it does, but not for a very long time.
Louise:	How could the leaves ever turn these colors?
Meredith:	They turn that way, 'cause I know why. Magic comes when it's fall. It turns the leaves to red and all colors. It gets very, very cold.
Michael:	It's like Terminator. The bad guy changed to different things, like the leaves, so nobody knows who he is. It's just like putting on Halloween costumes. Maybe somebody has the power to change the leaves.
Elysia:	The wind has the magic power. It makes the leaves change.
Michael:	I think the more the wind blows, the more the magic goes into the leaves and changes them.
Dan:	'Cause somebody gots magic.
Katie:	I know who does it; the wind and the rain and the clouds and the sun. God does it.
Michael:	I knew something was going on.

The Meeting

Jennifer Strange and Joyce Devlin are coteachers of 4- and 5-year-old children at the College School in Webster Groves, a suburb of St. Louis. Louise Cadwell has been working with the early childhood teachers at the College School as a studio teacher (our version of the *atelierista*). Brenda Fyfe is associate professor at Webster University and has been consulting with the College School teachers in a way that could be compared to the *pedagogista* in Reggio Emilia. This team of four met one day to examine conversations that Louise had facilitated with two small groups of 4- and 5-year-olds from the school. We had 1 hour to focus on this task, and during this discussion, we tape-recorded and took notes as we talked. We have learned never to have a meeting without keeping minutes and distributing these minutes as soon as possible after each meeting. Too often great ideas come from such a meeting of the minds and then are lost or never followed through because time passed and memories are distorted. Amelia Gambetti impressed upon us the importance of approaching teacher meetings as well as parent meetings with this kind of efficiency. An agenda is set in advance, and minutes are kept to help everyone remember what was accomplished, planned, and promised.

We began this meeting by taking parts and reading the conversations out loud. We have discovered that by doing this instead of just reading silently, we can sometimes better capture the feeling, tone, and dynamics of the conversation. After the readings, we asked ourselves, What do these dialogues tell us about what children already know, think, feel, question, or wonder? We reminded ourselves to complete an exhaustive list of the children's thoughts and to be careful not to project ideas into the conversation that were not explicitly stated by the children. Only after this was accomplished would we move on to planning for emergent curriculum.

Analyzing the Children's Conversation

We began with the question "What do children know, think, hypothesize, feel?" The conversation was lively. At first we just listed single ideas expressed by the children. Then we identified clusters of ideas or themes that connected ideas, such as the fact that both groups related leaf structure or leaf behavior to that of humans. They described leaves as asleep, dying, breathing, having bones and spines, having a body and skin. They said the leaves curl up when they are cold or tired. We noted that this kind of thinking is what Piaget characterizes as the young child's prelogical and egocentric beliefs in animism. We marveled at the intuitive thoughts of these young children.

A second category of ideas related to the falling of leaves. One described the falling as skipping and jumping. Another explained, "Its flying is its walking." One child said they are asleep when they fall. Others commented that the leaves fall down when it is fall; they fall down in the wind.

A third category related to comments about magic and power and change. Magic seemed to be a quickly accepted hypothesis that could explain the unexplainable (e.g., why leaves change color). One attributed the source of change to God. Another child thought about the change in the color of leaves as a kind of disguise. He likened this to Terminator's ability to change so nobody knows who he is. He said that somebody has the power to change the leaves.

We took a little time to reflect on the questions Louise used to provoke the children to think of analogies ("What do you see?") and express hypotheses ("Why do you think leaves fall?"). We noted that children were quite willing and able to think on these levels. We also noted that this was a conversation, unlike some earlier conversations, in which children were really talking to each *other* rather than just to the teacher. We observed that Louise had asked some pivotal questions that helped the children talk to each other. Frequently through the conversations it appears that children piggybacked on each other's ideas or continued a line of thought. This was a good indication that children were listening to each other. Though a few children had little to say, the relevance of their comments indicated that they, too, were listening and involved in the dialogue. We also knew that the prior experience these children had shared in collecting, observing, and drawing the leaves not only contributed to the ideas they expressed but probably gave them a sense of collective ownership of the topic and a respect for their own and each other's ideas.

Using Conversations to Inform Emergent Curriculum

Now we were ready to move on to curriculum planning. We knew that we needed to plan for several possibilities, possibilities that could help to make children's ideas visible and thereby help them revisit, reflect, reconstruct their thinking, and communicate this thinking to others. Although we have adopted a set of curriculum goals from Project Construct, a curriculum and assessment framework from the Missouri Department of Elementary and Secondary Education (1992), that guided our thinking about what is worth learning, we have tried to follow Rinaldi's (1993) advice about allowing curriculum to emerge in response to the children's needs and interests. We did not formulate specific goals for each activity in advance. Rather, we considered the ideas, hypotheses, and choices of the children and then projected possible activities that might help children answer their own questions (Forman, 1992a), test their hypotheses, and explore their ideas. We proposed ways that the project might evolve and then examined how these activities might support and integrate the goals of our curriculum.

We began with the first cluster of children's ideas: the relationship of leaves to humans. We thought that since the children talked about leaves having bones and spines, maybe we should consider helping them examine human or animal bones and spines and compare them to those of leaves. We could invite them to search for ways to look at human bone structures. We could ask whether they had ever seen pictures of their bones. This could lead to the possibility of finding real X-rays. One of the parents is a doctor; it is likely that he could help us in getting access to some X-rays. We could compare human bones with what the children have described as bones in leaves. We could ask children to then draw the "bone" structure of the leaves and the bone structures of people. This could enable us to talk with them about the discoveries or observations they would be making about similarities and differences. We would try to provoke conversation about hypotheses regarding form and function of leaf bones versus human bones. As children's questions emerged, we could encourage them to search for answers and sources for these answers (e.g., family members who know something about human bones or leaf structure; books or videos on the subject; local experts; collections of more leaves to examine firsthand; observations of leaves on trees). We could invite children to use their drawings as plans or designs for making skeletons or bone structures out of wire. This medium would enable us to think about how structures within leaves and bodies help support the rest of the structure (skin, muscle, organs). We might ask, Why do leaves have "bones"? Our goal would be to provoke thinking and a desire to know more about the form and function of leaf structures. We would be promoting a disposition to learn and a beginning understanding of the relationships of parts to the whole, how things work, and insight into the system of relations within and among living things.

The falling of leaves was a subject that stirred a great deal of excitement and a flow of ideas from each of us. We thought that we might remind the children of their ideas about leaves flying, jumping, skipping, falling down in the wind, and curling up. Then we could give them the opportunity to look at slides that were taken when they had observed this falling of the leaves. We could invite the children to dance with us in front of the projected slides to imitate and mime how the leaves fall. We could use scarves or other dress-ups and, with the children, select music that we thought suitable for our dance of the leaves. We might use the shadow screen to play with images of leaves falling behind it. Since we know that in the past year these children have shown great interest in writing and acting out plays, this experience might turn into a performance that children might want to script, practice, and perform for others. We might suggest composing or selecting poetry or songs to go with the dance of the leaves. If leaves are still falling outside, we might go there to observe the many different ways that leaves fall, to study how leaves fall when it is windy and how they fall when the air is still. If possible, we could plan to videotape these observations so that we might revisit this experience at another time or share it with other children. We might suggest that children take sketch pads along with them so that they could draw the path of the leaves as they fall. These sketches might be used later to help us choreograph our own body movements in the dance of the leaves and the flow of our scarves.

Louise remembered that once during her year of internship in Reggio Emilia, she observed Vea Vecchi take a small group of children outside one day and heard her say, "Look at how all those leaves have fallen. Do you see how the wind has created this kind of picture, by the way the leaves are arranged? Now pretend if you were the wind, how would you arrange these things?" The children played outside making patterns and constructions out of leaves. Sometimes they would cover their creations with plastic box tops to preserve them for a while.

The rest of us thought this idea was a great possibility for an experience that both adults and children would enjoy, and it would be a logical extension of the study of the effects of wind on falling leaves. It might lead to observations of other patterns in nature. It could help children think about spatial relationships among elements of a pattern (shape, texture, color). This kind of experience could help children develop stronger awareness of their environment and the beauty and complexity of nature.

So many ideas were pouring forth. As this happened, our own questions emerged. Does the shape of a leaf affect the way it falls? How far from a tree might a leaf fall? One teacher said that the leaves of ginko trees fall all at once (e.g., overnight) rather than over a period of days or weeks like other trees. She went on to say, "You can go down the street one day and the ginko leaves are all yellow; the next day they're all on the ground. It looks like it snowed ginkos." If that is true, we thought, wouldn't it be exciting to study a ginko tree with the children and try to predict when the leaves would fall? This observation could lead to an investigation of the many different kinds of trees in the school yard. We could try to find out whether different kinds of trees tend to shed leaves at different times, in early or late fall.

Finally, we decided to move on to the third cluster of children's ideas about power, death, and magic in regard to how leaves change color. It occurred to us that these ideas could easily be connected through most, if not all, of the experiences we had already projected. As we engaged in experiences related to the study of falling leaves, we could also discuss and observe color. Sources of information that we seek out in regard to leaf structures might also tell us something about the color of leaves and why the color of leaves change in the fall. As we observe the ginko tree to monitor the fall of the leaves, we will surely be noting the change in color that precedes their fall. We might encourage children to paint pictures of their theories about how leaves change color. We might encourage them to mix paints in order to match the many different colors observed. We might take walks to look for examples of leaves that have already changed color and leaves that have not yet changed, leaves that are just beginning to curl up and leaves that are beginning to decompose. We might decide together to represent these different stages through drawing, clay modeling, or other material. This would challenge the children to think about in-between states, thereby focusing more on the process of transformation. These graphic representations should enable the children to converse about their theories and consider each other's ideas.

At this point, our heads were swimming with the many possibilities of this project. We felt a need to reflect on how these experiences related to the goals of our curriculum. We had already discussed the value of several of the activities in regard to their potential for encouraging thinking about form and function, transformations and patterns in nature, and relationships of parts to whole. Though we had not yet talked about it, we could now reflect that, in all cases in which we helped children make their ideas visible (e.g., through various forms of representation such as drawing, construction, dramatic play, and movement—or any of the "hundred languages"), we were enabling them to better communicate and organize their thinking—to revisit, reflect, and recognize. The visible representations of children's ideas could enable them to discuss and defend their ideas with peers as well as consider each other's perspectives. We knew that if we supported children in asking and answering their own questions, we would be helping them build dispositions to be curious (e.g., about the physics of falling leaves or the relationships between bone structure of humans and the "bones" and "spines" in leaves), to take initiative (e.g., in seeking information or testing their hypotheses), and to exercise creative and critical thinking (e.g., in developing theories about why leaves change color). Several of the experiences would help children represent ideas and feelings through music and movement, construction, graphics, and words. Throughout this study, we would be building vocabulary and exercising the skills of discussion, debate, and listening.

We reminded ourselves of the advice that Amelia Gambetti had given us on several of her consultation visits: Though we had thought of a wonderful inventory of possible learning activities, we could go forward with them only if we could get the children to agree to pursue them. In other words, we needed to plan ways to use the documentation we had already collected to entice, provoke, invite, and/or negotiate with children in regard to the proposed learning activities. At the same time, we had to keep our ears and eyes open to alternative experiences or directions for the project that might come from the children. We remembered Rinaldi's (1993a) advice in *The Hundred Languages of Children:* that all of the work we had just done to (a) study children's ideas and hypotheses and (b) discuss and record the many possible ways that the project could be anticipated to evolve was "great preparation for the subsequent stages of the project—even should the unexpected occur" (p. 102).

We ended the meeting with a plan to meet again to discuss strategies for presenting one or more of our ideas to the children, to determine the roles each team member would play in regard to facilitating small-group activities, to identify tools (e.g., camera, camcorder, tape recorder, paper and pencil, etc.) and strategies to be used to document our ongoing observations of learning, to find time to analyze documentation, and to involve parents through documentation and other forms of participation or communication. As the project evolved, we would continue to examine ways to use documentation (e.g., photographs; slides; videotape; transcripts of children's dialogues; and children's drawings, writing, paintings, and constructions) to sustain children's interests and involvement in the project.

CONCLUSION

We all agree that planning for emergent curriculum is complex and time-consuming. It requires us not only to know principles of child development but to engage in an ongoing study of the particular children we teach. Children's conversations can be a prime resource for this kind of study.

We have come to learn that serious dialogue and exchange among children, teachers, and parents is critical at all levels. The guidelines offered at the beginning of this chapter focus on our work with children, but we are now realizing that the ability to listen, discuss, debate, question, probe, consider multiple perspectives, and wonder out loud must happen in our work with all members of the learning community. The skills we develop in practicing the kind of team study and planning just described transfer to our work with parents and children. As we get better at facilitating and participating in dialogue with children, we become better at doing this with adults. Through our efforts to put dialogue at the center of our curriculum, we are beginning to understand how to develop the "network of cooperation and interactions that produces for the adults, but above all for the children, a feeling of belonging in a world that is alive, welcoming, and authentic" (Malaguzzi, 1993b, p. 58).

14

The Challenge of Reggio Emilia's Research
One Teacher's Reflections

Donna Carloss Williams
Instructor, Ball State University, Muncie, Indiana

Rebecca Kantor
Professor of Early Childhood Education, The College of Education,
The Ohio State University, Columbus

In 1991, we had the privilege of participating in a study tour of the early childhood programs in Reggio Emilia, along with our colleagues from the A. Sophie Rogers Laboratory in Child and Family Studies at The Ohio State University. We went to Reggio with a wide range of emotions: excited to have this group experience as a staff (one more used to the role of host to our own visitors), curious, wishing to be challenged, and, admittedly, a bit skeptical of the amazing products we had seen on display in the traveling exhibit. We left Reggio with even more emotion: inspired yet overwhelmed by what we had seen and learned, and in conflict over how to use what we had seen without losing our own essential character.

What follows is an excerpt from a journal written by Donna Carloss Williams immediately following this excursion. While we have "traveled" even further from this beginning point in our explorations of the Reggio ideas over the 5 years since our trip, we still recognize the importance and difficulty of the first steps. We share this reflection to encourage others engaged in a similar process and to help others think about their own practices. This above all is what we learned from our visit to Italy: We visit others' programs, and we enter into a dialogue, not for the purpose of imitation but to be provoked to revisit our own understandings, engage in ongoing research and reflection, look forward and outward for resources and inspiration, and remain open to learning.

CONNECTING HISTORIES

After visiting Reggio Emilia's preschool programs, some elements of the approach there were an instant "easy fit" for us. An "emergent curriculum" (although the term *emergent* was new to us) has been implemented at the A. Sophie Rogers Laboratory School for over a decade. Long ago, the idea of preplanned teacher "themes" had been seen as a less productive means of facilitating children's learning than using their own ideas as the curricular focus. We had been "working from the ideas of children" (in fact, this is our program motto) successfully for so long that this element of the Reggio research felt quite natural to us. However, other elements were new and challenging.

The focus on socially constructed curriculum also characterizes a daily event in the lab school we call "group time," a planned context for working on collaborative projects. Each day, we plan our group time curriculum from an active learning, open-ended materials approach. We would bring materials as a starting point and suggest group projects, always with an eye for capturing the ideas and interests of the children. Thus, we, too, had seen the idea of collaboration as worthwhile. However, while the process was familiar, the time span for our projects was very different from the Italians'. Most materials we prepared were for the day's experience. They were appropriate, developmental, and born of children's input, but they were rarely done over time or in the depth of "study" we saw in Reggio Emilia. The entire project element was an exciting and challenging one to all of us.

Another aspect we saw as challenging was the element of representation across varied media. As part of our experiences, we had typically asked the children whether they were interested in writing narratives about what they perceived to be the experience's salient features. However, we had not considered other media (e.g., art) in this part of the process.

During our week in Reggio Emilia and on the plane trip back to the United States, our entire staff discussed whether our experience would change our practice. We all agreed we wished to use what we had learned in Italy in our classroom—but how? We began not with a blueprint but with the courage just to "try" to construct our own meaning from what we had seen in Italy. This dialogue has been ongoing for more than 5 years, but it began with the Water Project described here.

A TEACHER'S JOURNAL: THE WATER PROJECT

When I returned from Reggio Emilia, it was summer, school was in session, and it was hot. During our outdoor play, the children were making informal observations about water as they played in their small wading pools. Following our typical practice, I decided to bring some of those water experiences inside for our group time. (We have a mixed-age classroom of twenty 3- to 5-year-olds. Each day when we have our planned group time, we divide our classroom into two small groups—10 children in each group for the planned activity. I was the teacher/leader of the group of 4- to 5-year-olds.) Not as typically, I brought my camera, determined to watch and listen more attentively to the children's process to see whether any possibilities for extending the experience were suggested by the children in their actions and talk. I wanted to do a project at some point with the children, but I realized I could not just *put* some sort of project technique or method on the children's experience.

POURING: AN ENTRY POINT FOR A PROJECT

Our beginning experiment was simple. I brought containers of various sizes and one large, transparent tub and asked the children whether they would like to fill the tub and see what we discovered about the water.

At first, they were excited only about getting their pictures taken (see Figures 14–1, 14–2, and 14–3). I told them I brought the camera to record what they wanted about their discoveries. After each child had a picture taken, we became involved in pouring the water from the different containers, from varying distances above the tub, and with varying amounts of water. I got so involved myself that I often forgot to take the pictures. (Indeed,

FIGURE 14–1
Marcus drew the water that dripped over the container's edge.

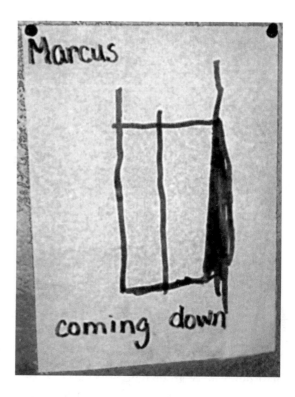

the photographs and the other documentation throughout the year were a source of joy, frustration, and validation of my memory loss!) Comments from the children included these:

Steven:	"Pour is like spilling."
Audrey:	"It makes waves."
Allison:	"Pouring high makes more bubbles, but close makes less bubbles."
Marcus:	"I got bigger water."
Alexandra:	"Little tiny containers pour like raindrops."
Thomas:	"The water makes kind of a hole."
Celia:	"If it's a small hole, not so many bubbles."

When the children felt finished, I replayed the group over and over in my mind. Where did they focus? What do I do next? If I bring the experience back, am I just doing it to be *my* first "project," or were *they* really as interested in this as I thought? I decided to go forward.

FIGURE 14–2
Bubbles made from water and "pouring into more water" were captured in this drawing.

BLOWING: A FURTHER AND DEEPER INVESTIGATION

They had seemed most interested in the bubbles and circles made by the pouring. I brought in water, straws, and funnels with the idea of creating circles and bubbles with "wind" (see Figures 14–4 and 14–5). I opened the activity by saying, "Yesterday, we discovered so many interesting things about the bubbles and circles in the water that I wondered if these things could help us discover anything about water too?" I almost held my breath—partly because I was so unsure of myself and partly because I feared I was beginning to "teach about water" rather than experiencing their learning about water. I feared that their interest was not as keen as mine and that I had forced this water exploration on them out of my own excitement about extended collaborative experiences.

I need not have worried. The children instantly put their *heads* in the water to blow bubbles. (On reflection, we thought this may have come from "blowing" experiences in swimming lessons many children were taking.) They used what I had

FIGURE 14–3
Steven was able to represent
water entering the container
and the motion under the
water line.

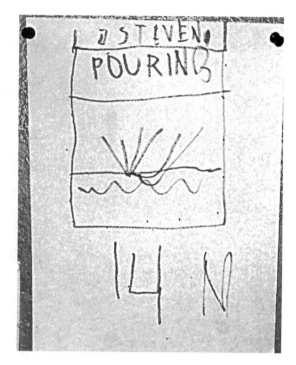

brought (straws, funnels, etc.) and got other things from around the classroom as well (tubing, paper cylinders, etc.). Although our group typically lasted 15 to 20 minutes, it was 45 minutes later before interest began to subside. Some of their comments were as follows:

Thomas:	[With mouth in the water] "It makes little circles and bubbles."
Marcus:	[With nose in the water] "Bigger circles."
Allison:	[With breath only] "Even little and big circles."
Thomas:	[With straws] "Smaller bubbles happen when you bend the straw."
Audrey:	[With paper funnels] "Bubbles are there but only wide."

There was more talk about waves and bubbles, but the children's most compelling interest was in what would happen to the water that was spilling out of the tub. Several children recited very accurate, detailed descriptions of the process of evaporation. Two were even "knowledgeable" about evaporation and weather. I decided the next experiment might involve these elements.

FIGURE 14–4
In another experiment, we tried blowing ("wind") on the water. With faces in and out of the water, straws, funnels, and a few additional implements (note the water pump in the center bottom picture), we blew!

EVAPORATION: THE CHILDREN'S THEORIES ARE REVEALED

I brought in paper towels and water and asked the children to predict where water would go if we wet the paper towels and left them out for awhile. In spite of their previous "recitations," *not one child* predicted that the water would evaporate. In fact, the group agreed that the paper towel would *never* dry, because "paper towels are something that soaks up water" (Alexandra). We wet the towels, children marked their own, and we recorded the day and time. The paper towels, of course, were dry when we returned the next day. The observations from the group were divided: Four believed the air was causal in the drying, and four believed the "clothespins and air together did it." Looking back, I am still surprised that I did not go forward with this exploration. I did put a few more wet paper towels up without clothespins for three of the children. These children later decided, "Maybe air just does it." However, I never really picked up on their cognitive dissonance with the "clothespin factor" (see Figure 14–6).

FIGURE 14–5
Alexandra worked hard to
document the ripples caused
by blowing into the water.

WAVES: WHAT GENERATES THEM?

I did notice that while wetting their paper towels, and for the third time, they were fascinated with waves. So, our next time together, I asked the children for their predictions about what generates waves. Most agreed an *object* was necessary to make this happen. Despite earlier experiences with both pouring and blowing where waves were observed by the children, neither was predicted as a possible wave producer. When questioned about what objects were best for wave making, "boats" were the most popular choice, followed by "hands." After experimenting with both, other predictions and choices were dropping crumbs into the water, blowing, and moving the entire container of water. Blowing was considered mildly successful in making "tiny, little waves" (Allison). Dropping crumbs into the water "just doesn't work" (Alexandra), and moving the whole container "does big ones" (Steven; see Figure 14–7). The summary causal factor was "fastness" (Thomas).

Again, in reflection, the children were showing me many other possibilities with waves that I just did not facilitate. They had decided "fastness" of motion was causal, and I went forward without further experimentation. Part of my decision making was

FIGURE 14–6
Steven sends the water vapor from the water into the air in this representation of evaporation.

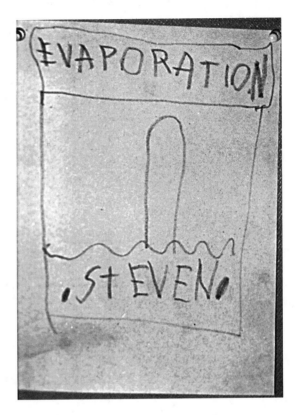

due to my lack of attention to their process and my resistance to the idea of doing a water "theme." As the experiences began to span several days, I was getting excited but also concerned. What was the difference between what I was doing and doing a thematic "water week"? Had I just taken the project idea from Reggio Emilia, or had I taken the understanding that children's process with discovering their own realities of the world could take time and collaboration? I was more and more unsure as I was simultaneously buoyed by how involved the children had become and how collaborative their conversations were. Despite my uncertainties, I went forward.

BOAT CONSTRUCTION: ONE PATH TAKEN

I lost the chance to proceed with wave making, but I did recognize their high interest in the boats they had used as wave producers. I asked whether they would be interested in making boats. They were very excited. Before we started, the children decided

FIGURE 14–7
Steven shows the water
rising from the surface in his
depiction of wave making.

we would need to have these elements in a good boat: "flat, edges, seats, a point, and it has to float." I brought aluminum foil as the first boat-making material. There was a high level of satisfaction with this foil boat making, though two disappointments came along with the discoveries:

> Steven: "It can rip."
> Alexandra: "If you put a lot of water in it, it won't work."

The children suggested future boat-making materials should be paper, plastic, and wood.

Following their suggestions, I brought construction paper next. Their only concern about paper boat making was that "even if it works, it will get soaking wet." There was a high level of confidence, because the group was so sure about "making edges" with paper. Marcus discovered the paper could float alone without shape or "edges." This discovery caused a surge of putting flat paper sheets in the water. Disappointment was coupled with frustration when the wet paper began to rip. The children's conclusion was "Foil is a material that can get wet and not be ruined. Paper isn't." (Thomas). Echoing this conclusion and the sentiment of the group, Alexandra said,

"Paper boats always fall apart." Discoveries were made, however, that were to impact future experiments:

> *Christine:* "Paper sticks to another paper."
> *Izzati:* "Putting it under the water gets it wetted easy."
> *Allison:* "If you put a little water on it, it floats still."

Following the children's suggestion of plastic, the next material we tried was plastic-coated paper (used for lining shelves). This material made a superior floater, and the children were quite impressed with the fact that it did not tear when it was wet. They were, however, very frustrated with shaping the material:

> *Alexandra:* "It doesn't bend well. Regular boats look more 'shapey.'"

Using their discovery of paper sticking to paper (the previous experiment) yielded the ultimate solution:

> *Celia:* "Making edges by placing another piece on top. It rolls up and sticks to itself."

They had previously decided that a *little* water in a boat was acceptable. This was the source of much experimentation, and it led to another discovery:

> *Catherine:* "Water can come in any hole in a boat."

Again, I believe there were more paper and plastic substances that would have been possible, but my concern about "how much is too much" was very primary in this first experience. I was, however, tentatively beginning to call this "our Water Project" with the children. I wanted them to begin to have a sense of the cohesive quality of what they had been doing. I was gathering quite a few photos now as well. I continued.

I brought wood next as the children had wanted. This was decidedly the favorite boat-making material. It did cause some questions about their previous conclusions:

> *Thomas:* "They float good, and they don't need *edges*."
> *Alexandra:* "You can't *fold* it, but it floats!"

These wooden boats were used the longest in play, and the group experimented more with water motion. Perhaps the choice to construct (as a group) a wooden boat would have extended their excitement, but instead I chose to bring in another material: clay.

Clay boats were the source of the richest conversation and problem solving. They were also the source of the greatest frustration and eventually spelled the end of the project. Some conclusions:

> *Christine:* "It has to be very flat."
> *Audrey:* "It has to be not heavy."

Alexandra: "Cracks let water in and out."
Catherine: "Water makes clay heavy."
Audrey: "If a boat floats, you know it's not heavy."

After the clay boats, the children clearly were finished with their Water Project. It had been 2 weeks long. Water is such a universally interesting material to children, and it had become a first-step "project" for us. I was elated. I already knew some of the errors in judgment I had made, but I was pretty sure I had not accomplished a water theme and so felt reassured. A theme is an integrated but preplanned experience that does not build on the unfolding inquiry process of the group. Integration and social construction are two different qualities related to curriculum design. Preplanning content feels more like a "monologue"; constructed projects feel more like a "dialogue."

REPRESENTATION AND DOCUMENTATION: NEW EXTENSIONS FOR THE TEACHER

After our water experiments, I ventured into another unfamiliar experience: to see whether I could facilitate their recording of their own experience. I had many photos now, and I mounted them with a simple, handwritten narrative of the experience (see Figure 14–8). It was unlike the beautifully done graphics on the panels I had seen in Italy, but it was the first such "panel" I had ever attempted or the children had ever seen. When I put it up, they surrounded it. They were amazed at viewing their own discoveries and called friends over to see the Water Project. (At the day's end, they brought their parents to see it as well.) This was as gratifying as much of the process itself. Their sense of accomplishment and mastery was obvious.

While gathered around this panel, I also showed them a handful of unmounted photos. I said, "These all remind me of the things we did during the Water Project. I thought we could use these materials (markers and paper) to record what we remembered about our project." Now, I *really* was unsure. I had always been taught to allow children to draw/create whatever their imaginations suggested. I had always resisted the idea of a teacher insisting on everyone drawing "the same thing." How close to that line was I now? Had I stepped over it? I decided to venture the risk. The results astounded me: They did not draw the same thing at all. Although their drawings were nowhere near the beauty of the children's art in Reggio Emilia, they were the most revealing drawings I had seen from these children.

REFLECTION

Looking back, this part of the project felt comfortable and appropriate after all. I was not directing the children's content or limiting their creativity (which I was afraid I was going to do); I was giving them a tool (a "language," in the Italians' terminology) to communicate what they had found out about water. Indeed, they were able to cap-

FIGURE 14–8
After our water experiments, I ventured into another unfamiliar experience. I mounted pictures of what the children had done together with a simple, handwritten narrative of the experience. When I put it up, the children surrounded it. They were amazed at viewing their own discoveries.

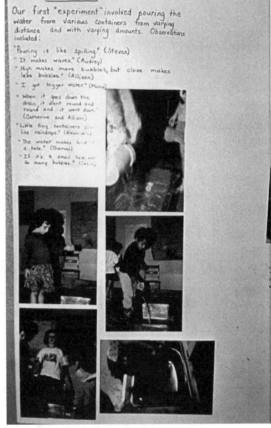

ture on paper what they had discovered: Steven captured pouring; Alexandra chose to draw the effects of flowing the water; Marcus even remembered water coming down beside the tub as well as the bubbles we had often seen; waves were also a subject for Steven, as was the evaporation process. I gave them the opportunity to further the dialogue by means of an additional language and that was the difference.

The evening after the group had drawn their pictures, I mounted them. Then, I sat in front of the bulletin board crying. My tears were from the joy in sharing the children's new experience, the sadness at not having given other children the "rights of their own potential," and the excitement of knowing that at that point in my career, I was beginning something new and exhilarating. In spite of my doubts and resistance, it felt so *right*.

15

There It Is! Exploring the Permanence of Objects and the Power of Self with Infants and Toddlers[1]

Nicole May
Lead Teacher, Infant-Toddler Program, A. Sophie Rogers Laboratory for Child and Family Studies, The Ohio State University, Columbus

Rebecca Kantor
Professor of Early Childhood Education, The College of Education, The Ohio State University, Columbus

Michele Sanderson
Director, A. Sophie Rogers Laboratory for Child and Family Studies, The Ohio State University, Columbus

---

[1] The research discussed here was the basis of Nicole May's project for her master's degree. She gratefully acknowledges the support and input of her advisor, Dr. Michael Glassman.

The intent of this volume, as well as the first volume edited by Joanne Hendrick (Hendrick, 1997), is for American educators to share with their readers their "first steps" in teaching the "Reggio way" so that others will be encouraged to explore the approach. Our introduction to the Reggio Approach occurred more than 12 years ago with a study tour of the city's schools. We have written about these experiences elsewhere (Kantor & Whaley, 1998; Williams & Kantor, 1997; Glassman & Whaley, 2000; Sanderson, 1999), describing the many ways that our views at the A. Sophie Rogers Laboratory School at The Ohio State University have been enriched and transformed by the work of the Italian children and their teachers.

Our school, which has been in existence since 1923, is a small program serving thirty children and their families. Our infant/toddler room has ten children ages 8 weeks to 3 years, while our preschool classroom has twenty children 3 to 5 years of age. Each room has a teaching team comprised of two full-time teachers and two graduate students, maintaining ratios of 1:3 for infants and toddlers and 1:7 for preschoolers. In addition to providing high quality care for the Columbus, Ohio, community we offer on-site training experiences for undergraduate students in early childhood education as well as research opportunities for students and faculty in child development, early childhood education, and related fields.

The underlying philosophy of our program draws from the idea that children, working together in groups, socially construct their knowledge of the world. Small group work has always been a mainstay of our preschool classroom and very naturally fits with the idea of in-depth project work. We were already familiar with engaging our preschoolers in small group investigations of particular topics of interest; however, our encounters with the work of our Italian colleagues challenged our thinking about the depths to which young children could carry their ideas. In particular we wondered about the viability of project work with infants and toddlers, what form it might take, and what meaning it could hold for them.

Looking back over 12 years of our experiences working together and exploring the highly complex pedagogical ideas of Reggio Emilia, we do not see a linear learning pathway with a single beginning. Rather we see multiple paths, some leading to new insights and greater understanding, others proving to be dead ends or missteps in our journeys to better understand young children and our roles as their teachers. Each of these paths contains a story, but of necessity only one can be shared here. While the particular story we have chosen is not literally from our first experiences, it does represent a beginning because our views of implementing project work with infants and toddlers were greatly expanded and enriched after observing and documenting parallel projects carried out by two children over an extended period of time. It marks the beginning of our insight that the compelling developmental work (e.g., understanding object permanence, agency, learning to walk, etc.) of infants and toddlers can be the basis for project work.

The educators from Reggio Emilia had oriented us to the importance of "small moments" that sometimes with an individual child or two can become projects in their own way. The well-documented project involving the toddler Lucia, her teacher, and her teacher's watch is one such moment (Edwards, Gandini, & Forman, 1998, p. 116).

As is often the case with insights, they become your own only when you (re)discover their meanings for yourself. In the "hiding story," Gus and Meredith explore the permanence of objects and the power of self. As the teachers followed their work, they discovered that projects are contained in processes and development as much as they are contained in materials and products, and their insights are reinforced in observing these rituals of childhood.

"THERE IT IS!" EXPLORING THE PERMANENCE OF OBJECTS AND THE POWER OF SELF: THE HIDING PROJECT

By 17 months, representation of the object has become more and more predictable. No longer written in disappearing ink, and not yet quite written in permanent marker either, practicing of control over reappearance and disappearance has made a record of experience from within. (Dunn, 1993, p. 335)

The Hiding Project with Gus

We cannot identify a clear starting point for "the hiding project" in which two children explore the ritualistic peek-a-boo game associated with the investigation of object permanence. Their developmental work is continuous—sometimes visible to their adults and sometimes not. Researchers describe peek-a-boo/hiding games, which may begin with mother-initiated peek-a-boo as early as 16 weeks, as a hallmark of infancy and toddlerhood that remains interesting to children through their third year (Dunn, 1993).

We can identify when this project began for the adults involved. We can identify the precipitating event, the "aha" moment when the adults in this story realized that the children were engaged in powerful, internal experiences that could be supported and documented as a project. This event took place at the sand table. The teacher, Michele, had engaged Gus (18 months) in play at the sand table. She caught his attention when she covered a plastic bug with sand, paused, and asked, "Where is it?" Gus stared at the place in the sand, but didn't try to recover the bug. Michele recovered the bug for him (brushed off the sand) and exclaimed, "There it is!" This evoked Gus' squeal of delight and celebratory dance when the bug reappeared. The sequence was repeated several times and drew the attention of Meredith (23 months). After several more sequences of "where is it?/there it is!" led by Michele, Meredith tried to take over as the one who brushed off the sand to discover the bug. Michele explicitly showed Meredith the steps of the game. She talked Meredith through the sequence, giving her the role of the discoverer. This too continued for a while. When Michele stood up to get the camera to document this small moment, Meredith took over the entire sequence—covering the bug with sand, asking, "Gus, where is it?," and

FIGURE 15–1
Meredith assumes the role
of "teacher" in uncovering
the hidden bug for Gus.

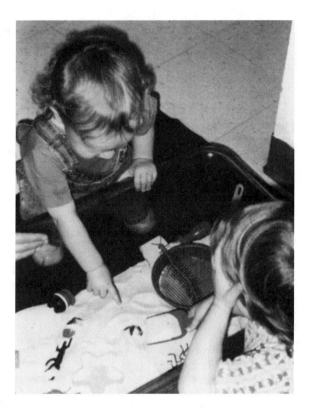

waiting for Gus to shrug his shoulders. As Gus stood by with anticipation, Meredith revealed the bug for him (Figure 15–1), which prompted him to squeal and dance in celebration. This game between Meredith and Gus was replayed often at the sand table over the next week-and-a-half.

Michele and Nicole remarked to each other on the transparency of Gus' experience of object permanence. They marveled at Meredith's discovery of her role as "teacher." A few moments after this interaction at the sand table, Gus initiated the hiding game with his teachers by covering his face with a plastic plate (Figure 15–2); Meredith initiated the game by hiding a pen in the binder of a teacher's notebook. The teachers wondered if they could support the interests of the children in the project style of the Reggio Approach.

This is the resulting narrative:

Soon after the day at the sandbox, the teachers noticed Gus playing hiding games both with Meredith and by himself, seemingly testing out his hiding theory, still practicing the idea of the permanence of objects. For example, several "busy-boxes" are available in the classroom. One morning, Gus picked one out and brought it to a chair. He pushed all of the buttons so that all of the animals popped up (Figure 15–3). He then shut the one door, which hid the elephant. He looked at

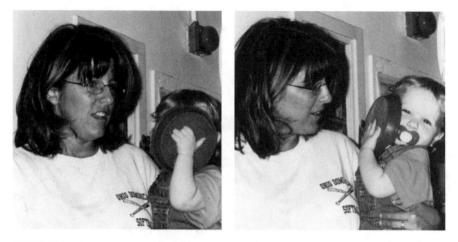

FIGURE 15–2
Gus' immediate initiation of another version of the hiding game gave impetus to the teachers' theory that perhaps this was the beginning of a project.

FIGURE 15–3
Gus tests his own hiding theory by popping up the animals in the busybox.

it, shrugged his shoulders, gestured with his arms as if to say, "where did it go?," paused, and then pushed the button to make the elephant pop up again. Again, Gus danced and squealed with delight at its reappearance. He repeated this for about 10 minutes. The teachers saw Gus repeat this activity with the busybox almost daily for about 2 weeks.

The teachers tried to support this exploration by planning activities that had other possibilities for hiding. For example, knowing that Gus liked to play with the plastic animals in the room, the teachers initiated a peek-a-boo game with the animals and a blanket. They covered the animals with the blanket with the expectation that he would find them. Surprisingly, while Gus was interested in playing with the animals, he seemed unenthusiastic about playing the hiding game with these objects.

While this and other teacher-planned activities failed to engage Gus in hiding games, he continued to explore the game on his own with various materials in the room. When he eventually moved to involve adults in his hiding games, they were ones that he had initiated himself. This seemed to be the key. Gus needed to be the initiator and the one in control of the game in order to be interested. As Gus initiated these games and the adults learned to be willing responders, Gus' control over the structure of the hiding game expanded. He started vocalizing in the "slot" for the words "There it is!" For example, when reading a lift-the-flap book with Nicole, he closed the flap over a picture of a duck and paused (Figure 15–4), waiting for Nicole to ask, "Where's the duck?" Gus then lifted the flap and vocalized "Da, da, da!" with the intonation pattern of the phrase "There it is!" that he had heard many times from the teachers.

FIGURE 15–4
Engaging Nicole in the hiding idea, Gus adds structure to the game as he intones "Da, da, da!" for "There it is!" upon discovering the picture hidden under the flap.

FIGURE 15–5
Gus increases his control of the hiding game as he alternately hides then "discovers" himself in this version with Michele.

Later in the same time period, Gus approached Michele wearing a red cap. He pulled the cap over his face and waited, prompting Michele to ask, "Where's Gus?" He quickly pulled the cap off his face and Michele exclaimed, "There he is!" They repeated this game several times (Figure 15–5). Gus then pushed Michele's hat over her eyes. He waited, pulled the hat off her face, and shouted "Da, da, da!" After a few more rounds of hiding Michele, Gus returned to hiding his own face. In these interactions, Gus was in control both when he was the hider (covering Michele's face) and when he was simultaneously the "hider" and the "hidee." This control was central to Gus' inquiry.

The Hiding Project with Meredith

Meredith too continued to show interest in the hiding games that were first noticed at the sand table by the teachers, but with important differences. At 23 months, Meredith clearly knew that a hidden object was still there, though she couldn't see it, and that she could retrieve it. In talking about the experience at the sand table, the teachers recalled seeing Meredith playing by herself at the light table a few days earlier. The teachers had placed small, colored-plastic fish and "Flubber," a gooey, sensory substance made of white glue, water, and borax, on the surface of the light table. Meredith covered the fish with the Flubber. The light from underneath made the Flubber translucent so that she could still see the fish. She would pause, pull a fish out, and say, "There it is!" She repeated this activity for about 15 minutes, varying the way she hid the fish (pushing the fish into the Flubber, draping the Flubber over the fish) until they were all covered. Then she would meticulously find each one (Figure 15–6). The teachers put this activity out daily that week, and Meredith spent time there each day with her private fish game. Interestingly, another toddler, Jonathan (19 months), tried to join her at the table, but Meredith became frustrated and wanted him to leave.

FIGURE 15–6
Meredith pursues the physical aspects of hiding, preferring to work alone at the light table when hiding fish under the Flubber.

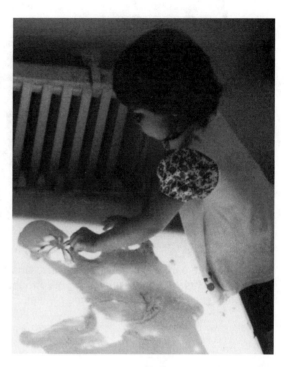

The teachers found objects for Jonathan to hide with his own pile of Flubber so that he and Meredith could work independently. At this point, Meredith seemed engaged in the physical aspects of hiding and retrieving objects and in being in charge of the game herself.

The teachers continued to try putting the Flubber and fish out for Meredith, and she continued to explore the activity but again rejected the idea of sharing it with her peers. However, when she subsequently had the experience at the sand table with Gus and Michele, Meredith's interest shifted to the social role that she discovered in her interactions with Gus.

After that first interaction with Michele, Meredith joined Gus at the sand table several times to play out the hiding game as mentor. In the weeks that followed, Meredith also initiated the hiding game with her teacher, Nicole. For example, Meredith would take a blanket to Nicole and motion that she was going to hide under it. Nicole, aware that Meredith was practicing the hiding routine, would ask, "Where's Meredith?" Meredith would pop out from under the blanket with great enthusiasm (Figure 15–7). Nicole responded, "There she is!" While Meredith engaged other adults in the room in her hiding game, she mostly used Nicole as her willing partner.

Eventually, Meredith used the teachers less and less for her hiding activities and was observed leading the game with her same age and younger peers. For example,

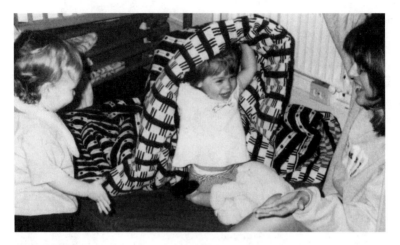

FIGURE 15–7
With her favorite partner, Nicole, Meredith investigates the social aspects of the
hiding game. Gus joins them, reinforcing his own theories as he observes Meredith
disappearing and reappearing under the blanket.

Meredith showed Harry how to play peek-a-boo around the telephone post: hide,
peek, find, and scream! The hiding game seemed to give her tools for social engagement with adults and peers and a place to explore a mentoring role.

Teacher Reflections

At the time that Gus and Meredith's hiding projects began, the teachers had been
deep in discussion about what constitutes an appropriate and meaningful project
with infants and toddlers. What are the entry points and the sources for such projects? Gandini (2001) acknowledges that many American educators struggle to re-
frame their image of working with infants and toddlers in the Reggio way.
Educators in the United States often ask the following questions: Is it possible for
infants to be involved in a project? How *does* one define a project for children less
than 3 years of age? (p. 63).

Many of the projects that our infant-toddler teachers had accomplished to this
point were more like the meaningful projects described by Malaguzzi in his interview
with Lella Gandini (Edwards, Gandini, & Forman, 1998): "First [a good project] must
produce or trigger an initial motivation to warm up the children. Each project has a
sort of prologue phase in which information and ideas are offered and shared within
the group. These will be used later to help the children to expand their intentions
along with the adults' intentions suggesting a final objective" (p. 90).

In fact, this kind of intentionality and group objective characterized many of the group projects that had been accomplished by our infant-toddler community, including an exciting "Mail Project" that had just culminated prior to the hiding project. The mail project had involved the whole group in writing, sending, and receiving mail. The focus of this project was on the reciprocity of communication, and on making visible the mystery of the mail process (Where does it go? How is it delivered?).

The older toddlers who had led the mail project had transitioned to the preschool room and were "replaced" by infants new to the classroom community. The teachers discussed how unlikely it was that this new younger group could engage in a project as abstract and group-oriented as the mail project. They found themselves turning to questions about the nature of project work with very young children. They agreed that they needed to offer experiences and activities for a while to observe, locate, and document the "threads" of interest in the room. The notion of "threads" was learned from colleagues at the University of Vermont Laboratory School (Gandini & Goldhaber, 2001), while documentation as an inquiry tool to uncover threads was learned from the Italians (Rinaldi, 1998).

This practice of observation and documentation led the teachers to Gus and Meredith's fascinating explorations of hiding games. Through trial and error, and through documentation and reflection, the teachers learned to expand their approaches to infant-toddler project work and to expand the conceptualization of their own roles in supporting that work. They learned that some child-led investigations can be supported with planned materials and experiences within the physical environment, but others, such as peek-a-boo, are better supported by sensitive, responsive adults in the social environment.

The teachers also learned to appreciate the nuances of a development (object permanence) and a social structure/cultural routine for supporting it (hiding games) that change and grow over a period of years. The hiding project opened up the possibility of investigations that are focused on individual children rather than the group, and the potential for developmental behaviors to be a source or "driving force" for a project. Meredith and Gus were both involved in the hiding project, each in her/his own way. For Gus, the explorations seemed to be rooted more in the physical world; Meredith's explorations were more about the social world and her agency within it. In ways similar to how toddlers parallel play with the same materials, these two children were engaged in a project with similar surface features, but they were exploring different personal lines of inquiry.

Thus Gus and Meredith led us to one answer to the question, "When is a project meaningful with infants and toddlers?" The teacher Cristina Bondavalli, in an interview with Lella Gandini (Gandini, 2001), eloquently articulates our discovery: "The questions and personal paths of the children become a project at the moment when the adult is capable of entering and staying within this game of making suggestions and proposals, having expectations about the path to take, then revisiting and interpreting the children's personal paths with other teachers." Thus, at the moment when Nicole and Michele realized they could enter and stay within the developmental games of Gus and Meredith, the work became meaningful as a project.

CONCLUSION

The writing of this chapter is another form of revisiting our experiences with the children. As we reflect upon what we have learned in this most recent step in our journey, we return to the wisdom of our colleagues in Reggio Emilia, as expressed by Carlina Rinaldi (1998), to capture and share what we believe to be the most important lesson reinforced in this project: the importance of learning how to listen to children. As Rinaldi (1998) remarks:

> We have always maintained that children have their own questions and theories and that they negotiate their theories with others. Our duty as teachers is to listen to the children just as we ask them to listen to one another. Listening means giving value to others, being open to them, and what they have to say. Listening legitimizes the other person's point of view thereby enriching both listener and speaker. What teachers are asked to do is to create context where such listening can take place. Listening is thus a general metaphor for all the processes of observation and documentation. (p. 120)

Learning to listen to our very youngest children is truly a refined skill that takes time and practice to develop. They communicate in a variety of ways that are not always as accessible as verbal language; their profound theory-construction is not always readily visible and the depth of their learning can be lost in the context of daily, caregiving routines. The challenge for infant-toddler educators is to practice daily listening in order to reveal and understand the interesting paths their children are taking—paths that have the potential to become projects in which children and adults learn together.

16

Embracing Snow
A Story of Negotiated Learning

Pam Oken-Wright
Teacher, St. Catherine's School, Richmond, Virginia

Children are powerful thinkers. They grapple with large and profound ideas all the time. What happens to people when they die? What makes a rainbow? What's happening where I can't see—inside a TV, to a baby before it's born, under the ground? Although it's certainly possible that children are asking for answers when they pose these kinds of questions, I believe that at least some of the time their intent is to initiate dialogue around theories they are constructing. In an environment where that natural and spontaneous expression of theory is appreciated and supported discourse around ideas abounds, a culture of conversation for the construction of theory develops. In the story that follows, one child's expression of theory about the source of snow—and the teachers' response to that expression—launched an in-depth investigation into the nature and source of snow. In a traditional curriculum, a study of snow might take a relatively straight path through concepts deemed "important to know about snow." In contrast, in negotiated learning (Forman and Fyfe 1998) children and teachers navigate the often winding path of investigation together, with an exchange of provocation and response, toward a deeper understanding of the aspects of snow that engage children's intellect and emotion most.

Investigations may begin anywhere; provocations may arise from many sources. The course of negotiated learning, however, begins with observation and documentation. Ideas flow in children's play, conversation, and representation. Teachers observe and document carefully to notice when a topic of play or conversation or representation seems to hold a certain energy or passion or longevity or pattern, all indicators of the possibilities inherent in the combination of topic, children, and timing. If, for example, the teacher notices tremendous energy around the news that the classroom was visited by mice in the night, and that energy and interest seem to be hanging on for a time, she might wonder, "What about this idea has so captured the children's imaginations?" She will know that though it is possible that the children are fascinated by the mice themselves, it is equally possible that the elusiveness of the encounter or the mice's sheer invisibility is at the center of their interest. Or that the children's passion could be borrowed from fear (which often seems to translate into a "plan" if it's pursued and supported). Perhaps we should say that in addition to one hundred languages there are one hundred possibilities at the beginning of every investigation. This is the nature of negotiated learning. Topics emerge, teachers document and wonder and provoke, children respond, and so on in an exquisite, often non-linear dance with layer upon layer of meaning. It *cannot* be planned, but it *can be planned for* through the teacher's disposition to observe, document, provoke, and think, through the preparation of the environment to invite the interactions and encounters through which children's ideas emerge, and through the development of a culture of conversation and construction of theory.

This chapter tells one story of negotiated learning, a relatively short-term (about a month long) investigation around snow. The setting is a classroom of sixteen 5-year-olds at St. Catherine's School in Richmond, Virginia. St. Catherine's is an independent day (and boarding for grades 9 through 12) school for girls. The Jr. Kindergarten children spend one year in the program, in a house off by itself on a suburban-type campus, with one teacher, one teaching assistant, and, as often as possible, a parent volunteer.

SNOW: FIRST PROVOCATIONS

It rarely snows more than a few inches in Richmond. When it does, though the adult world pretty much screeches to a halt, children's encounters with the snow are full of joy and wonder. It snowed 8 inches one January day this past winter, leaving short-term tangible traces but a long-lasting impression on the 5-year-olds in my class. The children's minds and conversations were full of images of and ideas about snow. When we came together for meeting on our first day back in school I asked, simply, "Tell me about snow." A minute or so into the ensuing conversation, Barbara offered, "I know how you make snow. You get water, and then you put snow inside of the water, and then it makes more snow."

Barbara's theory didn't exactly arise from nowhere. All year we had worked together to construct a culture of conversation and of co-construction of theory. The children were used to posing theories and inviting discourse. They were comfortable expressing their theories in the context of the group. And they had begun to "problematize" in the course of conversation, challenging each other, asking "what if . . . ," and offering provocation in the form of questions.

As it turned out, Barbara's statement served as the springboard for an investigation into snow that included construction of theory about the source and nature of snow and investigation into the nature of snowflakes, as well as the intersection of the two. As the investigation grew, the children's theories became more and more reasoned and plausible, and they articulated their ideas more and more clearly. Their first theories seemed to hold a sort of reciprocity between factual and magical thinking. Magical thinking often involves higher powers (in this case, God and Santa Claus) and magical agents such as dust, wands, angels, and so forth. Though their immediate thoughts were that God makes the snow or that it somehow comes from or through Santa Claus, the children tried to weave facts they'd heard into the framework of their thinking—elements of increasing plausibility. These are some salient theories from that first conversation.

God made the snow.

God collects the snow and dumps it down, maybe using a cup.

The wind brings the rain to God, and God gets the snow from the rain.

God gets the snow from the clouds and the clouds get it from the North Pole.

God makes snow from the white (of the clouds).

God makes some ice out of cold water, and then He puts it in a cup, and then He pours it out, and it goes down to the earth.

Santa Claus is the agent or intermediate source of snow.

Santa Claus found the snow in his backyard.

Snow falls from the sky into Santa's yard. From there it is distributed to the children's world.

The wind brought it to Santa's yard. (connections: wind → cold → snow)

Santa has special dust, and when he puts it down everywhere it turns into snow.

The elves make it, maybe with some special dust.

Luly proposed a theory, still magical but lacking the typical agent of magic: *The air makes it so cold that it [the air] turns into snow.* Luly's theory emerged multiple times throughout the investigation, and each time she adapted or changed it in response to other children's theories or new information.

After transcribing the tape recording of this conversation, my assistant, Jan Locher, and I studied it and mapped it in an effort to begin to understand the children's intent. What was it about snow that inspired the particular energy and unanimous interest in the topic? Noting the little dance between information and magical thinking in this conversation and wishing to provoke further thinking, we introduced the book *Snow Crystals* (Bentley, 1931), a collection of exquisite photographs of magnified snowflakes. Two children remained with the book for quite some time after the group disbanded, examining the photographs intently. We invited them to study the snowflakes even more closely by tracing some of them at the light table (Figure 16–1).

FIGURE 16–1

FIGURE 16–2
Documentation panel of one aspect of the investigation

REPRESENTING SNOWFLAKES IN MULTIPLE LANGUAGES: SNOWFLAKES AND SYMBOLIC THOUGHT

All during the next day the children continued to think about and represent snow and ice, cutting paper snowflakes and tracing them at the light table (Figure 16–2). In the studio, Laura and Liza declared their intent to make snowflakes out of clay. Then they just sat in front of their clay, apparently at a loss as to how exactly one *would* make a snowflake out of clay. Finally Laura went to get one of the pages from *Snow Crystals* to use as a referent (Figure 16–3). In the end, each child who took on the challenge of making a snowflake of clay chose a specific snowflake photograph to represent. But not one really stuck with the model. Rather, the children seemed to be representing their own theories about snowflakes through the clay (Figure 16–4).

Throughout this investigation the children continued to represent snowflakes in multiple languages. As they studied snowflakes in order to represent them, one or two children learned that every snowflake has six sides or points, like the hexagonal pattern blocks and overhead projector pieces with which they were familiar. Soon that small piece of information became a treasure, passed from child to child as they worked to represent snowflakes (Figure 16–5).

We came to realize that the children's work in representing snowflakes was an expression of their theories about snow. It seemed to me that these theories were more about the nature of snow and its relationship to the children's inner symbolic life, in contrast to our conversations that seemed centered on the mystery of the source of snow. For example, many of the children represented snowflakes with stars in the middle (Figure 16–6). When I wondered aloud about this association, one child explained, "I think the wise men, the star led them to Jesus, and it was Christmas when

FIGURE 16–3
Laura retrieved a page from *Snow Crystals* to help develop her model.

FIGURE 16–4

FIGURE 16–5
Using two pattern block pieces that she chose to use as referents, Mariah works to carve a hexagon out of a slab of clay for the center of her snowflake.

FIGURE 16–6

FIGURE 16–7

FIGURE 16–8

Jesus was born." Many of the children seemed to associate snow with Christmas, though I daresay most had never experienced a white Christmas.

The variety of languages with which the children represented snowflakes grew as the investigation continued (Figures 16–7 and 16–8). The children made snowflakes out of wire, drew them with pen and with chalk, and painted snowflakes with white paint on black paper. At one point the children represented snowflakes collaboratively with their bodies, inspired by one child's challenge. She sat on the floor, crossed her ankles and arms

FIGURE 16–9
The first version of a snowflake.

FIGURE 16–10
A second iteration. *"All snowflakes are different. This one is REALLY different!"* It made me wonder: Have I ever seen a three-dimensional snowflake?

FIGURE 16–11

FIGURE 16–12

and declared herself a snowflake. Others joined her, with intent to create one big snowflake. They called for us to capture their snowflake in a photograph (Figure 16–9) and then set out to innovate on that first formation (Figure 16–10). And right then, inspired by their own collaborative transformation into snowflakes, the children began to make snowflakes out of whatever they found in the vicinity—counting wands, parquetry blocks, lacing strings, and so on (Figure 16–11).

Later, using shadow as a language (portent of things to come!), two children constructed snowflakes with colored transparent shapes on the overhead projector. With a transition as fluid as that from body-snowflakes to found-object-snowflakes, the children began to frolic in the snow they'd made on the shadow screen (Figure 16–12). In addition to exploring snowflakes through familiar languages, after a while the children began to represent the idea through media new to them. While weaving snowflakes on

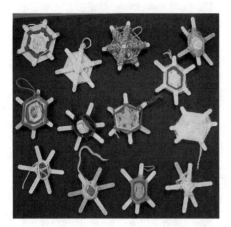

FIGURE 16–13

FIGURE 16–14
Documentation panel: The Source of
Snow

six-pointed "snowflake" forms made of Popsicle® sticks, the children were delighted to
discover that if one is careful with the weaving the characteristic hexagon emerges
(Figure 16–13).

THE SOURCE OF SNOW: CO-CONSTRUCTION OF THEORY

Meanwhile, the children continued to co-construct theory about the source of snow
(Figure 16–14) through conversation and representation.

> God makes the snow in a snow cloud.
>
> God sends snow to the snow cloud.
>
> The angels give it to God, and God brings it down to us and to the other
> people.
>
> Well, God has stuff to make snow, and God makes the snow, and Jesus
> helps Him make the snow, and then they call the angels to take the snow
> to the cloud.

Magic as an explanation did not satisfy the children for long. They began to
consider the attributes of snow as they entertained other possibilities.

> The air gets really freezing . . . really, really cold . . . and then it makes snow.

As an invitation to consider this theory a bit more I asked, "What is air?"

FIGURE 16–16
Caroline's snow theory drawing.

FIGURE 16–15

One child responded, "Made out of nothing." But another said, "I think that the air is made out of . . . God makes us and we breathe and the air comes out of us and all around us." (We make the air by breathing.)

My mom told me that there's a snow cloud that makes snow and it comes down to the ground.

Luly resurrected her theory, adding a color change: *The air gets so cold it turns into snow. When the air gets really really cold it turns white and that's snow.* Not everyone bought Luly's theory. One child argued, "One day it was really really really cold, but it didn't snow. And I was so cold that I weared sweater sweater sweater coat coat coat." Luly reasoned, "It had to be colder." We stopped the conversation while energy and interest were still high in order to invite the children to draw their theories about the source of snow (Figure 16–15). We encouraged the children to work in small groups so that the conversation could continue as they drew (Figure 16–16). When they finished we videotaped them explaining their theories.

Caroline:	There's little people in the clouds, and there's a block of ice cubes. They wet it. They mix it with water, and it makes snow. It turns into snow, and they put it in a cup, and they put it down.
O-W:	So they have ice cubes in the clouds?
Caroline:	Yes.
O-W:	Who are these people?
Caroline:	They're snow makers.
	At that moment Parker, who had already told about her theory drawing and who'd stayed to listen, interjected.

Parker:	Actually, there is something I forgot to draw. There's water in this. They mix it with the ice. (And Parker began to draw her revised theory.)
Caroline:	I forgot the water, too.
O-W:	Oh, you have more drawing to do. Do you want a thinking pen, too, Caroline?
Parker:	Caroline, are you the same theory as me?
Caroline:	Yup. They put ice in the water, and then they freeze it, and then it makes . . . snowflakes and it falls down.
Parker:	Mine was the same theory.
O-W:	Did you two collaborate on this theory?
Parker:	Yeah.
Caroline:	They made different kinds of snowflakes.

EXPERIMENTS: IF WE CAN MAKE SNOW, WE WILL KNOW THE SECRET OF THE SOURCE OF SNOW

The children collected large hunks of ice from the outdoor classroom—a treasure and a wonder in this Mid-Atlantic city. They wanted to preserve them, so we put them in the freezer. The children hypothesized that if we left the ice in the freezer long enough it might turn into snow. They remembered that in an earlier conversation Maddie had said that God has to snap His fingers for the transformation from ice to snow to occur. And so, for good measure, they snapped their fingers as they put the ice in the freezer. There was no immediate effect from the snapping, but the children were willing to wait for a day to see if there might be a delayed response. Alas, the ice did not turn into snow, even after an overnight wait.

The children's observations:

> It ran out of magic! It will NOT work if you put it in the freezer. Because ice stays ice. The freezer is not magic. The freezer will not make the ice come snow.

Whether the magic ran out or was never there, the children abandoned that possibility. Their thinking flowed to and settled into supposition about the mechanics of making snow from the human perspective (If we can make snow, then we can know how it is made naturally).

> I think when you get cold water and it turns into ice, and you put it somewhere overnight, and if you leave it out in the freezer overnight, I think that makes snow.

If you put ice into snow and put it in the freezer it will make snow.

From these ideas the children conceived three experiments. Perhaps one of these would make snow.

- ☐ Put snow on top of the ice and leave it outside.
- ☐ Put snow and water on top of ice and leave it outside.
- ☐ Mush spun wool and water together and freeze it for one night or 60 months.

There were still a few small piles of snow here and there outside, enough to perform the first two experiments. We hypothesized that the children's doubt in the likelihood of success of the first experiment—snow on top of ice—inspired the second experiment, creating a sort of cumulative theory: If this idea doesn't work, we'll add to the layers/complexity and maybe THAT will work. In contrast, the children seemed more certain that water plus white wool, frozen, would make snow. As they dropped water onto the bit of wool one child observed, "It's getting so small!" (like a snowflake?) and another, "It's turning into snow!"

THINKING ABOUT THE PROBLEM IN ANOTHER CONTEXT: EXPLORING THE DOME OF ICE

Hoping to inspire investigation into the connection the children seem to have made between ice and snow, we offered as provocation a large dome of ice in a water table, with droppers and salt water. The children's exploration of the ice over several days seemed to draw them toward comparison of the attributes of ice and snow (Figure 16–17).

When the children arrived at school the next morning they noticed that the experiments to make snow (ice + snow and ice + snow + water), left on the porch overnight, had turned into water and not snow at all. However, when we went to take the dome of ice, melted in the exploration of the day before and refrozen, out of the

FIGURE 16–17
"We made a big hole so we could study water, and we thought it would help us figure out about snow." A few minutes later: "I think I almost figured out how to make snow now. You have to put ice on something very, very soft."

freezer, the children noticed "snow" (frost) along the edge of the block. Both encouraging news and a new provocation! It is possible to make snow after all, though *how* is still a mystery! The idea resurrected, Laura and Kristen ran to the kitchen, thinking that perhaps there was snow in the freezer and that it got on the block of ice. But, no snow. Once again conversation flowed.

Lily:	Only clouds can make snow. We don't know how to make snow. We don't have the ingredients of the book of how to make snow.
O-W:	Who has the book?
Lily:	God.

Kristen offered a powerful provocation by suggesting, "Maybe . . . in your last class did you try to make snow?" I had to tell her no, that it hadn't snowed much last year and the topic of snow never really emerged. But Kristen's question inspired a new line of thinking. Experts were what we needed, the children thought! But whom to ask how it snows? Who might know? Moms, Dads, Grandmoms? Maddie offered, "My Daddy's magic. He can make snow." And someone suggested we ask "someone at the big school." In the end, the children decided to ask the fifth graders, the oldest children in the Lower School, how it snows.

The next day we held a general meeting and a small group meeting to prepare for our visit to the fifth grade. Though the goal of the conversation was to determine what exactly we should ask the fifth graders, the children continued to co-construct theory, now apparently driven to do so.

If we combine all our theories and those of the fifth graders, it will make snow.

Snow is soft ice.

The moisture in the clouds, when it gets very very cold, turns into snow. It's really really true. My mom told it to me.

I think when you're in fifth grade you learn how to make snow.

By the end of the conversation the children had produced a list of questions to ask the fifth graders.

- ☐ How is a real snowflake made?
- ☐ How does it fall?
- ☐ Who or what makes the snow?
- ☐ What makes a snowflake fall?
- ☐ We're trying to turn our ice into snow. How can we do it?
- ☐ Is there a pusher on the clouds that pushes them and then the snow falls down? (Lily already had an answer to this question: No one can stay in the air so it falls [gravity!])

- We don't have an ingredients book (cookbook?) of snow. Can you help us make an ingredients book to make snow?

- We need a book of all your theories of how to turn ice into snow.

- All our theories don't really work so can you help us make snow? Thank you for doing that. That's very helpful.

WHEN YOU ARE IN THE FIFTH GRADE YOU LEARN HOW TO MAKE SNOW

When we were ready, we visited Mrs. Cohen's fifth-grade class to pose our questions. The fifth graders promised to think about them and get back to us. Later that day I returned to the fifth-grade classroom alone and facilitated a conversation for the construction of theory about the source of snow with the older children. They continued the conversation in small groups after I left, and that night they wrote their co-constructed theories down. The next day the Jr. Kindergarten (JK) met again with the fifth graders, this time in small groups. The big girls drew and explained their theories to the 5-year-olds. In some of the small groups, the JK children reciprocated and shared their theories with the fifth graders. In others, the 5-year-olds challenged the thinking of the 10-year-olds. And in one or two groups, the little ones and big ones co-constructed new theories about the source of snow (Figure 16–18).

Wondering if and how the children's theories about the source of snow would change after hearing the fifth graders' ideas, we asked the children to draw their theories again. Some did incorporate bits of fifth-grade theory into their own and some did not. However, it was clear that the theories had evolved, and many of the children seemed to be quite a bit more articulate about their theories than the first time they drew and explained them. Lily's theory—not at all like that of any of the older children, by the way—proved to be a new provocation. Lily's drawing showed that a snowflake grows from a tiny piece of ice. Joined by more ice it gets bigger, then bigger. Then spokes come out of it. Then a star comes in the middle, then little dots come around the star, and there you have a snowflake (Figure 16–19).

FIGURE 16–18
The fifth graders in this group changed their drawing a bit in response to challenges from the 5-year-olds.

FIGURE 16–19
Lily's theory of the source
of snow.

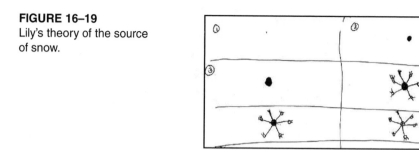

FIGURE 16–20
Snowflake Grows documentation panel.

Inspired by Lily's drawing of how a snowflake grows, we invited Lily to present it in a meeting during which we showed the children a brief video clip of a snowflake actually growing (time lapse photography), projected from the Internet onto a movie screen. Playfully, the children added their shadows to the continuous loop projection. Suddenly Kristen stopped and suggested that we could make a shadow puppet show of the growth of a snowflake. "One could do a tiny [snowflake] and big and big one and we could take turns putting ours up [on the shadow screen]!" And so began the "Snowflake Grows" project.

SNOWFLAKE GROWS: A SHADOW PLAY AND POWERPOINT® ANIMATION

After some negotiation, the Snowflake Grows small group affirmed Lily's theory that snowflakes grow in six stages (Figure 16–20). I am assuming that they chose six because of the six-sidedness of a snowflake. Their stages were similar to Lily's initial theory, with more spokes growing out of a central hexagon in each stage, and a star and dots drawn in the middle as detail on the last two stages. Then they organized the labor so that each child drew and cut out the snowflake at one of the six stages (Figure 16–21).

When the children went to the shadow screen to test the shadows of their representations, they discovered that the detail in the last two snowflake stages did not show in the shadow (Figure 16–22). Lily first thought to draw the dots and star on the shadow

FIGURE 16–21

FIGURE 16–22
The detail doesn't show in the shadow! Nor did it when the girls put the snowflake on the overhead projector bed.

FIGURE 16–23
Townley discovered that she could see the detail through a transparent object.

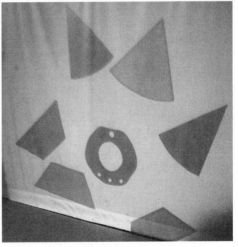

FIGURE 16–24

screen. She abandoned the thought, though, when asked what would happen when she moved the snowflake. Townley joined Lily in trying to solve the problem (Figure 16–23).

Townley's hypothesis was that if they put the snowflake on the transparent object the detail would show on the shadow screen. But it didn't. The children tried putting the snowflake onto a piece of cellophane, which is a bit more transparent. Still no detail showed. The children seemed stuck, so I showed them a plastic ring with holes in it and invited them to look at its shadow (Figure 16–24).

FIGURE 16–25   **FIGURE 16–26**

The children's first response was to put the snowflake *on* the ring on the projector bed. Where the snowflake did not cover it the ring's holes showed, but not the snowflake's details. And then Townley suggested poking holes in the snowflake. She poked one—and it showed in the shadow! She and Lily then poked holes along the rest of the detail (Figure 16–25) and the girls were satisfied. Townley declared herself a genius, and everyone agreed.

What interesting problem solving! Although the explicit intent was truth in representation of snowflakes, I think that the primary issue in this encounter was the nature of shadows. It occurs to me that shadows are quite magical to the children, that they are assuming that what they see can be transformed literally into a shadow, and that they are perplexed when it happens otherwise. It was a marvelous moment of disequilibrium. When what is expected does not occur, one's assumptions *must* be questioned. And so—discovery.

With a major problem solved, the small group was able to continue work on the shadow play. With technical support, the children photographed the shadows of the snowflakes, constructed and animated the PowerPoint® presentation, and added illustrations, titles and captions, music, and an author page (Figure 16–26).

THE SHADOW PLAY

The images in the shadow play are shadows of the same snowflake as it grows from a hexagonal piece of ice to a snowflake with a star in the middle and dots around it (Figure 16–27). Try to imagine the snowflakes dissolving from one stage to the next, accompanied by the Allegro from Vivaldi's Recorder Concerto in C major, the music the children chose for the play.

FIGURE 16–27
Note that the fifth stage had detail that the children did not punch out. It is interesting to me that this omission did not bother them but that it was important to them that the detail show in the last stage.

FIGURE 16–28
I know how to make a snowflake! First it turns into a dot. And then it gets medium every day. And then it grows a little bigger. And then it gets one stem, and then it gets 2 stems and bigger, and then it gets 4 stems. Then it gets 5 stems, and then it gets 6 stems, and then it turns into a snowflake! Liza

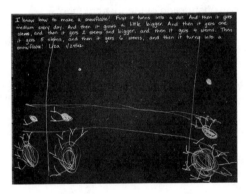

FIGURE 16–29
Stephanie drew a snowstorm in many colors, saying that the snowflakes have crystals in them.

Weeks after all the snow from the big storm had melted, the children were still thinking about snow. Children who were not part of the Snowflake Grows small group took on the construct and used it in their own exploration of the nature of snow (Figures 16–28 and 16–29).

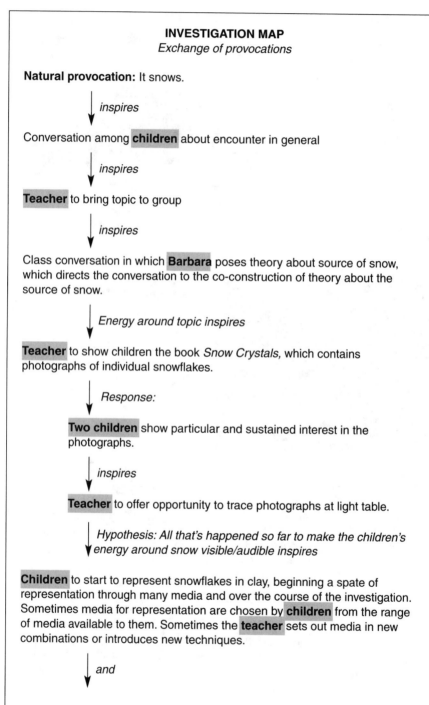

INVESTIGATION MAP
Exchange of provocations

Natural provocation: It snows.

inspires

Conversation among **children** about encounter in general

inspires

Teacher to bring topic to group

inspires

Class conversation in which **Barbara** poses theory about source of snow, which directs the conversation to the co-construction of theory about the source of snow.

Energy around topic inspires

Teacher to show children the book *Snow Crystals,* which contains photographs of individual snowflakes.

Response:

Two children show particular and sustained interest in the photographs.

inspires

Teacher to offer opportunity to trace photographs at light table.

Hypothesis: All that's happened so far to make the children's energy around snow visible/audible inspires

Children to start to represent snowflakes in clay, beginning a spate of representation through many media and over the course of the investigation. Sometimes media for representation are chosen by **children** from the range of media available to them. Sometimes the **teacher** sets out media in new combinations or introduces new techniques.

and

Teacher brings children's previous theories back to them, inspiring renewed co-construction of theory.

Children's continued interest inspires

Teacher to invite children to draw their theories; teacher records their explanations.

Children settle into the theory that if they can figure out how to make snow they will know how it is made in nature.

Children devise and perform three experiments to make snow. Experiments fail. Children revisit the issue. They decide to ask the fifth graders about the source of snow. Fifth graders prepare and present their co-constructed theories to the 5-year-olds.

Question: Will the children's theories change as a result of the work with the fifth graders? Will they assume the older children's theories, accommodate their theories to the fifth graders', assimilate the big kids' theories and co-construct new theories of their own—or be affected at all?

The **teacher** asks the children to draw their theories again and explain them as she records their theories. The children are far more articulate about their theories this time. **Lily** draws her theory that snowflakes grow from tiny hexagonal pieces of ice.

inspires

Teacher to show the children a video clip of a snowflake growing (citation of video in article).

inspires

Kristen to suggest they make a shadow play of how a snowflake grows. The next day a small group meets to plan the project. It is executed over several days. As problems arise the teacher facilitates negotiation but does not impose solutions.

The children produce an animated Power Point® presentation of the shadow play, "Snowflake Grows."

The extended period of investigation about snow and a brief reprise of snow-fall weeks later seemed to lead to increasingly sophisticated thinking about snow. One morning after the second, smaller snow, Kristen reported, "You know when it snowed? I saw how a snowflake is. I saw the hexagon inside the snowflakes. It had little strings of ice coming out. It looked like little ice crystals . . . I took a black piece of paper, and we let the snow fall on it, and it looked neat . . . I looked through it with my magnifying glass. The ones on the paper were different shapes. I was surprised about that. I thought snowflakes were alike."

In all they did in this investigation, the children had to consider every attribute of snow: its coldness, wetness, softness, whiteness, and intricacy, in trying to determine its nature and its source. The fifth graders told us that they had studied the source of snow in third grade. Yet their understanding of the process was really no deeper than that of the 5-year-olds. When children have wrapped their minds around an idea for a while (and construction of theory, particularly when done with others, is just that), they seem to develop a mental framework particular to that idea. Then when any information comes their way (for example, the fifth-graders' memory of being told that snow picks up particles of debris as it forms and falls), they have that framework within which the new information can reside. In other words, with the cognitive framework in place that bit of information *can* become knowledge, really learned. Otherwise it may remain an isolated piece of information, never transformed by understanding.

VI

Accepting the Challange to Change by Creating the Appropriate Setting

Of course, projects emerge best when provided with appropriate settings. Karen Haigh strikes an encouraging and practical note about how to do this as she describes the way the environment of her centers has continued to blossom since she wrote her initial chapter for *First Steps*. Undaunted by the fact that her centers include 44 classrooms and 15 family child care providers located in one of the most challenging parts of Chicago, she discusses many aspects of the environment ranging from color, windows, and furniture to room arrangement and documentation and offers numerous suggestions on how to achieve beauty combined with practicality.

Chuck Schwall provides many answers to Lilian's provocations about the feasibility of including an *atelieristi* as part of the educational setting. Illustrating that "where there's a will, there's a way," Chuck explains how an *atelier* or studio is set up at St. Michael School and how the studio teacher functions in relation to the "regular" classrooms there.

In chapter 19, Barbara Burrington and Susan Sortino describe how the staff at the University of Vermont came to grips with their desire to document everything the children did while also working within the constraints of a limited budget and, more seriously, a limited amount of time to devote to that process. Conceding that "no magic system was to evolve" (p. 227), they share with us their sensible recommendations together with examples from their experience of achieving success without losing their sanity.

SOME EXCERPTS FROM LELLA'S CHAPTER

About Space

The layout of physical space, in addition to welcoming whoever enters the schools, fosters encounters, communication, and relationships. The arrangement of structures, objects, and activities—often re-adjusted—encourages choices, problem solving, and discoveries in the process of learning.

It is also true that the centers and schools of Reggio convey a sense of well-being because they are simply beautiful. . . .

There is attention to detail everywhere: in the color of the walls, the shape of the furniture, the arrangement of simple objects on shelves and tables. Light from the windows and doors shines through transparent collages and weaving made by children.

About the Atelierista

A teacher who is trained in the visual arts works closely with the other teachers and the children in every preschool (and visits the infant-toddler centers). This teacher is called an *atelierista*, and a special workshop or studio, called an *atelier*, is set aside and is used by all the children and teachers, as well as by the *atelierista*. The *atelier* contains a great variety of tools and resource materials, along with records of past projects and experiences.

About the Power of Documentation

Transcriptions of children's remarks and dialogues, photographs of their activity, and children's representations of their ideas—using different media—are traces of observation carefully studied. . . .

Documentation is made visible and available through displays of panels and many other important means. For example, books and notebooks, illustrated daily or weekly diaries, small exhibits of children's artifacts, slide or video documentaries, audiocassettes, messages and letters, and so on.

SOME CHALLENGES FROM LILIAN

Physical features.   The arrangements and kinds of space available in the infant centers and preprimary schools of Reggio Emilia seem to be central elements of their work. How many of the elements of this feature can we realistically expect to adopt? How long would it take? How would the considerable costs be met? How essential are these physical features? Are they central to the nature of the Reggio Approach?

Atelieristi.   How many of us can hope to incorporate an *atelierista* into our programs? How could the cost be met? How much of the Reggio Emilia Approach can be adapted without the constant presence and expertise of the *atelieristi*? Or, for that matter, how important to the whole effort is the availability of an *atelier*?

Documentation.   The contribution of documentation to the work of our Reggio colleagues is also convincing and very impressive. How much staff time and energy does good documentation require? What kinds of additional resources would be required to yield such a high quality of documentation? How adaptable is this central feature to our situations? How much documentation is enough?

17

Reflecting on Changes Within Our Learning and Living Environments at Chicago Commons

Karen Haigh

Director of Programs, Chicago Commons Association,
Chicago, Illinois

In the time since the chapter in the book *First Steps* about Chicago Commons' child development program was written, Commons has continued to explore and interpret some elements of the Reggio Emilia Approach while experiencing a number of changes that have impacted the program. Examples of major changes we have experienced are as follows:

- ❑ Having begun with 7 classrooms, now all 44 classrooms at Commons are exploring the Reggio Emilia Approach. However, the exact number of classrooms continues to change as we continue to close and relocate sites.

- ❑ The number and type of classroom programs continue to change as we close centers because of gentrification and financial need and build new, larger centers. Types of programs include:
  - ❑ Early Head Start for children 0 to 3 years
  - ❑ Head Start for children 3 to 5 years; Subsidized Child Care for children 0 to 12 years
  - ❑ State Prekindergarten for children 3 to 5 years
  - ❑ Family Child Care for children 0 to 3 years

- ❑ There are currently 6 sites/locations serving 908 children:

ETC	3 classrooms/88 children
Emerson House	3 classrooms/74 children (soon to relocate)
Guadalupano Center	9 classrooms/194 children
New City Center	4 classrooms/108 children
Nia Family Center	13 classrooms/199 children
Paulo Freire Center	12 classrooms/198 children
Family Child Care	15 providers/47 children

- ❑ There is a core of central office and child development staff that includes myself as director, an assistant director, an education manager, three education coordinators, two studio coordinators, a parent involvement coordinator, a program monitor, and two administrative assistants. Because of unavoidable financial cutbacks, a social worker position and an additional education coordinator have been eliminated.

- ❑ There have been many very difficult adjustments as our central offices were relocated and Taylor House was closed, which necessitated moving 8 classrooms to three different locations.

- ❑ All of the centers have become NAEYC accredited and are in the process of renewing accreditation.

- ❑ Staff are much more involved with presenting public programs, as we have presented them more frequently to other schools and centers. We now hold at least two study tours a year during which such programs are presented.

☐ Like many other early childhood programs, the program continues to deal with staff turnover as a major challenge. We continue to support and extend a wide range of education and experience levels among our staff.

☐ The executive director, who had been with the agency for over 30 years, left the agency and was replaced by a new president and CEO.

☐ Many goals that were developed within the Chicago Commons chapter of *First Steps Toward Teaching the Reggio Way* have been accomplished.

☐ We continue to experience major changes in Head Start and subsidized child care as welfare reform and contract compliance issues challenge us to think about types of programming, eligibility requirements, assessment, and accountability.

☐ And lastly, we have made gradual yet dramatic changes in our environments.

Our goals for our environments, along with challenges, influences, elements, and changes we have explored along the way, will be shared in the rest of this chapter in hopes they will encourage and fortify the reader's determination to think about what might be done to improve the environments of their programs.

FACING CHALLENGES WITHIN OUR ENVIRONMENTS

As is true with many other programs, the environments at Chicago Commons present special challenges. Some of the special ones we must overcome include: old buildings that need a great deal of repair; staff's lack of knowledge and experience with building maintenance, repair, and renovation; finding willing and competent contractors to work with our environments; acquiring adequate funds for repair, maintenance, and renovation of existing buildings; and, perhaps the best challenge of all, keeping up with the many exciting ideas we develop to improve them.

I think it is important to view these obstacles, which sometimes feel insurmountable, as challenges to overcome, not as excuses for not moving forward. Another important insight gained is that it is vital to continue dreaming and planning *before* funding resources have been identified. This type of attitude is essential in order to "make things happen." Despite the fact that creating new environments takes an extraordinary amount of time and effort, make plans first rather than waiting around for funds and then making plans. We now have developed environmental plans for each site; many have changed at least six times, yet we continue to look ahead.

INFLUENCES ON OUR ENVIRONMENTS

Major influences have impacted and continue to impact our ever-changing and growing learning environments. Of course the programs of Reggio Emilia have influenced us to think about environments in new ways. I would say that the environments in Reggio have taught us to pay special attention to details (Ceppi & Zini, 1998; Gandini, 1998).

A second very powerful influence for us has been Anita Olds (2001), a psychologist who has devoted a great deal of time thinking about, presenting, and writing on the role of the environment with young children.

A third and most powerful influence when thinking about environments has been the result of staff looking at and experiencing a variety of environments together. Some of the environments we have experienced together in Chicago are the Botanic Gardens, the Garfield Conservatory, the Recycle Center, the Chicago Children's Museum, and the Art Institute. Together we have also visited unusual stores such as antique stores and Salvage One, a local business that sells unusual artifacts from old buildings. Time is usually provided for staff to reflect and dialogue together about the environment they have experienced and how it might suggest new ideas for our environment. Often these ideas are recorded and shared with other staff afterwards.

We have also explored special environments when participating in out-of-town conferences, such as visiting national parks, cathedrals, museums, and unusual stores. As a result we are much more open to gaining insight on ideas for environments from wherever we are.

A final form of influence has been formal professional development activities, such as a day-long or half-day inservice training on the environment, attending conferences, seminars, and workshops focused on the environment, and presenting at conferences on the environment. Staff have attended both the past Child Care Institute of Design by Anita Olds and the current Child Care Design Institute by Jim Greenman and Mike Lindstrom now sponsored by Harvard University.

OUR GOAL FOR THE ENVIRONMENT

I believe it is important to have a sense of purpose and intention for what one does, and why. Therefore it is essential that we consider our understanding of the role of the environment within our program. Discussion and dialogue about the meaning and understanding of words and ideas are essential for program development and growth.

Our goals for the environment are to create one that encourages and provokes a sense of wonder, exploration, and socialization, and that fosters connections with nature and culture. The environment is seen as living and forever evolving. Therefore thinking about the environment is an ongoing process. At times this statement will be thought about and reflected upon together during professional development experiences. In this way we are constantly revisiting and reinventing our thoughts about the role of the environment within our centers.

BASIC ELEMENTS OF THE ENVIRONMENT

As we revisit and reinvent our ideas about the environment, there are many environmental elements to consider, think about, and act upon. They include color; windows and transparency; entranceways and common areas; light, shadows, and reflections; nature; levels; classroom arrangement and boundaries; real furniture and real light; documentation and displays; identity and community; storage and organization of materials; and playgrounds.

Thinking About Color

Wall colors were one of the very first changes we made. I remember Lella Gandini saying that "the children should be the ones to bring color to the classroom," not the walls. So we spent months changing colors in classrooms and sometimes even hallways and offices. Often primary colors are used with young children, and in some ways they show a very limited amount of color variety, so we went from bright or more loud colors to softer tones. The softer tones made rooms feel more spacious and calm. We began to see the walls as backgrounds for the color the children and their work brought to the classrooms. Painting is a somewhat easy, inexpensive way to make immediate changes within an environment.

Thinking About Windows

We cut windows between rooms, in doorways, and even above doorways to give more of a sense of connection between inside and outside. Some may view windows as a distraction for children, yet we want children to be learning about the world—and what better way to learn about the world than to be able to see what is happening out in the world and even between rooms, whenever possible. Some windows were placed indoors so children could see and connect outward and others could see inward. In one particular classroom we created a wall of windows that led into a studio for children to work on special projects.

   A special challenge has been to keep windows free of paper clutter such as flyers, memos, and so forth. Windows are to look through, therefore they must be kept free of visual clutter. As time went on we got new ideas for windows. One idea was to put a large fish tank in a cut-out window space so children could look at fish and through the fish tank into another room at the same time. One can view two worlds at the same time, the world of fish and the world of children.

Thinking About Entranceways and Common Areas

We devoted considerable time and effort to thinking beyond the classroom to consider the entire center as a place to support children, staff, and parents. We are trying

What better way is there to learn about the world than to be able to see what is happening in the world and even between rooms, whenever possible?

to think about entranceways and the messages they give to those who enter. Some questions to reflect upon are:

1. Do you get an idea of what the building is for?
2. What messages about the sense of place do you want to give?
3. Who lives in this place?
4. Do you get a sense of the building's history and who the people are in it?
5. What are some of the values or philosophies of this place, or what do the people who live here think is important?
6. Is there a place to sit so one feels welcome to stay?
7. Is there something intriguing to explore?
8. Is there something interesting that connects to nature?

We changed the entranceways by asking each site to create a history panel sharing some information about the center and its history or highlighting assets of the community. Photos of all the families or staff within the program were mounted in the entranceway. Some centers displayed Loris Malaguzzi's poem, "The Hundred Languages of Children." Spanish-speaking centers displayed it in Spanish. We even thought of displaying floor plans for the color tiling of the center so people could see

Photos of family and staff
are mounted in the
entranceway.

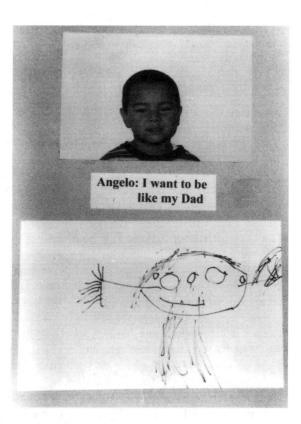

Angelo: I want to be like my Dad

the planned patterns for the building. Places that are more institutional tend to have few places for people to sit and feel comfortable, and the message seems to be "don't stay and hang around here." We thought about putting places to sit in the entranceway and throughout common areas so people would feel welcome and sit down. A chair or bench can give a very welcoming and comforting message. And the material the chair is made of can give a message of softness and comfort, or harshness. A group of school-age children was once asked to describe the new wooden classroom tables they got to replace the old Formica ones. To my surprise, the children said, "These tables are much softer." I have never thought of wood as being soft—but they did.

One center's entranceway has wooden benches made of logs and a large house-like structure to climb on, with a variety of hanging bells. Near the house is a series of small, round auto mirrors on the wall, a loom for children to work on, and a small basket of books on a small log table with small log benches. A chalkboard is on view as one enters. This is where teachers or parents can write a meaningful quote to share with others.

Common areas are much like entrance areas in that they are areas children walk through every day and have the potential to offer opportunities to wonder, explore, socialize, and connect with nature, identity, or community. In addition, common areas are where documentation of children's ideas, feelings, and meaning can be displayed for others to see and interpret.

We wanted to put items for children to interact with in these areas. We think of the whole building as space where children can wonder, explore, and socialize—not just classrooms. So we put a series of musical instruments in the hallway where children could play with them. There is an old bathtub with books and soft baby dolls in it so children can sit in the tub and look at books or read books to the dolls. There is some transparent plastic tubing installed in a hallway near a toddlers' room so children can put balls and items in the angled tubing to see what happens.

Some other items of interest we have placed in common areas are a series of boxes in a hallway where each opens up with a different kind of lock and has a different item to view in it after you open it. Each item is displayed on a mirror. They are simple items like a pinecone, seashell, and so forth. Another activity is a magnet table with a bench for two, as a bench for two encourages interaction with others.

Thinking About Light, Shadows, and Reflections

Light is especially important to people. People value light. People talk about being enlightened or seeing the light; we even refer to people as being bright. Light is important to us all. Children are intrigued with light, shadows, and reflections.

We began to think of ways to have interesting natural and commercial light in the centers. It is important to note that all types of light need not be the same. It is helpful to have different levels and kinds of light so there is variation in experience. Too many times centers or programs have the same kind of lighting throughout, which tends to feel institutional, dull, and monotonous; monotony begs for acting-out behavior.

Interesting lights and lamps were installed or purchased for classrooms and for the common areas. In addition, light tables or inexpensive light boxes (purchased at office supply stores) were acquired for programs. The big question with a light table or light boxes was, What do you do with them once you get them? One suggestion was for teachers to study and explore light along with the children. For example, investigating variations in light, transparency, and shadows throughout a space can raise questions and possibilities for further investigations.

Interesting lighting can also be used for nap time, a time when children may be experiencing great tension and anxiety. For instance, a lava lamp or a lamp with moving light can provide children with something to watch and a calming effect during a difficult time.

Mirrors offer opportunities for children to see themselves in many different situations and at different times of the day. Children can think about who they are and discover that they are still the same person even though they may look different or act differently. Mirrors can serve as a reference for children when making self-portraits with any variety of visual arts materials. Again variation of size, shape, and type of mirrors makes objects more interesting. Mirrors can be placed in many areas (not just the dramatic play area) of the classroom or center so children can experience what they look like when entering the classroom each day, or what they look like while drawing, building, talking to friends, and so forth. Auto stores tend to have very interesting, small, inexpensive mirrors that are easy to install.

Thinking About Nature

Jane Addams (1960) wrote about how children have a companionship with nature, and how imagination is connected with nature. Wishing on a star or imagining a pot of gold at the end of a rainbow are good examples of how children connect imagination and nature. Imagination is crucial for problem solving and essential for learning and living, therefore experiences with nature can enhance this ability to imagine.

Because we believe that nature is so important, we began to think of ways to make it a part of the children's experience. We especially wanted our children to have experiences with nature because they live in the inner city. So we tried to think of a variety of opportunities to bring nature into the center. Using a variety of healthy plants, fish, water, stones, rocks, leaves, seashells, and tree branches, we have made nature a focus and part of our environment.

The question to ask is, How can nature be brought into the center in new ways? Sometimes nature items for the center can be very simple, such as a basket of twigs or cut branches placed in the block area, or a basket of stones and shells used in the dramatic play area. Water tables can make great fish ponds. We have also tried some new, more permanent ideas such as embedding stonework into a countertop or creating a band of stonework within walls.

Thinking About Levels

Children enjoy encounters with different levels. Again, variation is important for making new connections. Low tables, the height of a coffee table, are often more easily used by young children for drawing and playing games as they can scoot up to and kneel at lower tables. Children, especially school-age children, also work well at drafting tables.

Risers offer a unique level, especially within block areas, to build on and leave constructions up while in progress but out of the pathway for being knocked down. Lofts are extraordinarily enticing to children because they can perch above and look out over the classroom. There can be comforting times in a loft with books and pillows. In addition, problem-solving machines like pulleys can be installed on lofts. Our lofts are mostly custom-made to fit individual classrooms, with various approaches such as a stairway at one end and a ladder at the other, or a ladder extended up through the middle of a loft. There are many innovative possibilities available when lofts are designed and built by those actually living in the center.

Thinking About Classroom Arrangement and Boundaries

We began to spend a great deal of time rearranging classrooms with particular focus on the relationships between **messy, active,** and **quiet** areas (Olds, 2001). Arranging classrooms can be taken for granted, but when considered carefully, classroom

Risers make an interesting area for block play to be created.

arrangement requires an amazing amount of time for thought and planning along with trial and error. It is really about designing space that is attentive to needs and interests of the children while paying special attention to curiosity, beauty, traffic flow, materials and their arrangement, interplay between areas and furniture, and many of the previously mentioned elements such as colors, windows, light, reflections, levels, and softness.

We also began to think of new ways to give an area a sense of boundaries. Often boundaries are "hard," such as the use of a line of furniture or a wall to give a sense of a separate area. However, softer boundaries can be used, too. Some softer and more interesting boundaries we have used include hanging pieces of cloth, umbrellas, mirrored Plexiglas®, large paper star-shaped lights, and trellises with hanging ornaments. Items like these are particularly desirable because many of our basic environments already feel hard; cloth and similar materials provide a gentler sense of being.

Thinking About Real Furniture and Real Utensils

We also spent a lot of time finding older, more homelike furniture and tools. We wanted to have unique and interesting furniture pieces that would create a different atmosphere, one more livable. We challenged each classroom to use at least one unusual piece of furniture—something not purchased in the educational supplies catalogs. So we went from small plastic couches to real wood-framed couches; from the usual children's furniture to antique furniture such as dressing tables, dining tables, accessory tables, dressers, and desks. At the same time, we did our best to purchase heavy-duty furniture for our school-age children because they can be quite hard on furniture.

We made a point of including familiar furnishings as part of the school environment.

We wanted the children to feel that they had the real items to play with (i.e., real kitchen utensils, real plates, pans), so we often went to the local stores for kitchen and home appliances. Furthermore, we wanted children to experience more items made of natural materials like wood and wicker instead of plastic.

Thinking About Documentation and Displays

More thought was put into what kind of documentation of children's work and ideas could be included. We began to put up larger documentation panels using the entire area, not just the part of the wall at children's eye level . We figured out ways to show three-dimensional work such as clay or wire. We allotted much time and attention to presenting children's work and experiences in an attractive and interesting way for children and adults. Often people believe there is one person who develops the panels, but over a period of years their development has really evolved into a group effort with everyone contributing their thoughts and action.

Thinking About Identity and Community

We realized how important it was for children to be able to explore who they are. We tried to display or show the many connections children have had individually and as a group in exploring ideas about who they are and with whom they are connected. To do so, we developed panels depicting the assets or history of the communities, or showing our special studies of a community such as: visiting children's homes, observing delivery trucks, exploring favorite stores on Chicago Avenue, looking at eyes in the community, seeing ways hands work in the community, looking at birds in the neighborhood,

looking at buildings downtown, and choosing favorite glasswork at the Garfield Conservatory's Chihuly Exhibit. We began to purchase furniture from a neighborhood store
that gets its furniture from Mexico. Since most of the children within that particular
program come from Mexico, this type of furniture helps our center make a connection
with the community and their ethnicity.

Thinking About Materials and Organization of Materials

We also began to think about organizing and storing materials for children in a different manner. We grew to realize that all storage containers do not have to be made
of plastic. All shelves do not have to be jam packed. We acquired containers made of
wood, woven baskets, wire, glass, ceramic, and some kind of plastic transparency.
Children's books were sometimes displayed in beautiful baskets. We began to acquire
unusual, attractive hooks on which to hang items.

Thinking About Playgrounds

The time and effort spent on our indoor environments influenced us to change our
outdoor environments. We have renovated four existing playgrounds and created an
original playground at our new Paulo Freire site. We worked with an architect who is
familiar with licensing regulations to plan playgrounds, and then hired landscapers
and carpenters to create them with special features like hills, sections with bushes or
trees, sandpits, houses to hide in, outside studios, and water sources. Interesting objects are included for children to interact with, such as column capitals for children to
sit on or stone pieces with shapes or colors embedded in them, and for younger children, a set of stairs to climb in order to drop items into a basket placed below.

Conclusion

The environment plays a powerful role and can influence people in a variety of ways.
Environments can limit us, challenge us, expand us, support us, heal us, excite us,
calm us, relax us, and teach us. Environments can convey physical, mental, and emotional messages. People are not victims of their environment, nor are they masters of
it. People are partners with the environment (Venolia, 1993). The challenge for all of
us has been to find how we can plan, think, and work to partner with the environment
so children, parents, and staff can live and learn together.

Some Hopes for the Environment for All Children

- ❏ that all children experience beauty
- ❏ that all children are given many opportunities to connect with nature
- ❏ that all children experience uncluttered environments that are organized in a thoughtful manner
- ❏ that all children experience reflections of culture and history that represent the children, parents, and staff of the particular center

- ❑ that all children and their work (not the bulletin boards or walls) become the main colors of the classroom
- ❑ that all children are given opportunities to encounter, interact, and exchange among themselves and with other classrooms
- ❑ that all children are given opportunities to explore and experiment with interesting materials in an atmosphere of discovery
- ❑ that all children are offered opportunities to know themselves, to express who they are, and to share their experiences and ideas in many different ways
- ❑ that all children experience having walls that speak for them and their life

Questions to Reflect Upon When Thinking About the Environment

- ❑ How can the environment be welcoming?
- ❑ What kind of message does the environment give as one enters the center?
- ❑ How can the environment have beauty and harmony?
- ❑ How can the environment help children and adults make connections with nature?
- ❑ How can there be natural light and interesting commercial light?
- ❑ How can the environment be uncluttered?
- ❑ How can the environment be organized in a thoughtful manner?
- ❑ How can the environment reflect the culture and history of a particular group of children and adults from the center?
- ❑ How can the environment show the children and their work to be the main colors in the center?
- ❑ How can the environment allow and encourage social interaction in which children have encounters, interactions, and exchanges among themselves?
- ❑ How can the environment encourage exploration and experimentation within an atmosphere of discovery and serenity?
- ❑ How can the environment offer opportunities for children to see themselves in many different ways?
- ❑ How can the walls speak for the children?

18

The Atelier Environment
Recognizing the Power of Materials as Languages

Charles Schwall
Studio Teacher, Consultant, The St. Michael School,
St. Louis, Missouri

I am a studio teacher[1] at The St. Michael School in St. Louis, where I have worked since 1993. I work full time with three preprimary class-rooms: a 3- and 4-year-olds' class, a 4- and 5-year-olds' class, and a full-day kindergarten. I began studying the Reggio Approach in 1992, resulting in several trips to Italy, frequent presentations at conferences, and work as an educational consultant in schools and other organizations. I hold studio art degrees from Washington University (MFA) and the Kansas City Art Institute (BFA). In addition to my role as an educator, I am an artist with a concentration in painting.

The St. Michael School is an Episcopal School for children of all faiths, enrolling about 110 children, three years old through sixth grade. The school is one of three that form the St. Louis–Reggio Collaborative (the other schools are Clayton School's Family Center and The College School of Webster Groves), and our staff is in dialogue with other educators interested in the Reggio Approach.

WHAT IS THE ROLE OF THE ATELIER?

Educators in Reggio Emilia often speak about connections between values and education (Rinaldi, 2001, p. 38). Choices we make in our schools reflect our values, and these values become part of the culture that forms the school. To establish an *atelier* in a preschool is a choice based on values. It is a choice that increases the teaching potential of the environment and supports children's experiences with visual languages.

The *atelier* is a specific context, often a separate area or room, for the use and understanding of materials. It gives children opportunities to explore and become experts with materials in a place that is designated for this purpose. As the classroom teachers and *atelierista* use the *atelier* to organize experiences, they develop their knowledge by observing children's learning through materials.

The *atelier* is also a place of research. It provides a setting for teachers to actively participate in observation, documentation, and interpretation. As a center for documentation tools and strategies, the *atelier* promotes documentation as communication in the school community.

Loris Malaguzzi (1998) spoke of the school as a system of relationships and interrelationships. The *atelier* is a workshop for relationships among materials, experiences, ideas, theories, emotions, new understandings, and multiple ways of communicating.

---

[1] The terms "studio teacher" and *"atelierista"* are used interchangeably and have the same meaning. "Studio teacher" is often a more accessible term for people in the United States, yet still implies a role unique from the traditional art teacher. In reference to the environment, the word "studio" can be used as an alternate to *"atelier."*

CREATION OF THE ST. MICHAEL SCHOOL ATELIER: INTENTIONS, BARRIERS, AND SOLUTIONS

Our head administrator, Ashley Cadwell, was very committed to having an *atelier*, along with a full-time *atelierista*, working with the three preprimary classrooms. This choice was one of many changes in our school as we began learning about the Reggio Approach. We wanted the *atelier* to be an amiable place that children and teachers would enjoy, as well as an attractive space that would communicate our values. As we began considering the physical environment of the *atelier*, we had many intentions to achieve and obstacles to overcome.

The first intention was to have the location of the *atelier* in close proximity to the classrooms. Children's interests and experiences frequently have their origin in the classrooms. Pedagogical connections between the *atelier* and events in the classroom are supported by the closeness of the two spaces.

An area between the 3- and 4-year olds' and 4- and 5-year-olds' classrooms was selected to become the *atelier*. The location was agreeable, but the space needed many improvements. A parent with a background in architecture drew the initial plans. We began by transforming the wall that connected the *atelier* to the 3- and 4-year-olds' classroom. Windows were installed in this wall, creating an openness between the two rooms. Another parent, a freelance builder, did the actual construction. Once this was complete, the *atelier* immediately seemed connected to the preschool environment (Figure 18–1).

While adjacent to the 3- and 4-year-olds' classroom, the *atelier* is only a short walk across the hall to the 4- and 5-year-olds' classroom. The kindergarten room is located on the third floor of the school building; therefore, connections to this class are maintained by frequent communication between the *atelierista* and teachers, by the children's daily use of the *atelier*, and by making the *atelier* visible through documentation in the kindergarten classroom.

The second intention was to create a quiet, well-defined work space for small groups of children. The *atelier* is a place for groups of children to work together with one teacher over an extended period of time without interruption. During the first year, our *atelier* space did not have its own doors but opened into the 3- and 4-year-olds' classroom. Noise traveling between the *atelier* and the classroom was a problem for both rooms. To solve this problem, walls with doors were constructed, and this made the *atelier* a more quiet and self-contained space (Figure 18–2).

The third intention for the *atelier* environment was flexibility. The three classrooms may have very different connections to the *atelier* during the course of several days. For example, the 3- and 4-year-olds might be weaving with natural materials while the kindergarten class collaborates on a large mural. These various situations often dictate how the *atelier* space is arranged and used; therefore, the elements and components of the studio need to be rearranged to fit many circumstances. Components in the *atelier*, such as a large work table, two easels, and a light table, can be rearranged and changed as needed on a daily basis.

FIGURE 18–1
A view of The St. Michael School *atelier* looking in from the 3- and 4-year-olds' classroom. The windows were installed to create an openness between the two rooms.

FIGURE 18–2
The St. Michael School *atelier*.

Flexibility also relates to storage space. Children may want to leave their work set up at the end of a work session and return to it later. Our *atelier* is a small room, approximately 11 × 25 feet. Its size limited the space for materials, as well as storage of children's ongoing projects. A long row of floor-to-ceiling shelves was installed along one of the interior walls, and a freestanding wire shelf was placed in the middle of the room. Also, shelves were created by the windows that look into the 3- and 4-year-olds' classroom. These changes enhanced the space for children's ongoing work, as well as for materials.

A fourth intention was to achieve a pleasing quality of light. At The St. Michael School, both of the preschool classrooms and the *atelier* are located in the basement of the school building. Because of this, there are few natural light sources. The *atelier* space has no access to daylight, necessitating a strong dependence on fluorescent light. After lighting was researched, high-quality fluorescent bulbs that simulate natural light were installed in the *atelier,* as well as the rest of the preschool. Also, "grow" lights capable of sustaining plants were added to the atelier to give another quality of light.

I feel we achieved success in regard to the issue of lighting. Several years ago a mother whose son was attending the preschool desired to create a studio environment for her son in the basement of their home. She often came to me for ideas, inspiration, and troubleshooting. One day, she came into the *atelier* and announced that she was discouraged. The results of her efforts were just not measuring up to her expectations. We were discussing the issue of lighting, and out of frustration she exclaimed, "Chuck, I just don't have the natural light that you have here!" At this point, I gently reminded her that The St. Michael's *atelier* had absolutely no natural light and that we were standing in a basement. This anecdote illustrates that high-quality results can be achieved, even when a location is less than ideal.

THE ENVIRONMENT, AESTHETICS, AND LEARNING

The presence of the *atelier* introduced aesthetic issues into the entire culture of the school. By recognizing aesthetic qualities as connected to and part of daily life, these qualities have the potential to help facilitate learning experiences. The aesthetics of the environment are life values that can be connected to educational values. For example, transparency, an aesthetic quality, can make an environment very attractive. Through the use of windows, transparent screens, or shelves that are open, a room can become inviting and pleasant to inhabit. But transparency can do even more when applied to a space that educates. On many occasions at The St. Michael School, 3-year-old children, after having watched kindergartners through the studio windows, will ask to participate in similar activities. Transparency can reveal the mystery and content of what is happening in a room in beautiful ways and, in an educational setting, give visibility to children's learning.

When attention is given to the aesthetic qualities of the environment, connections between these aesthetic elements and the daily life of the school can occur.

Transparency, for example, combined with other elements such as color and light, can become media used by children. During a project about the changing seasons, children in our school made colorful drawings of leaves on acetate and placed them on the windows of the preschool entryway. In this context, transparency became a medium.

In another situation, an oil burner that scented the classrooms with beautiful aromas became the beginning point for a project about scent and fragrance. Children's fascination with how the oil burner worked caused teachers to notice the potential of fragrance in learning. New experiences were organized around this topic. The result was an investigation that lasted several months and supported children's theories about scent and smell (Cadwell, 2002). Once aesthetic qualities are recognized in the environment, and are acknowledged as part of the normal process of living, they have the capacity to play an important role in children's learning experiences.

THE ATELIER AS CONTEXT FOR MATERIALS IN THE SCHOOL

It is essential that the contents of the *atelier* offer children many materials and languages with which to express and communicate. Everything that children carry inside themselves—their thoughts, knowledge, creativity, emotions, dreams, fantasies, wonderings, and ideas—is all very precious and rich. Materials provide unique ways of expressing and communicating. John Dewey summarizes this thought in his book, *Art as Experience*:

> Because objects of art are expressive, they are a language. Rather they are many languages. For each art has its own medium and that medium is especially fitted for one kind of communication. Each medium says something that cannot be uttered as well or completely in another tongue. The needs of daily life have given superior practical importance to one mode of communication, that of speech. This fact has unfortunately given rise to the popular impression that the meanings expressed in architecture, sculpture, painting, and music can be translated into words with little if any loss. If fact, each art speaks an idiom that conveys what cannot be said in another language and yet remains the same. (1934, p. 106)

Here, Dewey articulates the idea that each medium has its own unique values, possibilities, and ultimately, individualized communication. He also suggests that the languages of art, materials which communicate through the senses, are often devalued in relation to spoken and written forms of communication. The *atelier* can restore value to the languages that are based on the senses.

Children interact with the materials in their environment to communicate their ideas and feelings. They will have different sensitivities to various materials based on their individual personalities, attitudes, and knowledge. This is at the heart of the reason for an *atelier*. It causes us to reconsider the types and quality of materials we offer to children.

Collections of many types of materials, often in clear containers or open baskets, occupy the shelves of the *atelier* at The St. Michael School (Figures 18–3 and 18–4). These collections vary greatly in nature and in use and are maintained by teachers and children on a regular basis. It is important that there is a wide range of variation and difference in properties among the materials available to children. For example, natural objects such as leaves, sticks, pinecones, dried flowers, and small stones are contrasted next to collections of various types and gauges of wire and small metal objects, beads, and buttons. Materials can be arranged according to purpose (i.e., looms can be placed next to fabric, paper strips, or other weaving materials). Children often participate in the preparation of materials. For instance, they might roll tissue paper into small shapes, or fold pieces of paper and cardboard for later use. Tools are also stored on the *atelier* shelves. Clay tools, pliers for bending wire, scissors, hole punchers, rulers, measuring tape, and many other tools are available in open containers or clearly labeled boxes.

Placing materials and tools in locations that are easily accessible fosters respect while suggesting possibilities. The *atelier* has many open shelves, so children can take things out and put them back on their own (Figure 18–5). One shelf, in a location

FIGURE 18–3
A freestanding wire shelf, located in the center of the *atelier,* provides many types of materials to children.

FIGURE 18–4
Collections of many types of materials, often in clear containers or open baskets, occupy the shelves of the *atelier* at The St. Michael School.

FIGURE 18–5
One shelf, in a location children can easily reach, contains drawing materials such as various markers, soft drawing pencils, colored pencils, pastels, and charcoal.

children can easily reach, contains drawing materials such as various markers, soft drawing pencils, colored pencils, pastels, and charcoal. On a shelf directly below this are paper trays filled with drawing paper of various sizes, colors, and shapes. Visibility and accessibility help children to know what types of materials are available, and send the message that the materials are for their use. When children understand that materials and tools are for them, they view themselves as autonomous, powerful, capable, and trusted to be protagonists in their experiences.

DECENTRALIZING THE ATELIER: MINI-STUDIOS IN THE CLASSROOMS

Mini-studios located in each classroom give children further opportunities to learn through materials, techniques, and symbolic languages. Loris Malaguzzi addressed this issue when he described the importance of decentralizing the *atelier* (Gandini, 1998). By creating mini-studios, spaces in each classroom that have a similar purpose to the *atelier,* the teaching potential of the school environment is again increased.

The materials in the mini-studios are similar to those in the *atelier,* but can be adjusted to the ongoing initiatives and personalities of each classroom. One year teachers and children in the 3- and 4-year-olds' classroom used their mini-studio to launch an investigation of wire. After teachers and children evaluated the inventory of wire and related materials available, parents and children improved the collection by bringing in items found at home. For several months, the mini-studio was the central location for children's explorations with wire. As the investigation evolved, wire experiences also took place in the larger *atelier.*

The fact that this experience began from a context in the classroom is significant. Teachers and children had the freedom to hypothesize and organize experiences, and the mini-studio became a pedagogical resource for their inquiry. The *atelier* is not meant to be a secluded, privileged place, but an expansive element that invigorates the entire school. The influence of the *atelier* becomes tangible throughout the school community when attitudes usually associated with it, such as creativity, exploration, and high expectations of materials, are present in all areas of the classroom and the school.

THE ATELIER AS A PLACE OF QUESTIONS

In Reggio Emilia, an attitude of research is applied to children's work with materials, and this is one of the reasons why their work is so compelling. The teachers in Reggio don't repeat what has been done in the past in an unconscious manner. Instead, they relaunch experiences with an "attitude of research" (Rinaldi, 2001) and with the full intention that the new work will contribute fresh insight. Reggio educators fully expect children and teachers to contribute new knowledge to new situations. This point of view is sometimes referred to as a permanent research. At The St. Michael School, we have tried to apply this same attitude of inquiry in our work. When we decide to begin a research, teachers agree together about areas to focus on and develop initial questions. These questions are refined, adjusted, and updated at any time as the research progresses. From the beginning, teachers are co-learners with the children.

For example, understanding the potential of the language of clay has been an ongoing initiative at our school for several years. Some initial questions that framed teachers' thinking were: What do teachers observe children doing with clay? What are some strategies children use when building with clay? How can adults be attentive to different ways children begin working? These questions were the framework for the inquiry and supported the experience as it evolved, and also helped teachers discover some of the ways that children use clay to explore, create, play, invent, make meaning, and communicate.

AN EPISODE WITH CLAY: FLANNERY'S LIONS

At The St. Michael School, children spend time getting acquainted with clay. They have many opportunities to investigate its properties, engage in play with the material, and explore a variety of building techniques. The language of clay is part of the daily life at our school.

Several years ago, a group of 4- and 5-year-old children became interested in making animals with clay. They enjoyed talking together about animals they might create, discussing the qualities of their favorite animals, and representing them in clay. Their curiosity about this topic continued for several months and into the kindergarten year. The teachers documented many of these experiences with particular attention to the unique strategies and solutions that individual children used to represent an animal. The following is an episode from these experiences.

A group of four kindergarten children are working with clay in the studio. There is a large block of clay on the table, from which the children can take clay as they need it. A variety of clay tools are available for the children: ribbon and loop tools, wooden and plastic knives, small rolling pins, ball stylus tools, and a jar of slip, used for joining clay parts together. Each child has a small base of plywood covered with cotton canvas on which to build.

The children each begin talking about what they would like to build with the clay. One of the girls, Flannery, tells me that today she wants to make a family of clay lions. She begins working and, within a short time, she has produced several small clay lions. During this time, I am engaged with all of the children and therefore observe only some aspects of how this has happened.

FIGURE 18–6
"First you make the legs. You make them really fat. You stand them up before you put the body on. To make the body, you roll it."

As she continues to work, I ask her, "Flannery, would you tell me about your lions? I am very interested in how you made them. I'll write your words down in my notebook, so we can remember what you did." The other children remind me to make notes about their work also, and I assure them that I will. I also mention that I will take some photos of everyone's work. While acknowledging the importance of everyone's work, in this situation I stay focused on following what Flannery is doing.

Flannery begins to make another lion. Using her hands, she carefully makes four small cylinders, and stands them up, placing them on the base in a rectangular arrangement.

She says, "First you make the legs. You make them really fat. You stand them up before you put the body on."

Taking a larger piece of clay, she makes another cylinder, this one longer and wider than the previous four. She takes her time as she uses her hands to roll the piece of clay into just the right shape for a body. Flannery explains, "To make the body, you roll it" (Figure 18–6).

Next, she uses slip to join the finished body on top of the four legs and adds, "... and then you stick the legs on." The lion's body is now strongly attached to the four legs (Figure 18–7).

FIGURE 18–7
". . . and then you stick the legs on."

"And then you make the head," she says, after pulling off another piece of clay and rolling it into a small round shape.

The details of the face are added with her fingers and some of the tools on the table. Describing her use of a ball stylus tool, she says, "Then you make the nose. It is a circle. I use a 'poker' to make the mouth, and to make the eyes" (Figure 18–8).

She rolls a smaller coil of clay for the lion's mane. The mane is gently wrapped around the lion's head, with the face showing through in the center. "You stick it to the mane using slip," she adds.

With the head completed to her satisfaction, she attaches it to the body. She makes one final clay coil, connects it to the lion's back, and announces, "Then you make the tail—and you are all finished!" (Figure 18–9).

Flannery's experience of making clay lions did not occur in isolation, but was supported by a network of relationships. On that particular morning, I observed her intention to build a lion family. This intention was composed of many elements: playfulness, seriousness, her prior expertise and confidence with clay, a desire to make the lions, and the freedom to try. She was supported by teachers who were curious about her work, an awareness of other children's clay animals, and an environment in which clay was valued. Flannery's desire was fulfilled by the material of clay; the idea, act, and medium were joined together in the experience of creating the lion family.

FIGURE 18–8

"Then you make the nose. It is a circle. I use a 'poker' to make the mouth, and to make the eyes."

FIGURE 18–9

"Then you make the tail—and you are all finished!"

Observation and documentation play key roles in the learning process. The choice to document Flannery's work was made in connection with the teacher's original questions about children's work with clay. In this case, notes and photographs were used to record close observations of Flannery building with clay. Documentation strategies have been used extensively in Reggio Emilia, and we have found them to be essential in the schools of the St. Louis–Reggio Collaborative. From the teachers' point of view, it is valuable to study children's interactions with materials. As adults construct their understanding, they uncover each material's potential and become more in harmony with children's knowledge. Consequently, the role of the materials in the school increases, as adults realize that children's knowledge and understanding of materials can teach the teachers.

CONCLUSION: THREE REFLECTIVE QUESTIONS

1. *What were turning points in your thinking about the role of the* atelier?

The *atelier* is a tool, but not a prescriptive tool. Experiences take us on paths that are often unexpected, unforeseen, and surprising. This is fundamental, and we, as adults, must constantly learn and relearn it. Children continually discover ways of communicating with materials that are not preconceived. These examples are all around us if we take the time to notice them. To expose these treasures, we must pay close attention to the seemingly small events in the daily lives of children. Learning to give value to these daily events was a big turning point for me.

2. *What from Reggio has inspired you as an* atelierista *here in the U.S.?*

We are deeply indebted to the educators in Reggio Emilia for the concept of the *atelier* and their development of it. To study their work, I believe, challenges us to think differently about what is possible in our own schools. For those of us interested in this type of work here in the U.S., studying the contexts of our schools and having the courage to find our own solutions remain imperative.

3. *How does an American art teacher move in the direction of the* atelier?

Try to move away from isolation by seeking connections between the art studio and the classrooms. Listen to the teachers and discover ways to collaborate with them. Pay close attention to the experiences children and teachers are involved in, and use your expertise with materials to support them. Think of art not as an object or a product, but as integrated in children's experiences.

Make a research of, and document, any part of your life at school that you feel compelled to know more about, especially your environment and the children's use of materials. Document what the children do and what you do. Interpret this documentation with the teachers, and use your findings to guide further decisions. This cycle of observation, documentation, and interpretation can be a very powerful catalyst for change. If you can't change all of the things you want to change about your situation, realize that change is gradual and focus on the elements you can influence.

19

In Our Real World

An Anatomy of Documentation

Barbara Burrington
Head Teacher, UVM Campus Children's Center[1]

Susan Sortino
Lecturer, UVM Department of Early Childhood Education

We have learned that a system is a kind of living organism; it will evolve and change many times.
(Burrington & Hobbins-McGrath, 1995)

[1] The authors would like to state their profound emotional and intellectual respect for the educators of Reggio Emilia, Italy, and for the children whose voices they so eloquently represent.

Of course we document. Our mothers raised us in a culture of documentation. They were the matriarchs of the American form, an intuitive form that exercises a natural impulse to remember and represent. Our mothers made photographs of everything. There are albums for specific children, each decade, all the marriages, and every grandchild. Somehow, between raising a total of 11 children and 150 cows, growing gardens and keeping immaculate households, our mothers managed to record on the back of each picture the names and dates and enough information to give the photo a reason.

They saved anything—newspaper clippings, school photos, report cards, Sunday school diplomas, obituaries, and even teeth were tucked away. All events were documented, but the artifacts alone only begin to tell the stories. The images and artifacts are by-products of the meaning that we made in our lives. They are like words in the language of our families, fragments of memories. They represent and evoke the time, place, thoughts, and feelings of those particular moments, and we revisit these documents and artifacts of our childhood again and again, with our parents, our siblings, our friends, and our own children. Our mothers' efforts to document life recorded a history of everything up to now. Their photograph albums, scrapbooks, and neatly folded files are like the documents of archaeologists. They reflect our families' experiences, culture, and values. Yet their artifacts tell a story that is incomplete, for without words, without a narrative, there is only a shadow of an anecdote with no particular shape, without substance. No one would know about our secret hideouts, our untold desires to change our names and run away from home to become surfers and cowgirls, how we defined friendship, or about our late night Ouija® games by candlelight.

Teachers have it easier than archaeologists and mothers because, if we are so inclined, we can draw on a wider array of resources to document children's growth and behavior. In the classroom we can observe children in their daily interactions and we can accumulate various artifacts they have made. In the case of verbal children, we can ask them about the meanings of what they are doing, and we can interview parents too. When these rich resources are pooled together, the resulting *documentation* supports, elaborates, and informs our understanding of the children, thereby making our findings more trustworthy and our practice more engaging and responsive.

At the Campus Children's Center at the University of Vermont, this responsiveness is an essential cornerstone of our teaching philosophy. It means mobilizing our knowledge of child development with our understanding of our particular children—hypothesizing about where to go and continually observing and adjusting our course as we review the accumulating documentation. It means interpreting our observations and throwing back new encounters with a degree of uncertainty, which is probably the most difficult step, especially for teachers who are just beginning this approach to being with children.

Responsiveness requires a lot of practice and, as one teacher at our school said, "it takes a lot of investment in your practice!" It also requires consistent work on accumulating all the forms of information that fall under the heading of *documentation* because documentation empowers responsiveness.

BUILDING THE INTERNAL STRUCTURE

Documentation is key to a practice which genuinely unites thought with action, belief with ritual, philosophy with pedagogy, and perhaps aesthetics with the mundane.
(Lauren Lawson, UVM Preschool Teacher, 2000)

Since 1992 we have dedicated ourselves to exploring the role of documentation in our teacher education program at the University of Vermont (Gandini & Goldhaber, 2001; Goldhaber, Smith, & Sortino, 1997) and at the Campus Children's Center at the University of Vermont. Over the course of those ten years, we have learned that "exploring the role of documentation" cannot be separated from understanding the role of the teacher. We could not engage in documenting the life of our school without redefining ourselves and changing our own identities. We have been seriously considering and growing our own processes for observation and for doing documentary work because we understand and believe deeply that by documenting our work with children we became more responsive, effective teachers. Documentation gives us access to our encounters with children and helps us apply our knowledge as teachers in our actual context with our particular children.

TAKING THE FIRST STEPS

Initially we didn't have a particular *system* for doing documentary work. Our practice was evolving; our values and priorities were changing. Early in our experience we were buried under our own data. We literally had baskets, piles, cabinets, notebooks, and tables full of our observations and the accompanying artifacts—photos, stories, sketches, and videos. We had to have a method of deciding what to document, determining who would use it, and subsequently understanding our processes and tools for gathering our data and sharing our thinking. At the same time that we were trying to develop our systems, we were deepening our knowledge and respect for the people and the work in Reggio Emilia. We familiarized our students and ourselves with the more formal Reggian process for doing qualitative research as a means of beginning to utilize our observational work, our anecdotes, and our personal stories and experiences.

We were influenced by a lot of people and places, including the documentary work of James Agee and Walker Evans (1941), Wendy Ewald (1985), and Robert Coles (1997); the writings of Corrine Glesne and Alan Peshkin (1992); the exhibit "The Hundred Languages of Children"; and by the work of one another. As a staff, we were very motivated by our desire to create a rich and meaningful environment and to honor our developing identities as a community of educators and "carers." In these early years, when we were developing a mechanism for thinking about our observational work, documentation gradually developed into a strategy for approaching questions. Differences in our points of view became resources for our evolving system.

TAKING THE NEXT STEPS: TEACHING AND DOCUMENTING—THEY'RE BOTH ABOUT RELATIONSHIPS

Teaching is some kind of connection between people, not rules on a piece of paper; a teacher teaches you how to learn principally by learning himself.

(John Taylor Gatto, 2000)

No magic system was to evolve for us. We remembered our constructivist roots: "Constructing knowledge requires collaboration" (Piaget, 1973). Collaboration for us conveys the value we place on relationships as essential to the construction of learning. It is a healthy way to exercise and consider the inherent conflicts that occur when things are considered from multiple points of view. We know from our observations of children and teachers in the classroom that collaboration provides pleasure and increases action. We recognize these opportunities too in our own experience of researching and writing together.

Propelled by a deep desire to create a meaningful process within our context and to find meaning in the humanness surrounding us, we dedicated time to sharing our stories, to thinking critically together, and to reflecting on our own practice with one another. We constructed opportunities to share experiences by taking advantage of overlapping times in our schedules, we devoted staff meetings to dialogue, we stole evenings to be together, and we placed our observations in common areas (Figure 19–1) and wrote responses and questions to each other's analyses. We took advantage of our particular context by creating continuing education courses at the University as a more structured means of processing together, constantly looking for and ultimately finding common ground among our emerging systems. We engaged ourselves in cross-disciplinary work, reading and taking courses and workshops that informed us about photography, graphic design, visual anthropology, advocacy, qualitative research, and pedagogy. We offered readings to parents and engaged them in our conversations. We asked for written feedback about our documentation and their experiences with what they were seeing.

Our willingness to discuss our frustrations and celebrations about documentation conveyed a trust that built even stronger connections among us all. We were developing as a staff, recording the history of our school, improving the quality of our interactions, and increasingly viewing ourselves as something more than "teachers." We were becoming researchers, advocates, intellectuals, artists, activists, ethnographers, carers, cultural geographers, writers, and overall, teachers as people who can make a difference in the world. Documentation afforded these relationships and provided a place for us to enjoy life as teachers, realize our own sense of agency, and offer children a sense of theirs as well.

"Children are natural scientists and, *given the opportunity*, will engage in their own experimentation and problem solving."

(Chaille and Britain, 1994)

The natural world and the quest for learning have the power to captivate each one of us, especially the very young. There is an enticing call for us to take a closer look, to examine, experience and revel in new discoveries. Lucien shows us just how strong the lure of nature and discovery can be. His eyes are immediately drawn to a tree and show us the intensity of his curiosity. He touches the tree, feeling the texture, discovering that pieces of the bark come off. Naturally he brings the bark to his mouth to explore it further. (under the watchful eye of a teacher.) When he drops this piece of bark his attention falls to the wood chips below. Perhaps with the initial intention of picking up the small piece of bark, he reaches his fingers down into the wood chips, making yet another discovery. Using all of his senses and with undivided attention Lucien continues to explore this element. The curiosity and scientific agenda of the young child is inspiring. It reminds us how critical it is to honor and support these moments of inquiry and total engagement.

October 2000

FIGURE 19–1
The natural world and the quest for learning have the power to captivate each one of us, especially the very young. There is an enticing call for us to take a closer look, to examine, experience, and revel in new discoveries. Lucien shows us just how strong the lure of nature and discovery can be. His eyes are immediately drawn to a tree and show us the intensity of his curiosity. He touches the tree, feeling the texture, discovering that pieces of the bark come off. Naturally he brings the bark to his mouth to explore it further (under the watchful eye of a teacher). When he drops this piece of bark, his attention falls to the wood chips below. Perhaps with the initial intention of picking up the small piece of bark, he reaches his fingers into the wood chips, making yet another discovery. Using all of his senses and with undivided attention, Lucien continues to explore this element. The curiosity and scientific agenda of the young child is inspiring. It reminds us how critical it is to honor and support these moments of inquiry and total engagement.

FACING AND SOLVING REALITY ISSUES: UNKNOTTING OUR OWN DILEMMAS

Most teachers in the field whom we speak with tell us that what seems extraordinary to them are constraints that reflect budgeting—both time and money for documenting, and finding the physical space to do it. In the real life drama of early care and education, these elements of practice are very real. Physically, our center is located on the ground floor of a square, brick and concrete building that combines dormitories and classrooms. Our classrooms were originally designed to be "suites" for housing undergraduate students. Transforming them into amiable environments requires an ongoing commitment to our vision.

Outside each room are two Homasote® boards that teachers use to share current and ongoing work and documentation. Inside each room there are daily journals and message boards with current anecdotal observations, news, and "great quotes" by children. Our Parent-Teacher Advisory Group maintains a center-wide board for all parents inside the entryway.

We have converted a portion of our storage room into a place for meeting and working on documentation. It is far from elegant, but practical and accessible.

Time is also a finite part of our reality and given our myriad responsibilities to various groups of people, we live the dilemma in our unique way. The center is open year-round, 50 hours a week. We supervise undergraduate student teachers year-round and receive many visitors from all over the U.S. and Canada. Consequently we are always busy, never bored, and we have become expert at talking to one another on the fly; writing notes; asking good questions; and taking turns presenting our project work, replete with questions, to one another during our weekly staff meeting. When it came to considering time and documenting, we used to wonder if the Italians ever slept! Of course, we know they do. We know too that you just have to be awake with more passion.

Though we exist within a university, the Campus Children's Center is a self-sustaining "business." Our center has to generate a profit, or at least break even, in order to exist. So we understand the money question and recognize that documentation can be costly. We take full advantage of our local copy center and their discount to schools, as well as "half price color copy days." We publish "wish lists" for families that include film, paper, and photo processing (always doubles!). Parents can contribute what they want, and they do. Thanks to our participation in a generous federal grant called Preparing Tomorrow's Teachers to Use Technology, each classroom is equipped with a digital video camera, laptop computer, scanner, and printer. Everyone learns to use the technical media to enhance, extend, and support their documentation. Keeping electronic folders is an excellent method for saving, retrieving, copying, moving, and emailing information. Additionally, we find that typing up our analyses helps with our composition. This is increasingly true for our students, many of whom learned to "write" at a keyboard.

FIGURE 19–2
An array of preschool
classroom notebooks.

While computers and digital video cameras are costly and may require special funding initiatives, paper and pens are not. Documentation, as evidenced from our stories, is a search for understanding (Gandini & Goldhaber, 2001) and that understanding, though complex, can happen and happen beautifully without technical equipment. In our work with children, we are continually seeking and constructing ways to move between places of abstract thought and internal processes to graphic forms of representing our thinking, so there are infinite artifacts to consider.

We write daily anecdotes and transcripts by hand. We require ourselves to initial and date what is written, attach an artifact when possible, and to make certain that the context has been recorded as well. Anecdotes are kept in baskets and on a regular basis, teachers sort the material by categories or "threads."

"Thread" is the term we use to describe an emerging theme seen in children's narratives, representations, play, questions, interests, and passions. Thread can also refer to an inquiry or interest that emanates from a teacher or phenomena. Based on the practices of cultural anthropologists and their use of fieldbooks, we determined that transferring our data into notebooks supported an extremely accessible system. Each classroom maintains a large thread notebook that makes visible what is occurring in the classroom. If an investigation becomes intense, and subsequently its section of the notebook becomes so prolific it outgrows its allotted space, the data graduates to a notebook of its own (Figure 19–2). Following *The Cycle of Inquiry* (Gandini & Gold-haber, 2001), we begin to frame questions regarding the meaning of what we are hearing and seeing. Analysis refers to moving our thoughtful observations of daily life to carefully considered interpretive comments. Our projections emerge from multiple sources, but ongoing threads are a primary provocation.

STORIES FROM THE FIELD

Fortunately we cannot offer a recipe to follow to make good documentary work, since the process must evolve authentically to reflect its own historical context. We can, however, offer stories that have emerged from within the framework of our developing systems. Embedded in each of these vignettes is the approach to documenting that was used by the teachers who lived the events. Our documentation is written with particular audiences in mind—our children, families, students, visitors, and campus community—and reflects our assumptions about their knowledge, attitudes, and interests. By sharing brief excerpts of ongoing investigations and methods of documenting them, we hope to conjure the call to document in others.

Eli's Huge Sea Monster and Little Snake—January, 2002

This encounter unfolded during the first week of Linda Johnson's student teaching in the preschool classroom. In an hour-long meeting with her mentor teachers, she shared the large pastel drawing by Eli (3.5 years of age) and her personal feelings about what had occurred in the classroom. The documentation was conceived and composed from that dialogue. The drawing was cut out and mounted on brown craft paper (Figure 19–3), along with the following narrative and a color copy of a photograph of Eli.

Eli is 3-and-a-half years old. For as long as anyone can remember, he has always been deeply interested in mighty creatures. When he was barely a toddler, he would enter the classroom with his favorite toys from home: a polar bear, an alligator, a whale, dinosaurs, and snakes. At the same time, Eli transforms himself many times each day into a puppy. Eli the puppy is very playful and funny. He is kind and nurturing. He is loyal and devoted to his masters. Eli moves seamlessly through his roles and narrates for us the understanding he is building about relationships. Eli knows that all living creatures share the characteristics of being alive and the feelings that he experiences. He tells us that something can be big and strong and at the same time, kind, funny, and helpful.

As Eli passionately drew his Sea Monster, he growled and roared. Linda, his teacher, responded to the sounds of the Sea Monster by expressing some anxiety and Eli turned the pastel-crayon toward her face, still growling. Linda pleaded for "Help!" Eli took action. He drew a little snake in the corner of his picture. He made tiny, snake tongue-licking sounds

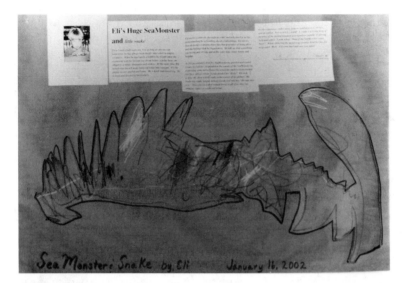

FIGURE 19–3
Eli's huge sea monster.

and told her, "He can save you." This evasive action seemed ironic to all of us since we imagine snakes as scary and lethal. In our experience, snakes have come to symbolize evil, trickery, and deception. Not so in Eli's world! A snake is a living thing, a member of the animal kingdom and therefore capable of offering help and solace. Linda asked, "What if the Sea Monster comes back?" While slithering the pastel-crayon away from her face, Eli responded, "Well . . . I'll come back and save you again."

Sewing Stories—Barbara Burrington and Lauren Lawson

Our preschool has been using sewing for many years. We have documented many projects where children have chosen sewing to access their representational thought and expression (Figure 19–4). For a long time, children's sewn objects, along with their drawn patterns and reasons for being, were shared on a wall outside the classroom to announce to all who entered that there was a group of competent sewers on the other side. Children's narratives are embedded in the teachers' analysis and together they weave a meaningful context for other people to understand the value of what the children are engaged in. Since the children select sewing and fabric to best represent their thinking, anecdotes and artifacts related to sewing can be found in many different threads and investigation notebooks. Here are excerpts from ongoing documentation related to sewing.

The act of sewing feels like "real work" and enhances children's feelings of competence. Since sewing is a great interest of many adults, it provides an opportunity for children to

FIGURE 19–4
Matilda's (3.8 years old) drawn pattern of her cat "Daisy" and her sewn construction underway.

work side by side with grown-ups and share a common, rewarding experience. Young children in the preschool have demonstrated the ability to develop sophisticated skills with regular practice and dedication.

"I think sewing is like grown-up work," comes from Emily, whose mom is an avid and talented seamstress. Many of Emily's favorite "spinny" dresses were homemade with handpicked soft fabrics by Mom. Emily has been closely observing her mom sew for years, gathering specific information about how sewing "works." Her extensive observation phase proved very valuable when Emily surprised herself with her hidden, yet profound sewing talent. The first time Emily picked up a needle to make a beanbag, she made neat, even stitches all in a row and found her experience both joyful and rewarding. She proudly showed her creation to her mom and explained, "I was good at sewing and I didn't even know it."

Lexi makes the connection between sewing and surgery. "My dad likes to sew too—he sews people's skin back together who've been hurt and he fixes them." Lexi understands that sewing can mend and repair—it is a "healing" art. "I used to be a man and now I'm a sewing man."

Jack feels that his ability to sew has altered his identity. He has discovered that being a good "sewer" is one of the primary attributes that makes him proud to be Jack. "I love to sew because I love making things."

Maddy understands that sewing provides her with a tool to construct things that are beautiful and functional. She has created beanbags, several decorative pillows, many *tooth-fairy pillows in preparing for her baby teeth to fall out, and several purses to hold special treasures close to her body.*

Kevin sees the relationship between sewing things for his mother and bringing her joy. He makes her things out of purple fabric because it is her favorite color and he wraps each one and attaches a love letter.

Visual Messages, Metaphors, and Memories: Children Remember Important Things—Barbara Burrington and Lauren Lawson

The majority of our children enter the center when they are infants or toddlers. For many years they have watched the teachers watch them, take photographs of their play, and write down their words. They understand that teachers document because we value their work, and they notice that the camera emerges from the cupboard when "important" things are happening. As the children revisit older documentation, they learn that photography and written language create useful traces of past events and preserve memories. Intrigued by the possibility of turning the camera around—so to speak—and observing our world through the eyes of the children, and inspired by readings about spaces as areas of meaning (Holloway & Valentine, 2000; Nabhan & Trimble, 1994), we decided to try to support the 5-year-olds in creating their own visual narratives relating the particular meanings they had built at school. We organized the project as a culminating event in their preparation to graduate to kindergarten, and exhibited the photographs they made, along with our reflections, on graduation day.

Organizing our cycle of inquiry.   We wrote our questions and had conversations with the children to consider each question: What is a memory? What are your memories? What have been your favorite experiences? What brings you joy? Who are the most important people in your lives at school? What are your significant places? How can you use images to represent an aspect of yourself? How can you tell a story through a photograph or a series of photographs? We read and told stories about other people's remembering.

The project.   This project has supported children in thinking about memory, identity, and visual literacy through the process of constructing an artistic commentary on their lives. They have created something that has deep meaning, history, and aesthetic value. Each child's work reflects a personal narrative based on their own experiences in this place, with these people, over the course of time. The children began by writing "shooting scripts" or photo plans outlining their ideas of specific images that might illustrate and convey their life's experience at school (Figure 19–5).

The process.   With the generous support of families, each child was provided with a disposable 35mm flash camera to capture and make visible their thinking. The children's shooting scripts helped them to slow down and to be mindful, intentional, organized, assertive, and successful in their photographic processes. The children were very engaged while they were shooting their film and the five days necessary for processing the film seemed like an eternity. When the photographs finally arrived, the

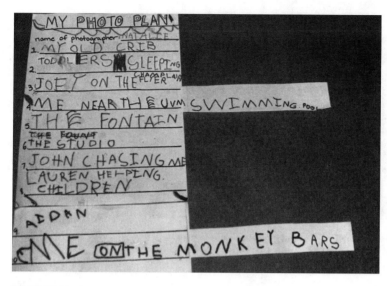

FIGURE 19–5

Natalie's (4.1 years) "Shooting Script." It reads:

1. My Old Crib (where Natalie slept in the Infant room)
2. Toddlers Sleeping (recalling a dramatic thunderstorm that had awakened her from sleep when she was a toddler)
3. Joey on The Champlain Flyer (a classmate who loves this local train)
4. Me Near the UVM Swimming Pool (she felt she was a "great" swimmer, recently mastering swimming)
5. The Fountain (an important icon on the UVM green and the focus of a project Natalie was part of)
6. The Studio (the *atelier,* where Natalie often did her "best" work)
7. John Chasing Me (a good friend and a favorite game)
8. Lauren [her teacher] Helping Children
9. Aidan (her infant brother)
10. Me on the Monkey Bars (a big physical challenge that she saw herself "excelling" at)

children were asked to spend time considering their prints, engaging in reflective dialogue, and critiquing and interpreting their work (Figure 19–6).

Looking back. The project cast the children in their new role as graduating preschoolers, elucidating their thoughtfulness, sophistication, and symbolic competence. In this exhibit we asked the children to bring their ideas together, to consider multiple points of view, to challenge one another's thinking, and to perhaps change their minds! The children knew we were paying close attention and that the work was important—important because it carried meaning, it was real, it was part of a culminating event, and it would be shared with families and friends.

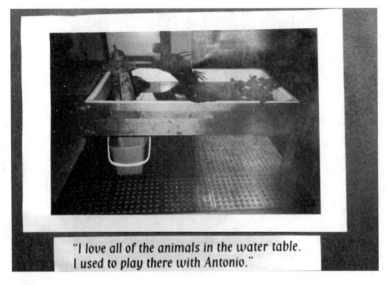

"I love all of the animals in the water table.
I used to play there with Antonio."

FIGURE 19–6
A photograph and commentary by Jake (5.4 years old), recalling a favorite place to play with his best friend who had graduated a year earlier.

Looking ahead.   We can learn from these children because they are mirrors for all of us. Our concern for them is a kind of self-concern to realize a better world at school, with children and for children. Their images and stories convey the universal importance of being connected to the natural world, of having a sense of freedom, peace, and love, and for creating solidarity among people. Their work reminds us that places are areas of meaning and that the meaning resides not only in the present, but also in the stories of the children who came before them, and in the ongoing history of our little school.

A NOSTALGIC FUTURE

> *If future archaeologists find fragments of our work, we hope they*
> *may consider them art and put them under glass.*
> (Staff, UVM Preschool Vision Statement, 2000)

Perhaps it harkens back to the ways of our mothers, to the mantles, walls, and tables that hold framed images of memories that reflect who we are, that recall where we have been and the bridges we crossed to get here. Wherever the root took hold, the notion of a nostalgic future, attributed to Loris Malaguzzi (Ferrari, 2001), resonates deeply in us and resonates deeply in the life of our little school within a much bigger school.

FIGURE 19–7
Jake discussing his photographs with a teacher and a classmate.

The documentation on our walls and in our archives is a visual and literary account of events, ideas, projects, learning, people, and community. It represents our history. Our documentation marks the passing of time, honors relationships, celebrates moments, and conveys the inner thoughts and feelings of children and their teachers (Figure 19–7). We are more present in our daily encounters because we have an identity that is part of something larger. The images of strong, competent, thoughtful children remind us that we have an immense responsibility to the future.

What is very clear to us is that the decision to utilize documentation—to make it part of who we are as a learning community—has changed our identity and practice forever and, we believe, for the better. We are constantly evolving solutions to the questions we have about making the best use of our time, resources, and space. It is good to ask the questions and then move on and do the work. We learned that you can hide behind constraints for a short moment only, otherwise the inability or lack of desire to enter the documentation process becomes the primary issue, and that is a much deeper issue that one can address only in his or her own pedagogical heart.

VII

Accepting the Challenge to Change on a Larger Scale

 Karen Haigh already provided us with one description of meeting challenges on a large scale when she told us about the 44 classrooms she has in her care in Chicago. Now Sandy Miller and Sonya Shoptaugh describe an even larger experimental project attempting to extend the Reggio Approach into public education in four elementary schools in Ohio. This four-year project, which met with varying degrees of success, reminds us once again of Lilian's cautions about the nature and difficulties of achieving change when confronting an entrenched system of education.

SOME EXCERPTS FROM LELLA'S CHAPTERS

Educators in Reggio Emilia have no intention of suggesting that their program should be looked at as a model to be copied in other countries; rather, their work should be considered as an educational experience that consists of reflection, practice, and further careful reflection in a program that is continuously renewed and readjusted.

Bearing these facts in mind, the educators in Reggio Emilia are pleased to share their experience with other educators in the hope that knowledge of the Reggio Emilia educational experience will stimulate reflections on teaching, helpful exchanges of ideas, and novel initiatives in other schools and in other countries, for the benefit of children, families, and teachers.

LILIAN'S CHALLENGE:

Change is systemic. Here Fullan (Fullan & Miles, 1992) agrees with our Reggio colleagues—that all parts of the system must be involved in the desired changes simultaneously. He points out that change must focus not just on structural features, policies, and regulations, but on the deeper issues of what he calls the culture of the system. Such a stipulation presents overwhelming challenges for U.S. early childhood educators.

   All large-scale change is implemented locally. Change cannot be accomplished from the distance, but must involve all those who will implement the innovative practices as well as the larger and more distant agencies involved.

20

Reflections on a Journey of Inspiration
Teacher Change in Public Education

Sandra M. Miller[1]
Director, Office of Early Childhood Education,
Ohio Department of Education, Columbus

Sonya Shoptaugh
Educational Consultant, New York, New York

---

[1] This chapter is dedicated to all of the teachers who participated in the project.

In the spring of 1996, the Martha Holden Jennings Foundation offered the Ohio Department of Education's Office of Early Childhood Education an opportunity to advance quality early childhood practices by instituting a professional development program aimed at teacher change. This effort was to be achieved through the study of the Reggio Emilia Approach to education. The Reggio Approach was selected as the framework for study because of the emerging interest of a host of teachers wanting to know more about project work, documentation, and the role of the environment as the third teacher. It was also believed that the underlying beliefs of the philosophy of the Reggio Emilia Approach—collegiality, public demonstration and sharing of practices, documentation of the work and learning, and perhaps most importantly the belief in the potential of children—could serve as the backdrop for critical examination of our own beliefs, practices, and understandings of children, teaching, and learning.

One of the requirements of the Foundation and the Office of Early Childhood Education was that the schools selected represent public educational settings across Ohio. As with many publicly funded projects, it is important to demonstrate what is possible across all educational settings and where the uniqueness within each context may reside. While funding through the Foundation for an early childhood project continues, the use of dollars for this particular professional development initiative was for 4 years.

Each school selected for participation was located in a different part of the state, and the children within these schools represented a broad economic spectrum of families ranging from upper- or middle-class homes to children on free and reduced-cost lunch programs. Children with disabilities and children who were considered gifted were included within the classrooms of the teacher participants. Since the Reggio Approach is a preschool model, the decision made was not to work with an entire elementary faculty but rather to create "schools within schools" with a few of the teachers from the primary classrooms. The range of grades across the four schools was preschool through second grade. In one case, the project impacted all kindergarten classroom teachers the first year, and added first-grade teachers in the second year. In another school, all preschool teachers and their assistants, a total of eight classrooms, participated in the professional development program.

THE PROFESSIONAL DEVELOPMENT PLAN

The professional development plan for the first year was designed in collaboration with Lella Gandini, U.S. Liaison to Reggio Emilia, and with the general approval of Amelia Gambetti, Educational Consultant to the U.S. The intent of the first year was to immerse the participants in the elements of the approach through monthly 1½-day whole-group meetings. The plan included presentations by Lella Gandini, Louise Cadwell, Jennifer Azzariti, and Sonya Shoptaugh. All of these individuals had worked closely with Amelia Gambetti and were considered to be well versed not only in the elements of the approach but also in the underlying system and actions necessary to implement the elements.

The teachers were told that we would study the elements of the approach as a group but that the strategies for implementation were to be integrated into the existing work within the local and unique interpretation of each school setting. While *The Hundred Languages of Children* (Edwards, Gandini, & Forman, 1998) served as the main text for study, a number of articles that reflected similar philosophical stances or teaching actions within our own U.S. educational history were also provided to highlight the similarities in philosophy or suggestions for teaching strategies.

All of the participants were also required to meet weekly in their home schools for at least two hours to discuss what they had learned at the whole-group meetings, spend time analyzing readings for understanding and interpretation, and determine ways to support each other to accomplish project work and documentation. For the first year, all teachers were required to keep a personal journal, and as a group within each school they were to take notes of their weekly discussions. Both were to serve as a trace of their personal journeys as well as gain an understanding of the course and development of teacher talk.

The support to teachers for the first year of the professional development plan was provided by a team of three consultants. One consultant represented the Ohio Department of Education and served as overall project manager, a second consultant was contracted for services because of her knowledge of the approach and the work that she achieved toward implementation within her own program, and the third consultant was hired to provide a project evaluation and at times facilitate group dialogue. The team made monthly visits to all of the schools during the first year to hear the concerns of the staff and to help make connections between theory and practice when asked.

YEAR ONE: THE SELF THAT TEACHES

For the first year, the professional development plan was conceptualized as two parallel paths: One was directed at understanding the Reggio Emilia Approach and the other focused on revealing similarities and differences between our own educational system (i.e., John Dewey and project work; issues of assessment) and that of Reggio Emilia. The decision was made with Amelia Gambetti to provide the teachers with a solid base of knowledge about the Reggio Emilia Approach by using the stories of the educators as they engaged in implementation. The organizing staff felt it important that the ways in which we learned about the approach modeled collegiality, inquiry, and support. These actions are implicit within the work of the Reggio educators and it was believed that through this framework we could become a community of learners.

The concept of a community for this project was more akin to that of communities of practice (Wenger, 1998) where mutual engagement, joint enterprise, and shared repertoire "hold the key to real transformation—the kind that has real effects on people's lives" (p. 85). Learning to dialogue with each other without judgment, discovering ways to question each other that were respectful and non-threatening, and finding ways to connect with each other across all four schools and not just with staff within each school setting were considered important outcomes of the project design.

In addition, the concept of a community of learners is a philosophy and a value that is realized through an infrastructure of support, communication, and action research, fostered by small schools, team teaching, and pedagogical coordinators. Needless to say, an infrastructure such as this did not exist at any of the schools. The development of a community of learners was to become the infrastructure for support and communication for the group. We had yet to discover what was possible within each school context.

After the third month of whole-group exploration concentrating on one aspect of the Reggio Emilia Approach, our own questions about belief and practices began to emerge. Why do we do what we do in our classrooms? What are our beliefs about how young children learn? How do we engage with families and why do we do this? What does it mean to teach and to learn? Examining beliefs through group discussions and debates about the decisions, actions, and practices of curriculum and teaching by using slides of classroom design and our developing notions of documentation panels was new to many of these teachers. Moving from private teaching actions to public forums of discussion—sharing, questioning, challenging—was difficult and sometimes emotional for the majority of the participants (and met with resistance from some).

It was through the first year of exploring the philosophy of Reggio Emilia and the unique make-up of the group that the tension between a professional and a personal identity began to emerge. First, there were differing levels of understanding of the approach, from teachers who knew nothing about it to a few who had attended conferences for at least two years and were devoted fans of the approach. Second, there were different motivations for participation, from the desire by some teachers to understand project work and documentation to other teachers who were struggling to understand the intentions of their administrator as to their required participation. And finally, there were teachers who were ready to implement or try aspects of the approach and others who liked things just the way they were. Regardless of why teachers were participating, all believed that they were doing good work inside their classrooms. They had no reason to believe otherwise.

It was through the tensions that we discovered how deeply teaching was viewed as a personal set of actions—I am what I teach and how I teach (Palmer, 1998). The first year provoked confusion, tension, anxiety, wonder, and imagination that were personal aspects of teaching. For any change to take place and be sustained requires a critical self-examination of "identity." Do I want to engage in this process? If not, why not? What might I learn about self? About my actions? What might be revealed to others and particularly to myself? "When you love your work that much—and many teachers do—the only way to get out of trouble is to go deeper in. We must enter, not evade, the tangles of teaching so we can understand them better and negotiate them with more grace, not only to guard our own spirits but also to serve our students well" (Palmer, 1998, p. 2).

YEAR ONE: ISSUES OF TRUST, SECURITY, AND SIGNIFICANCE

The push for self-reflection (why do I do what do?) and group dialogue revealed three themes that gradually emerged over the course of the first year in response to the personal and professional tensions. Issues of trust, security, and significance, while not stated overtly, were revealed through teacher talk at the whole-group meetings and at the local school meetings.

Establishing trust takes time. As a whole group, we all were in the infancy of our relationships with each other across the four sites and of our developing concept of respect for the contributions of everyone within the project. Relationships are essential to trust—knowing who the other is, where they are coming from, and why takes time. Parker Palmer (1993) writes of trust as truth that is revealed through personal relationships. Truth or trust requires "careful, vulnerable listening for how things look from a (this) standpoint and that and that, a listening that allows us not only to know the other but to be known from the others' point of view" (p. 67).

It became evident that among the individual schools as among the group, trust was a local issue too. This project was "experimental," and while the principal could certainly justify the philosophy of the Reggio Emilia Approach to other staff, the bottom line remained—will the children learn, will they pass the test, will they meet goals on an Individualized Educational Plan?

Second, the process of change requires "security." The teachers wanted to be assured that they had the freedom to explore the ideas of project work, the use of media, and new forms of inquiry, and that their jobs were not on the line. The teachers wanted to explore new practices that would not be questioned by administration and by the other teachers in the building. Security also meant that within this community of learners, the space for sharing would be safe, supportive, non-judgmental, and non-competitive (Wenger, 1998; Palmer, 1993).

The social climate—the acceptance and support by the other staff—often played an important role in the change process. The school principal, as building leader, is required to attend to all teachers and their issues. This meant that they had to deal with social repercussions emanating from some of the non-participating teaching staff, who viewed the project as controversial and inconsistent with district philosophy. Therefore, offering silent support was perhaps the easiest way to provide support to the project teachers since it caused the least attention back inside the school. Over the course of the second year, while the principals did not overtly demonstrate decreased support, they did not explicitly encourage the continued actions by the project teachers.

And finally, the teachers needed to know that they were significant. The process of change, of asking teachers to constantly examine what they believe and to reveal (either publicly or to themselves) the paradox between belief and action, brought about many feelings of self-doubt and anxiety, raised questions of self-confidence, and highlighted the connection of the personal and professional self—that the two are not separated at the school door. The teachers wanted to be respected for their risk-taking, valued for their hard work, and recognized as "good teachers" not only by those of us who were "in charge" of the project but also by their colleagues. The desire to be recognized as "good teachers" in the midst of change was important to all of these educators. A "good teacher" in the eyes of self is a "good person" and most reform efforts implicitly challenge the self that teaches because they ask for change.

YEAR ONE: CONCLUSIONS

Deborah Meier suggests that there are five qualities demonstrated by teachers who may move schools toward a more democratic and collegial working style. These teachers possess a self-conscious, reflective stance about how they themselves learn and a sympathy toward others who reflect on their teaching. They have an appreciation of differences among the teaching staff, a willingness to work collaboratively, a passion for sharing interests, and the perseverance, energy, and devotion to getting things right (Meier, 1995). Yet, these kinds of teacher behaviors require atypical school structure and organization: a system that offers teachers time to be with each other throughout the day and offers a wider sense of educational community and responsibility to teachers so that, collectively, they may help students achieve the standards, the benchmarks, and the objectives on the test. Such actions cannot be achieved inside individual classrooms and behind closed doors. In the closing chapter of *Inventing Better Schools*, Phillip Schlechty wrote, "Much of the variance in performance of all organizations and of the people in those organizations has to do with the properties of the systems themselves rather than with the attributes and motives of individual men and women" (1997, p. 221).

The words of wisdom regarding our first year of change were summed up by the teachers themselves. In placing before our teachers the image of a teacher envisioned through the elements of the Reggio Emilia Approach to education, the teachers asked that the consulting team:

❑ Give full attention to their stories, listen to and value their struggles, and recognize their histories.

❑ Take time to understand the person within the teacher and the teacher within the person.

❑ Foster communal ways of working but support their own individual growth, strength, and creativity.

Loris Malaguzzi, the visionary behind the Reggio educational approach, believed that education was about reinforcing each child's identity through recognition from peers and adults. It is through this recognition that each child would come to feel a sense of belonging and the self-confidence to participate in the activities of the school. As consultants, we had to ask ourselves whether we were recognizing our teachers—confusing or clarifying images of their identity—and we had to come to terms with our responsibility for complicating the issue. In our haste in the first year to impart information about the Reggio Emilia Approach, we had not given the teachers the recognition they deserved.

YEAR TWO: CURRICULUM AND TESTING FROM A NEW POINT OF VIEW

It was clear that we could "learn" about the principles of the Reggio Emilia Approach to education, but we would benefit from someone who had practical experience in implementing it. Sonya Shoptaugh, former educator at the Model Early Learning Center, Washington D.C., agreed to serve in a consultant role for the overall project and also worked in depth with a group of teachers from one school to help them translate the principles into action.

In this section, the ways in which Sonya brought her knowledge and skills to teachers within one of the elementary schools will be highlighted through her reflections and notes. In doing so, the struggles and rewards of trying to implement the Reggio Emilia Approach within a public education setting are made visible.

> Sonya writes in September of the second year of the project, *"With the teachers who were involved in the project last year, we are looking at what they are doing in the classroom and beginning to make connections between the theory and the practice."* Sonya does this through questions: *"How do we have conversations with children? What does it mean to listen to children? What does it mean to document? Why do it? How might we do it? How do we work collaboratively? How do we use the environment as another teacher? How will we organize the experiences to make use of inquiry, media, tools, techniques? What does it mean to make decisions with children? With parents? With each other? With administrators? With the larger school community?"*

Sonya's notes reveal that through the year-long professional development plan of the first year, the following actions were evident:

> The image of the child: *"The question of 'What image of the child do we have?' has . . . in turn, directly affected their interactions with the children. They ask many questions of the children in order to understand. . . . I find an increased level of attentiveness to who the children are."*
>
> Small group work as a learning strategy: *"The teachers have begun to explore how they can support the development of relationships and facilitate the learning by organizing experiences where the children are able to work together in small groups."*
>
> Planning: *"We are involved in shifting our definition of planning from the adult-dictated, before-the-fact lesson plan, to an organization where the teachers formulate hypotheses of what could happen on the basis of their knowledge of the children and of*

previous experiences. Along with these hypotheses, the teachers formulate objectives that are flexible and adapted to the needs and interests of the children. Planning then becomes understood in the sense of preparation and organization of the space, materials, thoughts, situations, and occasions for learning." Sonya readily admits this way of planning is challenging.

Organization of the physical environment: *"There are documents on the wall which share the experiences taking place, the thoughts and questions of the children and the teachers. To be surrounded by images of themselves—how does this affect the children's and teachers' sense of belonging and well-being? In order to create such documents, the teacher has to look closely at what she is doing and why."*

Ongoing professional development: *"To enter into a style of teaching which is based on questioning what we're doing and why, on listening to children, on thinking about how theory is translated into practice and how practice informs theory, is to enter into a way of working where professional development takes place day after day in the classroom."*

Sonya's challenge was to continue to introduce the elements to teachers new to the project in the second year and to build on and deepen the understanding with the teachers from the first year of the project. But Sonya quickly came to recognize the complexity of the school-entrenched ways of being and doing that were persistent and pervasive.

Adopting the elements of the Reggio Emilia Approach required a shift in how teachers and administrators engage with each other in the daily life of the school. Working within a framework of relationships, communication, and collegiality requires a commitment to creating conditions within school life that foster and support new ways of working together.

"The concept of moving forward 'together' was one that we needed time to understand. I sensed an atmosphere of isolation and separation. For example, teachers had limited knowledge about what their colleagues were doing and why. Through different attempts such as changing our organizational structures, dedicating time in meetings to share our experiences in the classroom, writing reports, and working together on joint projects, we have started to shift the atmosphere in the schools more toward collaboration."

Sonya was coming to recognize the culture of public education. The culture of any organization is the result of the meaning given by the participants, and public education has a long history of a particular culture (i.e., individual classrooms, individual work, everyone experiencing the same activity) supported by the system. "Much of who people are and what they believe is a product of the interaction between the self and the social structure, history, and biography" (Schlechty, 1997, p. 137). While we can create systems, change them or modify them, systems also shape how individuals act and feel.

"How do we translate some of the basic ideas of the Reggio Emilia Approach in a system based in isolation rather than collaboration? The challenges are enormous; however, the

teachers continue to be available to try. Because many people are watching, there is an added pressure to do the required work and then the work related to the project. We are still trying to see how we can integrate more the experiences of traditional elementary school with the Reggio Approach, formal academics with project work, assessment forms with documentation. In this way, we hope to support the shifting of thinking in ourselves, as well as those who are watching us."

YEAR TWO: CHANGING THE ENVIRONMENT

The elements of the Reggio Emilia Approach that are most "transportable" are initially realized symbolically. Changes in the environment, the use of "project-like" work, the use of media, and the creation of "documentation" panels were the most common elements of the Reggio Emilia Approach found in the classrooms of the teachers. Designing the environment to reflect the culture of the classroom community and to serve as a resource to children was the change that was desired and attempted by most teachers. Yet it was revealed that change in the classroom environment, while at times dramatic inside the classrooms, was difficult and complex in terms of articulating the underlying reasons for the change—a cultural shift in thinking. Changing the environment did not mean changing the way in which one practiced the art of education.

In one conversation early in the school year, Sonya was invited into a classroom where one of the teachers new to the project stated "I like my environment just the way it is and I'm not changing it." Sonya replied, *"You don't have to change anything you don't want to change . . . but will you share with me what you do like about your environment?"* Two months later they were still discussing the classroom, but the talk shifted from what to do with the space to ways of thinking about the spaces for purposefulness and meaning. The teacher discovered through conversations with Sonya and through a subtle change in thinking about the classroom to that of creating learning spaces, that her room could afford different meanings and provocations for the students and for her teaching style. All the prodding in the world to change the environment could not have had the impact on the environment that this self-discovery did.

YEAR TWO: OVERCOMING ISOLATION

The concept of isolation takes many forms inside schools—from closed doors to isolated and autonomous teaching. Sonya wrote, *"The teachers have been rather far away from each other in many ways."* As Sonya moved from room to room, she slowly started to offer the teachers ways to connect—from sharing ideas about a possible project, to brainstorming ways to collect conversations from children and ways to connect "rooms." *"We are starting to dig holes through them (our walls) with our ideas and who knows how much openness we will be able to create."*

Two teachers decided in the second year to "combine" their rooms. Structurally each room was self contained, but they organized the spaces to reflect a unity of materials and experiences. One room held materials for math and science, experimenting, moving, and creating with objects. The second room was designed to support literacy activities. By team teaching, these teachers had to discover new ways of thinking and presenting the required curriculum content, ways to organize small group experiences with 44 children, and ways to schedule the day so that one could observe the other and take notes or photographs when needed.

Organizing the two rooms in this way made visible the abilities of all of these children to handle themselves well across this new vision of learning spaces. The design of the space, materials, schedule, and time—with two different teachers working collaboratively—while challenging, brought about new ways of seeing the children as learners, doers, and constructors of knowledge.

YEAR TWO: VENTURING PROJECT WORK

The concept of a "project" was exciting and overwhelming at the same time. How will we know a project is a project? What will we document? How will we document? *"We have begun spending time talking about projects, how to listen to children, where to go with experiences, and how to document."* Countering the concept of project work was the necessity to provide for mandated coverage of the curriculum, pupil performance objectives, and the course of study. Within public education settings, these educational constructs are real and cannot be ignored or dismissed.

Sonya again provided guidance by suggesting that *"the kinds of questions that a teacher asks influence where a conversation with children may go."* As the following example illustrates, the kinds of questions a teacher asks can relate to content standards that are required as part of the first-grade curriculum and embody the Reggio Approach as well. After an analysis of one of the science objectives in the course of study and analyzing children's interest against the curriculum requirements, the teachers were able to see differently how *"the interests of children and the course of study could walk hand in hand."* Sonya was clear in her notes that *"this way of teaching (project work) requires the teacher to have an ability to listen closely to the interests of children, possess a knowledge of the required course of study, and then link the two together in meaningful and authentic ways."*

For example, early within the school year, the teachers realized some rainstorm puddles could be used to fulfill a district requirement about the water process and that this requirement could be achieved via project work. Through the technique of children sketching their theories of the system of water, the teachers discovered that the children already knew a great deal about the water process but did not have the language to describe what they knew. They also discovered that some of the ideas about the rain were imaginative, such as children's notion of rain as the result of the devil making God cry. This new twist of the water process provided for a lively discussion among the children, but the teachers reported with good humor that they felt frozen—God inside a public school? In the end the teachers honored both versions of the children's understanding of the system of water, the factual and imaginative.

It was only when the teachers began to have conversations with children—real conversations with children—that the concept of project work in light of curriculum mandates took on a new meaning. What questions might lead us to come to know what children know, what children want to know, what interests they have? What materials do we have to support what they want to know? How are materials organized and offered to children? How is the environment designed to support explorations and conversations and openings for discussions? Sonya made a date to walk through the room and examine it "through the lens of the course of study" and also through the lenses of richness, robustness, and potentiality.

The journey into the Reggio way of presenting content—by following children's ideas and interests and attending to the curriculum requirements, by asking the children to sketch what they know and then revisiting these original sketches throughout the study, by designing more engaging studies of different aspects of the water process and planning for more thoughtful questions to get at in-depth understanding—provided an enormous amount of information for the study of children, of learning, of teaching, and of sense-making. Learning how to work together, how to observe, how to listen, and how to provide support to the children and to each other was coming alive inside this classroom.

This kind of teaching required the teachers to know the curriculum content and objectives stated in the more formal, district-required structure. It is through systematic and intentional questions aligned with curriculum requirements, and careful and annotated records of the observation and documentation of children engaged in the work that teachers found they could not only meet the course objectives but in many cases surpass expectations of required content results by providing the hidden benefits of project work such as problem solving, creativity, and collaboration. By studying the State Department of Education's grade-by-grade and district content requirements, the teachers felt confident that they could meet the requirements of their district and at the same time honor the interests of their children.

YEAR TWO: DEALING WITH THE QUESTION OF ASSESSMENT

It was not too long before the question of children passing a standardized test emerged in relationship to the concept of project work. How do we provide more opportunities so that the kind of thinking required on tests will occur within the daily organization of the day and the experiences offered?

> "With our beginning inventory of skills and strategies for test taking, we ask each other, 'How do we know the children have these abilities?'. . . assessment, observation, documentation . . . more questions. How do we know what children know? Why do we need to know this? For what purpose are we using this information? How do we share

what we interpret children know with their parents, other teachers, and with the children themselves? Why do we share what we share? How does this influence how we and others view children's capabilities? And on and on. . . ."

Working with these classroom teachers within the public schools, Sonya recognized that *"we must support these children in the context of their reality—which is our reality. That means test taking, curriculum requirements, the teaching of skills and strategies."*

One after-school conversation was sparked by confusion over the multiplicity of tests that often asked for the same information but in different ways. The teachers clearly recognized the value of providing all of the children whatever instructional support they needed, either through intervention services or after-school programs, but most often each request for information or justification became a burden rather than an asset in terms of developing teaching plans. Again Sonya listened carefully to the teachers. The decision was to look at each assessment and to examine it to understand better what was required of each—what information was needed for central office reports and what information was needed to support a referral for intervention or after-school services. How could teachers organize their time differently to collect this information? How could the teachers collectively help each other get what was needed for the assessment or report and learn more about each child in the process? How could a series of well-designed tasks be used to collect information for more than one assessment?

This conversation sparked the design of one professional development meeting in which all of the teachers took the fourth-grade proficiency practice test for reading. Each teacher took the assessment and then through grade-level discussions determined what skills the children would need in preschool, kindergarten, and first and second grades. In addition, by studying the proficiency tests of prior years, the teachers were able to examine the structure of the questions, the selection of vocabulary, and the required tasks to determine comprehension ability. What was revealed was that the nature of the test was one of problem solving. Armed with this knowledge, the teachers could discuss collectively the ways in which teaching strategies and targeted lessons could provide children with the required test-taking skills and experiences. A problem-solving approach to learning is useful not only for taking tests but also for teaching reading and math, for a scientific approach to inquiry, for conflict resolution, and for project work. This activity turned a perceived problem into a learning lesson for everyone.

When the two teachers who were teaming reviewed their students' "off-year" scores (end of the second grade) with the principal and then compared them with other student scores, it was evident that many of the students working with the teachers in this project outperformed many of the non-project children. (Since the focus of the project was on teacher change, and student outcomes were not used to measure teacher performance, there is no formal record.) Knowing that their children were doing as well as all other students only reinforced the teachers' belief in this way of working. Educational standards and increased expectations of students are the result of knowing the children and the subjects well and having a passion for the ways in which one teaches and engages with learners.

While many teachers may question the use of standardized and formal testing procedures with young children, the simple task of deconstructing the tests to understand what is being asked of children to know better how to help children achieve the necessary skills not only proved useful but also supported many of the actions that the teachers were striving for in teaching the Reggio way. Sonya and the Reggio educators have often challenged us to understand what is before us.

YEAR THREE: MAKING THE REGGIO PHILOSOPHY MORE VISIBLE

The goals of the first two years emphasized continuously examining the elements of the Reggio Emilia Approach and delving into inquiry, observation, and listening as ways of digging deeper into the meaning of teaching and learning. During the third year, the teachers were ready to create the identity of the school and make visible the philosophy of their new ways of working together.

While the teachers still had questions about the environment and project work (going deeper), they were now concerned with the images that they wanted to project to the community. Sonya helped each school in the project begin to examine the messages that they wanted to share. "*What do we value for children? For children with disabilities? For families? For the staff?*" She helped each school discover their unique identity through values, history, cultural diversity of the children and families, the educational philosophy and traditions of the school, and the relationship with the community and in particular with parents.

Within one school, the teachers decided to explore the concept of an identity of a school through four small workgroups that addressed each of the above big ideas of identity. They began to collect artifacts: photographs, newsletters, examples of curriculum, news clippings, prior celebrations, maps of the area, mission statements, the history of the school song and mascot, individual teacher collections, and interviews with parents and school administration. The objective was to create documentation panels that shared not only the history of the school but also the history of these teachers within this project. The desired outcome was to show connections, growth, and change over time that were part of the culture of the school. It was also one more way of making visible to teachers within each school but outside of the project the work that these teachers were doing inside the classrooms and beyond their own school.

In doing this, the teachers moved from thinking of their individual identities in this school to the meaning of their collective identity in a place called school. Each school wrestled with this in its own way, but the desire was to communicate to the wider school community the sense of unity that had grown among these teachers within this project.

YEAR THREE: UNDERSTANDING
THE CONCEPT OF "INTENTION"

Sonya also introduced the concept of "intention." She wrote, *"Inside the discussion about identity resides the sharing of intentions. There is a reciprocity between identity and intention."* Sonya helped the teachers uncover their intentions, either through individual interests as she visited the classrooms or through group conversation. These individual intentions became the framework for the teachers to write for mini-grants to support their research into ways of implementing these intentions.

One teacher wrote of her intention to explore the role of the adult working with children identified with special needs. She was interested in understanding her role related to supporting, enabling, and taking over in order to make it easier for the children. She also wanted to know when and how she provided scaffolding techniques to let the children discover their own potential, create ideas to be shared among peers, and construct projects on their own. Writing of initial observations of her research, she stated "The more deeply I reflect upon the role of the adult, the more complex it becomes."

> In her observations of intention, Sonya wrote, *"In the sharing of our intentions, what we value oftentimes moves from the tacit to the explicit, and our interests, values, and identity have the opportunity to become more conscious to ourselves and others. Through the community sharing of self, the community identity changes and evolves and influences the evolution of self (personal and professional). The intention offers to us, self and community, a motivation to an openness to change over time."*

Through intentional study, the teacher described above realized the complexities of teaching.

YEAR FOUR: CHANGES AND SURVIVALS

In the fourth year of the project, Sonya moved out of state and was no longer part of the team on a regular basis. In addition, major personnel shifts within three of the four schools began to interfere with the overall project design.

New leadership in one school and a mandated curriculum with strict adherence to its organizational framework in another impacted the evolution of the work. The result was that some teachers accepted positions in another school district and one teacher retired. In the third school, three teachers transferred to another school with the curriculum supervisor, who was newly assigned as principal. In her role as curriculum supervisor, this individual had provided much of the leadership for the project. The move of these four individuals resulted in a slowdown of efforts in the original school.

Within the fourth school, the teachers that had aligned themselves most with the philosophy of Reggio Emilia continue to study together. They continue to work to create an environment of support and challenge and use project-based design to attend to curriculum requirements and children's interests. They continue to incorporate media as a tool for thinking and find time to create documentation panels. Most importantly, they find ways to engage with other teachers in discussions of their work either through an informal process within their school or through membership in Ohio's Reggio study group. Now, two years beyond the end of the original project, the membership of teachers within this school continues to grow. They too have new leadership that requires concise articulation of their purpose and the ways in which they address curriculum content to help all of their children meet the standards. However, the administration recognizes the hard work of these teachers, the impact of their group study and discussions, and the willingness of the teachers to directly address issues that impact their teaching and the learning of students.

MAKING CHANGES: WHAT WE HAVE LEARNED SO FAR

The process of change at the level of the individual and at the school level is a complex one. Any change efforts, no matter how small as in the case of this project, will touch the political and social networks and culture of the school and will impact teachers at a personal level (Brown and Moffett, 1999). All efforts to introduce change in teaching and learning produce tensions in all arenas of school life and all must be addressed. While this may be viewed as a leadership issue—an administrative issue—teachers as leaders also play a critical role in the responsibility for and ownership of confronting, addressing, and dealing with tensions, particularly when the source of the tension involves issues of teaching and learning that are of personal and professional significance.

All of the teachers within the project tried and found many different ways to increase the number of ways in which they could spend time in their colleagues' classrooms or meet to collaborate on project development or documentation panels. To do this the teachers had to commit to creating conditions that fostered relationships, communication, and collegiality.

The underlying concepts that supported the change—trust, honesty, security, and significance—were addressed as the years progressed. Perhaps more importantly, three years into the project it was acknowledged that external forces cannot create the safe place for dialogue, change, innovation, and risk-taking. Rather, the safe place is developed and nurtured as teachers slowly create their own communities of learning and of shared practices.

While the pressure to change can come through a variety of forms, such as state and district mandates, new leadership, poor test scores, incentives, grants, and initiatives such as this project, real change, as Parker Palmer (1993) points out, comes from caring for the students, caring about the subjects that you teach, and also from caring about the conditions, "inner and outer that bear on the work teachers do" (p. 182).

If the process for real change and transformation begins with self, schools must create the space and time for teachers to engage in self-examination and critical reflection of their practices through dialogue with peers within a community of acceptance, and the administration must view these teacher actions as critical to continuous improvement efforts. Fullan and Hargreaves (1991) point out that change requires new forms of relationships, the creation of systematic ways of initiating and sustaining the dialogue about content, increased attention to sharing and discussing teaching strategies, and the development of a safe and supportive atmosphere to test out ideas and hypotheses about new learnings.

SUMMING UP

Reflecting upon her time in Ohio working within public education settings, Sonya wrote,

> "At first glance, for many educators it seems the philosophy of the Reggio Emilia Approach won't fit, won't work, can't work in public education contexts. They are right; the Reggio Approach doesn't fit in our context if we expect a direct transportation.
>
> "However, it is not about copying Reggio, transplanting the approach, or squeezing it into our structure from the outside in. Rather it is about using Reggio as our inspiration. It is up to us to design and construct our own interpretations. How this evolves will depend on the school culture, the surrounding community, and the personalities of those involved.
>
> "Some schools that I've visited have on their bulletin board 'In dialogue with the Reggio Emilia Approach.' But it feels more like an argument, a wrestling match. Having a relationship with the Reggio Approach is like a marriage; you're in it for a lifetime and while it's a most meaningful connection, there are times you wish you never met. It's not easy. Not easy at all. In fact, it can be downright drag'em out difficult, and also one of the most worthwhile, nourishing adventures we could ever have.
>
> "Why should we consider such a challenge in public education settings? Because children deserve a place where they can express themselves at their highest level, educators are entitled to be fulfilled by their work, and parents have a right to be integrally involved in the education of their children. When we stop trying to 'do Reggio' and start taking a close look at the values Reggio has at the foundation of its system, we can begin to notice the values that speak to us."

Some of the values that Reggio demonstrates daily are those that speak an international language: democratic participation; the centrality of children and childhood; high standards for children, parents, and teachers; the value of imagination and creativity as integral to intellectual development; and systems of interconnections that are the infrastructure for achievement for all.

In the public schools involved in this project, the teachers found the courage to reveal their reality and examine it from a new vantage point. By bringing themselves back again and again through reflection and group dialogue to questions of values, the teachers began to embrace teaching from a position of learning about the children, themselves, and their peers. The journey of self-reflection and public dialogue is not easy, as Parker Palmer points out in *The Courage To Teach* (1998), but the renewed passion and commitment to teaching and the sense of one's own creativity and contribution to others make the choice to do so worth the ride.

VIII

Creating a Vision for Future Change
Where Do We Go from Here?

 Because *Next Steps* is primarily an encouraging, "how-we-are-doing-it" kind of book, the authors have focused on various steps they are taking to implement the Reggio Approach in very down-to-earth ways.

But, as educators, they agree that we must also think beyond the individual steps we are taking and do our best to advocate more broadly for quality care for the children we educate. The four contributors to this final chapter, Judith Allen Kaminsky, Margie Cooper, Jeanne Goldhaber, and Karen Haigh, suggest many practical ways to advocate for that better quality exemplified so clearly by the Reggio Approach.

A FINAL EXCERPT FROM LELLA

The good news is that several educators in the United States have proceeded to consider and study deeply the philosophy, strategies, and practices of the educators of Reggio Emilia and re-construct or re-invent them. As they work they are doing their best to always keep in mind the background, context, environment, and cultures of each preschool or center, and the parents, teachers, and children who are involved there. This volume contains the narratives, reflections, and creative thoughts of a number of these educators. What they can relate to other educators, and also to the educators from Reggio Emilia, is about the value and force of ideas that are rooted in the conviction that education has to be deeply rooted in the respect of people and their relationships.

THE FINAL CHALLENGE FROM LILIAN

This brings me to my final round of questions. Since all real change must be implemented locally, the responsibility for change is placed right on our own doorsteps. It pushes us to take stock and ask, Where are we now? As potential implementors of the Reggio Approach, what should we be thinking about now? What should or can each of us do now?

21

Experiences in Advocacy
Expanding the Role of the
Early Childhood Educator

Judith Allen Kaminsky

Editor, *Innovations in Early Education: The International Reggio Exchange,* Merrill-Palmer Institute, Wayne State University, Detroit, Michigan

Margie Cooper

President, Inspired Practices in Early Education, Inc., Roswell, Georgia

Jeanne Goldhaber

Associate Professor, Early Childhood Pre-K Teacher Education Program, University of Vermont

Karen Haigh

Director of Programs, Chicago Commons Association, Chicago, Illinois

In numerous ways, Reggio Emilia reminds us of what we believe in and demonstrates the feasibility of our common goals. Yet our motivation to grapple with what Reggio Emilia has to offer also draws support from something less apparent but perhaps more important in the long run, and that is the growing conviction that there is something genuine to be gained in more clearly defining our roles and goals as educators and citizens. The relevance of Reggio Emilia to the field of early childhood education in the United States corresponds to our growing understanding of the linkages between educational practice and the larger sociopolitical context, between our personal ethics and our professional responsibilities. To that end, the most critical step in learning to 'teach the Reggio way' is to move to an expanded role of early childhood educators as advocates for a new image of young children.

(New, 1977, pp. 225–226)

In Rebecca New's chapter on advocacy in *First Steps Toward Teaching the Reggio Way,* she challenges American early childhood educators to reflect on their roles within and outside the classroom, and to expand their roles as advocates for a new image of childhood and education in their communities. The experience of the Reggio Emilia educators serves as a provocation to empower and inspire teachers, administrators, parents, and community members to work for quality care and education for young children. Our colleagues in Reggio Emilia have shared with us their struggles and their strategies, their philosophy, and their practice to inspire us to understand our own values and our own culture. In this way, we can develop experiences for children, teachers, and parents that reflect our beliefs and those of our communities.

Many early childhood educators in the United States and Canada have accepted the challenge and the responsibility of this expanded role. They are reaching out into their communities to communicate the depth of their work and the reasons behind the choices they have made. They have worked to develop relationships with the members and leaders of their communities to establish communication and understanding about the value of early childhood education and care that is respectful of children, teachers, and parents.

This chapter features the stories of educators in Illinois, Vermont, and Georgia: Karen Haigh of Chicago Commons Child Development Program in Chicago, Jeanne Goldhaber of the University of Vermont in Burlington, and Margie Cooper of Inspired Practices in Early Education in Atlanta. I believe that exploring their experiences in advocacy and the process of their growth can inspire possibilities in other communities. Hopefully, the sharing of their stories will make the initiation and development of these kinds of relationships seem less daunting and intimidating to those who have yet to take this step.

Karen, Jeanne, Margie, and I have collaborated on some questions that each could address to explain the process of developing community relationships and the numerous factors that influence that process. These questions concern the following areas: the development of and motivation for relationships with community leaders and policy makers; strategies used to communicate the principles behind their work; the roles of teachers and families in the advocacy process; the role of documentation in communicating with families, community members, and policy makers; the advocacy role of "The Hundred Languages of Children" exhibit; connections with state early education initiatives; and the goals, plans, and implementation of the leadership delegations to Reggio Emilia.

KAREN HAIGH: THE POWER OF COLLABORATION

What is advocacy? What is the relationship between advocacy and early childhood education and our programs? These are ongoing questions in my mind and questions I like to ask other people so we can think about what we mean by advocacy. What is the relationship of advocacy to the care and education of young children? What is leadership's role in advocacy? These are very big questions that we tend to take for granted and assume we have a common understanding. I think more about the advocacy roles of administrators, education coordinators, and consultants than teachers because teachers are so busy in the classroom. How can we connect with people who impact public policy for children's care and education? How can we draw public attention to our work and to the children for whom we are working? That is our charge and none of us, teachers, administrators, or parents, is good at that. None of us is trained to do that in our education or our work experience. My participation in study tours to Reggio Emilia has caused me to think about drawing public attention to our work. That is the biggest challenge.

Possibilities for Drawing Public Attention to Our Work

Advocate for Quality During the Week of the Young Child.   A perfect example is the Week of the Young Child. I believe the Week of the Young Child should be a time to try to communicate with people who don't understand or care about issues concerning care and education for children. I think it is a way to invite them to be informed and involved. Every year during the Week of the Young Child, we have events at our sites and every year, our sites invite our parents to come to the program to do a special activity with the children. How is this connecting to those people who make decisions about children in order to encourage them to be interested in children's issues? It is very difficult to motivate our staff to invite community members and policy makers into their programs. I don't believe the National Association for the Education of

Young Children (NAEYC) strongly emphasizes the importance of this type of advocacy during the Week of the Young Child. NAEYC generally suggests the usual parent-child activities that don't do anything to advocate for our programs. We have to learn how to connect to community leaders. Our legislators might be interested in supporting our programs if they knew something about them. I believe that teacher education and administrative education is weak with regard to advocacy. Yet I don't want to totally focus on education, because in Reggio I don't think they go to classes to learn about advocacy. They learn about advocacy in their programs. In the United States, we don't emphasize advocacy in education or practice.

Advocate for Quality by Encouraging Teachers and Parents to Become Advocates. One important way that we work with teachers and parents in thinking about advocacy is through monthly meetings. These meetings are not a Head Start requirement or a requirement of any kind. They are voluntary and in addition to all the other meetings we have each month. In these meetings, we go to a different site each time, and the parents and teachers tour that site so they become familiar with all of the different Commons sites and communities. A teacher makes a 15–20 minute presentation on current explorations or studies in the classroom so everyone is able to connect with an experience that's evolving with children and teachers. The third part of each meeting's agenda is discussing particular questions together. One year, we asked: What is your image of the child? What do you think is the public school's image of the child? What is society's image of the child? Discussion around these questions can continue for months. We gather the notes from the meetings, read them, and try to think of other questions that could develop from the conversations of these meetings. I see this as advocacy.

Other questions we've discussed are: What are the goals for children in the program from a child's point of view, from a teacher's point of view, from a parent's point of view, from a future employer's point of view? Some area employers came to the meetings when we discussed these questions and we asked them: On what skills can the schools focus to help a child be a good employee? This year, we asked what we thought was a simple question but turned out to be a big challenge: What is the government's role in child care? When we asked this question, we got a lot of blank stares from the parents. We realized the question was too overwhelming, so one of the coordinators suggested asking: What is the child's role in society? What do you think was the child's role in society 200 years ago? 100 years ago? and now? These questions led to a very fruitful conversation about the evolution of the role of children. From that discussion, we led into the government's role regarding children and child care, in particular.

We learned how to stay focused on our questions during these meetings and our reasons for asking them. At one meeting, our coordinators asked the question: What is a quality program? That led to discussion about education in the public schools. After the meeting, I met with the coordinators, and we had to go back and think about: What is our goal in discussing a quality program? We decided it was to look at quality child care, not quality elementary education. The reason we wanted to discuss the government's role in child care is because we knew that state child care cuts were coming. We felt it was important for us to think about why we want to advocate for child care and why it is important to fight these cuts. But it's essential to remember how slow and tedious this kind of process is, and how you have to go step by step and little by little. When you want major change to happen fast, the process falls flat on its face. You have to be very patient, very thoughtful, and very well planned. You have to keep evaluating each step of the process of moving forward. It's not easy. But when you move slowly and continually evaluate and adjust your movement, you do see some pretty amazing changes when you look back over time, perhaps two years or so.

I've learned a lot about the cultures of the Hispanic and African American parents during these discussions. For example, it's been a real struggle to involve the Hispanic parents in advocacy. We've been organizing parents to go down to Springfield [Illinois's state capitol] to help object to cuts in child care. Yet the Hispanic parents can't believe all the services that are offered to them in the United States compared to Mexico. They can't believe that they have child care and only have to pay a small co-payment for these experiences for their children. So it's very hard to get them involved in advocacy issues. I didn't realize that's how many Hispanic parents felt until I heard them talk about child care in this country. I believe that these discussions are really important for administrators, coordinators, teachers, and parents to think about. They help us to understand each other and where we're coming from, and give us more of a sense of where we might go together. This is one area that has evolved and is evolving, in terms of parents' and teachers' roles in advocacy.

Advocate for Quality by Documenting Children's Learning Experiences.   Another arena concerns the opportunity for teachers to gather documentation to display so people can be provoked to think about children in new ways and to see the complexities and abilities of children, particularly low-income children. Through the process of assembling documentation of learning experiences, teachers become aware of children's powerful thoughts, ideas, and feelings, as do parents and visitors (sometimes legislators) who make decisions about programs. So documentation plays a major role. We're also trying to put together a book on literacy in response to the push toward children learning the alphabet through drill-and-skill types of activities. We want to try to capture moments the children are learning about literacy in other ways. We've spent the last year trying to capture photos and children's and teachers' words related to the literacy development essential to the children's ability to learn how to read. I want this book to make a strong impact on whoever reads it so they'll think carefully and thoughtfully about how literacy development emerges within children.

Advocate for Quality Through Learning Tours.   Another way that parents are learning about advocacy is through our learning tours. We've asked a panel of parents to field questions from our learning tour audiences. They get up in front of 50–100 people and answer questions about their children's program, explaining what they think about it to those who aren't familiar with the program. Perhaps someday we will ask parents to become more involved in reaching out to the general public, but this is a beginning step. Some of the questions that people from other states ask are very challenging. I think the fact that parents are participating in this panel is remarkable. I see this as another aspect of advocacy. I believe that teachers and parents within our program have become advocates or are becoming advocates through experiences that cause them to think and reflect about so many issues related to the care and education of young children. Hopefully, parents will become advocates not just for their own child or only while their children are in the program. I hope they will come to see the importance of child care and education for all children.

Development of Leadership Study Tours to Reggio Emilia

I'd like to discuss the evolutionary process of the two leadership study tours. The idea initiated with Margie Cooper and Jeanne Goldhaber. The three of us realized we were all working on developing relationships with community leaders and policy makers so we decided to pursue the idea of a study tour to Reggio Emilia specifically for these people. I don't know why I wanted to do this. I'm not very political and haven't historically been very aggressive about communicating with legislators. We've been exploring Reggio at Chicago Commons since 1993 because it's an amazing way to respect teachers, children, and parents, and it's an extraordinary framework for reflective professional development for teachers to try to understand what they're doing and why.

I have not spent a lot of time promoting this philosophy in Chicago or in Illinois. Educators in this area have gradually learned from their colleagues around the country about the work related to the Reggio philosophy that we are doing at Chicago Commons. It's taken many years for that to happen. In fact, last month, the city of Chicago Deputy Commissioner in charge of Head Start and child care contracts came to visit our program for the first time, and we talked about our work at Chicago Commons. She was very respectful of what we were trying to do, and we discussed the future of child care in Chicago. She is interested in going to Reggio in the future. Developing these connections and relationships takes time, and you have to be patient. I believe that if Chicago Commons can develop this kind of potential for our children and our program, others can as well.

The First Leadership Study Tour.   I did not know how to strategically approach community leaders and policy makers for this leadership tour. I learned that when you don't know how to do something alone, find someone to do it with you. I would never have pursued this without Margie and Jeanne. When I knew that they were working on the same efforts in their states, I felt I could do it. It's very powerful to know that you have comrades who are working on the same thing that you are. It gives you an energy that you wouldn't necessarily have if you were doing it alone. I decided to seek out comrades in Chicago. I called a friend who has been involved in Head Start for years and is politically astute, and asked her for advice. I also called two people whom I knew had the potential to be key collaborators and were familiar with my program. One was the director of Ada McKinley, a program working with low-income children much like Chicago Commons, who was very connected to a lot of people in Chicago. I also called the executive director of the local NAEYC affiliate who had seen our programs and was very impressed with what we were doing. I asked them if they would be willing to help me identify a group of people in leadership positions and try to interest them in our Reggio-related work and this leadership tour. All three agreed to join this effort, and we met to strategize how we were going to proceed. We identified people in Chicago and in Illinois from three groups: legislators/government administrators, funders, and university educators. Again, our collaboration made possible what I could not have done alone.

We mailed invitations for a symposium that would include a site visit, a presentation by Lella Gandini, and a presentation by me about our exploration of the Reggio philosophy at Chicago Commons. As a result of that symposium, two architects committed to the leadership delegation: one works with Chicago Commons and one with other child care programs. Two educators from Chicago Public Schools agreed to go to Reggio: the Director of Early Childhood Education and the Director of the Early Childhood Demonstration School. Two people from the Illinois Facilities Fund, a non-profit organization that works to fund and build child care centers in Illinois, committed to the leadership delegation: the executive director and one of the key project directors. One administrator who works at Ounce of Prevention and at the Erikson Institute also decided to participate in the leadership study tour. Ounce of Prevention is another key grantee for Head Start in Chicago. Then there was a funder from the Tribune McCormick Foundation in Chicago who went to the World Forum and the study tour to Reggio that followed. Since the 2001 leadership tour was a part of the World Forum study tour, she joined our group in Reggio. Most of our group was incredibly moved by the experience. For one member of the group, it was necessary to visit a few of our programs after her return for her to believe that this was possible in the city of Chicago.

Only eight people from Illinois participated in the first leadership tour, but those eight people have since made an impact in thinking about Reggio in Chicago. We have developed a wonderful relationship with the staff of the Illinois Facilities Fund, who are very supportive and respectful of our work. The Ounce of Prevention representative on the study tour has called to request presentations about our experience with the Reggio philosophy and has asked us to consult with her on some of their initiatives. We've also been asked to do a three-session class on the Reggio philosophy for the Erikson Institute this summer. This is the first time we've been asked to participate in the Erikson Institute's professional development program. Most significantly, the Chicago Public Schools have asked us to consult with their early childhood program regarding exploration of the Reggio philosophy. We are now consulting with five Chicago Public Schools, ranging from two to four classrooms each.

In addition, the funder from the Tribune McCormick Foundation brought a board member of a key advocacy group, Voices for Illinois Children, to see Nia Family Center. They were both very appreciative and respectful of the work we are doing.

This board member was also able to visit La Villetta School during a trip to Italy. When she returned, she called me immediately and was very anxious to work together on some sort of initiative related to the Reggio philosophy in Chicago. So you can see, one thing leads to another in a step by step process.

The Second Leadership Study Tour.   I relied on the support of those people from Chicago who had gone to Reggio in 2001 while planning for the 2002 leadership tour. I called three members of that delegation and the Voices for Illinois Children board member, who suggested contacting the organization's executive director because he was so knowledgeable about child care and education issues and advocacy. When we met to strategically plan for the study tour, the question arose, "What does curriculum have to do with public policy?" I realized we have to portray the Reggio approach as a philosophy about working with children, teachers, and parents, because if we say it's a curriculum approach, child care advocates don't listen. This question caused me to think about how I explained our interest in this philosophy and why we are organizing these study tours. How would I explain it to a legislator? I decided that an exploration of the experience of the Reggio early childhood program is a way for people who make policies about care and education for children to think about quality.

We decided to have a meeting at Nia Family Center, where people could tour the site and communicate with a panel of those who participated in the 2001 leadership tour or a previous study tour to Reggio. We carefully chose the panel, aiming for political diversity. We chose our architect, the Tribune McCormick funder, the Ada McKinley director, and a university professor. The moderator was the Chicago Public Schools Chief Deputy for Education. The panel discussion went on for a long time and the dialogue was excellent. For the first time, a state legislator came to the meeting. During the site tour, this legislator saw documentation of letters from parents about the child care cuts, an issue about which she would be deciding! Having a state legislator at this meeting, visiting one of our sites, was a major stepping stone in this process.

We sent out letters inviting the people who attended the meeting to the leadership tour to Reggio. This time, we would try to acquire funding for government employees and legislators. Because we had some good momentum, including the Chicago Public Schools project, Margie and Jeanne were very supportive and gave us 20 slots in the leadership tour. Ten people from Chicago Public Schools committed to the leadership delegation: the Chief Deputy of Education, the Director of Professional Development for Early Childhood Education, four principals, an early childhood specialist, and three teachers. Some of these people had visited our sites and we had cultivated their interest.

We were hoping to have four legislators on the 2002 tour. I called the Day Care Action Council (the leading advocacy agency in Illinois) and asked for advice on whom to ask. I also asked their executive director if she wanted to go. The Day Care Action Council recommended four legislators, Republicans and Democrats. A Republican state senator and a Democratic state representative decided to join the leadership delegation, as well as a Columbia College professor. The assistant director for subsidized child care for the state of Illinois agreed to go and then dropped out because of child care cuts. The funding we expected to get fell through and we are waiting for word from another funder. It's like a game of chess. You have to keep changing your strategy. But I am so excited about this group. This leadership tour is a way for policy makers to learn about Reggio's history and ideas about quality and about respect for children, parents, and teachers. It is also a way that we can learn about ourselves.

Initially, I would have never predicted that Chicago Public Schools would want to explore Reggio. We were interested in exploring what could happen as a result of our collaboration, by encouraging them to think differently about school and children. I also hope that advocacy groups like Day Care Action Council and Voices for Illinois Children may begin to think in new and expanded ways about what quality could be and how to respect children, parents, and teachers. This 2002 leadership tour could be the beginning of developing relationships with legislators who want to understand and support high quality care for children.

We're one of the richest countries in the world, so shouldn't we have the highest quality care for our children? During the rally against child care cuts in Springfield, I heard people say you can tell the quality of a society by how they treat their children, especially their young children. If this country is supposed to be so rich and so powerful, shouldn't the quality of care and education for children be rich and powerful, if we really want competent and productive citizens? I am hoping that we can begin thinking about this with teachers, parents, legislators, advocates, and other leaders in Illinois. Together we can talk about ideas, issues, and possibilities concerning assessment and the education of poor children. Together we can talk about the importance of professional development for teachers. That's what I'm hoping. I like the idea that we'll be connecting with other people in the United States who have some of the same questions and different questions, some of the same perspectives and different perspectives. We're all fueled by the energy of diverse perspectives.

JEANNE GOLDHABER: A VISION OF POSSIBILITIES

The ways I've looked at the early childhood programs of Reggio Emilia have changed over the years and seem to radiate out from an egocentric point of reference to increasingly more distant concentric circles. My first trip to Reggio Emilia was in 1991 and I went with a very personal agenda. I wanted to see for myself what George Forman, Carolyn Edwards, and Lella Gandini had described to me, what I had been reading about, what I had seen documented in "The Hundred Languages of Children" exhibit in Washington, D.C. in 1990. When I returned to Reggio in 1993, I went with a lens that I hoped would inform our work in our teacher preparation program and on-site Campus Children's Center, a lab school and full day, year-round program for University of Vermont faculty, staff, and students. Still later, I wanted the Campus Children's Center teachers and even some of our students to experience the programs of Reggio Emilia firsthand, so that together we could construct a vision of how we wanted our program to evolve. Seeing how powerful this experience was for us, I began to organize small delegations of Vermont educators to join the study tours, hoping that Vermont's early childhood community could work together to build our own Vermont vision of early care and education.

Initial Efforts to Strengthen Community Relationships

After many trips to Reggio Emilia, I realized that these programs aren't just about pedagogy but are as much about the power that a group of committed citizens can wield if they are persistent and have a vision. I also began to see that the Vermont community shares many of the characteristics of Reggio Emilia. Both have long histories of progressive political leadership, active citizen participation, and a strong sense of community. But what Vermont doesn't have is an integrated, comprehensive, and universally accessible system of high quality early education and care. So in 2000, I invited several influential community leaders to join the U.S. spring study tour to Reggio Emilia. I hoped that by experiencing this municipal early childhood system, they would come away with a sense of what could happen when a community dedicates itself to articulating its own definition of the best practice and care it can offer its youngest citizens.

The community leaders who participated in this study tour included a Vermont state senator, a dean of Education and Social Services, and the Vermont Deputy Commissioner of Human Services. Because of the size of our state, I either knew these people or they knew of me since I've worked in Vermont early childhood programs for nearly 30 years. So my invitations were personal, and that remains the common thread throughout the Vermont story. Most community leaders who have gone to Reggio Emilia were either invited or urged to go by a friend or colleague who had gone before, or were convinced through conversation with former delegates that seeing these programs firsthand would support the development of a high-quality system of early education and care in our state. In fact, from this point on, the Vermont story must be told in the first person plural since all subsequent initiatives have been the work of many. These initiatives wouldn't have happened without the emotional and very practical support of educators throughout the state.

Developing the 2001 Leadership Delegation.   The idea of organizing a delegation designed specifically for community leaders and policy makers emerged from conversations with the participants of the 2000 study tour as well as with Margie Cooper and Karen Haigh. When we approached Reggio Children about the possibility of a leadership delegation, they suggested we join the three-day study tour that was to follow the World Forum on Early Education and Care in the spring of 2001. While this would not be designed specifically for community leaders, we believed it would be an interesting option that could appeal to non-educators.

Together with the Vermont delegates of the 2000 study tour and others, we phoned, e-mailed, and wrote invitations to office holders, legislators, state department administrators, early childhood advocates, business people, administrators of large early childhood programs, faculty and administrators from higher education, and early childhood advocacy/legislative groups. Those who accepted our invitations included a member of the Vermont Business Round Table, the Vermont Commissioner of Education, and the Director of the Governor's Commission on Women.

Developing the 2002 Leadership Delegation.   Like our participation in the 2000 study tour, the 2001 experience generated spirited conversation and renewed investment among the Vermont delegates about issues related to early education and care. They urged me to try to organize a community leaders delegation for the next year, and began a list of leaders to invite. Margie's and Karen's delegates' experiences were similarly productive, so that together we once again submitted a proposal to Reggio Children for a Community Leadership Study Tour the following summer. Thanks to the generous spirit of Reggio Children and its teachers, families, and children—and Margie's coordination efforts—we returned to Reggio Emilia in 2002 for a three-day Community Leaders Study Tour. Vermonters from the state Department of Education, the Department of Human Services, and the business sector were included in this most recent delegation. We have just returned from Italy and have scheduled a meeting at the end of this month to discuss the study tour and how we want to follow up on our experiences.

Outcomes and Inspirations from the Leadership Study Tours

As a result of these delegations and the discussions that followed, other less grandiose but possibly even more effective strategies to raise the level of quality and accessibility of early education and care in Vermont have emerged. A community group in Burlington has organized to make young children more visible in what is essentially a college town. They have met with the mayor several times and also organized a small exhibit documenting a program for young children that they run in City Hall Park during the summer. One of the teachers from the Campus Children's Center made small panels for child-friendly businesses in Burlington, thanking them for their welcoming attitudes toward young children, and presented a panel to the mayor as well. The chair of our department and I presented some of our center's documented investigations during a conference for school superintendents. A network of teachers inspired by the Reggio philosophy (RIVET) is engaged in a statewide teacher research project looking at young children's understanding of their Vermont communities and the natural world. A RIVET teacher displayed panels from her program during her community's Town Meeting Day, a true Vermont phenomenon. Our Commissioner of Education and a UVM faculty member presented the RIVET work to the Vermont Senate Education Committee. We've also organized "Autumn Tours" for policy makers to visit and learn firsthand about early education and care in their communities, and are organizing them this fall for local candidates for public office.

Last summer at our first RIVET reunion, we wrote a strategic plan that we will revisit this summer. We've made progress on many of our projections. The success of the strategic plan may suggest that the leadership delegations can serve as an effective agent of change, but what matters is whether we manage to influence the quality of life for all young children in Vermont. Only time is going to tell us that. When we started looking to the programs of Reggio Emilia to inspire a Vermont vision of early childhood education and care, we conceptualized it as a long-term project. If it took the citizens of Reggio Emilia 30 years, we would surely need at least that long to create our own inspired system. So while our advocacy efforts may or may not include leadership delegations in the future, they will definitely continue and will reflect the inspiration of the citizens of Reggio Emilia. Perhaps in 2025, we will be writing a chapter celebrating the world-class system of early education and care in our little state of Vermont!

MARGIE COOPER: EXTENDING THE DIALOGUE

My first visit to Reggio Emilia was as an Ohio State graduate student in June 1991. An encounter with "The Hundred Languages of Children" exhibit in my hometown of Dayton had piqued my interest in the Reggio educational philosophy. Interestingly, Jeanne Goldhaber and Karen Haigh were delegates on this same study tour. During the course of our work on this chapter, the three of us realized we were all on that same trip so many years ago. This discovery has caused me to wonder how much of our personal and professional evolutions may go unnoticed for very long periods of time. Did it take a certain passage of time in our three respective lives for each of us to decide to work in new and broader ways with community leaders as well as teachers? What is our understanding of the role of time in the course of our own learning? Why did it take ten years for me to "know" that a fundamental aspect of what we call the Reggio Approach is its connection to and relationship with its own community? What about professional relationships? Would any of us have had the courage to challenge our thinking and push ourselves out of our comfort zone without the support of others? With these unanswered reflections, the story of my journey with community leaders begins.

Initial Interest in the Reggio Philosophy in Georgia

I maintained an almost private interest in the Reggio educational philosophy during most of the 1990s, attending many conferences across the country, returning to Reggio several times, meeting new colleagues, and maintaining my relationships with Ohio colleagues whose statewide initiatives through the Martha Holden Jennings Project continually served as a source of inspiration. At the beginning of the decade, I was a new resident of Georgia and a new mother. In time, I developed relationships within my neighborhood community and the early childhood community of Georgia. By 1994, I was volunteering as the annual conference chair for the Georgia Association for Young Children (GAYC) and was surprised that few were aware of the field's growing interest in Reggio. By 1997, I began to focus on efforts to host "The Hundred Languages of Children" in Atlanta. In 1999, a small group of us joined together as a not-for-profit organization, Inspired Practices in Early Education, to support the exhibit work. As the year 2000 dawned, we were awaiting the exhibit's arrival in November. There was a growing interest within the professional community about Reggio, partly as a result of our work but mostly as a result of the natural passing of time and the growing availability of written materials about the Reggio philosophy.

Impact of "The Hundred Languages of Children" Exhibit

During the 1990s, there was a dramatic increase in interest in early childhood care and education in Georgia. During this time, Georgia became the first state to finance universal pre-K programs for the state's 4-year-olds; it is presently supporting efforts to offer financial incentives for teachers to obtain formal education degrees and for centers to adopt practices correlated to higher quality, such as lowering teacher/child ratios. The work of Inspired Practices continues against this backdrop, guided by a mission to strengthen Georgia's vision of what is possible for young children.

We have felt our way along our course, but hosting "The Hundred Languages of Children" exhibit during the NAEYC 2000 annual conference was truly the basis for our current work. It was through the oftentimes desperate work of trying to raise money, find a location for the exhibit, and develop supporters that many relationships were founded and/or strengthened. The lasting impact of the exhibit was the positive energy that encircled the work involved in hosting it. Through that positive energy, a conversation developed about a higher vision for children, and many gained a greater understanding of what is possible through the strong images of the exhibit. The exhibit was also the place where we first reached out to a large number of community leaders by inviting them to a reception a few days before the grand opening. From an invitation list of approximately 150, jointly created by the exhibit committee, we welcomed approximately 50 special guests.

Project Infinity: A Specific Example of the Exhibit's Impact.   Another aspect of the exhibit's impact was very specific. Our new project working with three schools materialized from these schools' fascination with and affinity for what they experienced through the exhibit. While we had a preexisting relationship with one of the schools, two of the schools made contact with Inspired Practices for further professional development following the exhibit's closing. Relationships strengthened over a period of months and a complex experiment named Project Infinity was conceived. So, in the school year immediately following the hosting of the exhibit, we embarked on an experiment that challenges our ability to form a strong learning community between volunteers from Inspired Practices and three separate schools with very different histories, demographics, and facilities.

Project Infinity is so named because we think our work will last forever and that its inherent possibilities are infinite. We say in our work together that "Reggio" is shorthand for the deep study of teaching, learning, children, and community. This characterization reminds us that we are not interested in copying or implementing "Reggio." Our goal is to learn together and support one another as each school strengthens its own identity and becomes its better self. We find that we have to constantly challenge ourselves to consider our work together in the widest pos-sible terms. We make conscious choices not only to converse about and study our practice, but also to question ourselves about our personal connections and the schools' connections to the community. We are wondering about ways to put the schools in the minds and experiences of those in the community who may be in-terested in supporting our work and our values regarding early care and education.

Building Relationships Within the Georgia Community: A Long-Term Benefit of the Exhibit.   Though still in its infancy, Project Infinity is fairly well defined and organ-ized. The experience of the exhibit also resulted in the less defined and organized work of building relationships with and among community leaders. Like Jeanne and Karen, I found myself wanting to create an inspiring experience for those in our state whose point of view can contribute to charting a new course for early childhood policies and practices. For many years, I have felt that if these people could see the systemic com-munity accomplishments and rich practices of Reggio, they would raise their own ex-pectations of early care and education in our state. In 1999, with the help of Reggio Children and Angela Ferrario, we began to organize Georgia delegations within the annual U.S. study tours, initially to build enthusiasm for the exhibit project and later to build enthusiasm for a stronger vision of the possibilities for children, teachers, families, and communities in our state. The delegations of 1999 and 2000, with a com-bined total of 45 participants, included just a few community leaders. During the 2000 delegation, Jeanne and I began to talk about some of the lessons we were learning through our work with community leaders. By 2001, through continued collabora-tion with Reggio Children and Angela Ferrario, Jeanne, Karen, and I were given an opportunity to bring about 25 community leaders from our 3 respective states to the study tour following the World Forum conference.

Strategies for Sustaining and Nurturing Community Relationships

Since 1999, seventy Georgia delegates have participated in study tours to Reggio. Our leadership delegates have included university faculty, early childhood agency direc-tors, and elected officials. Through the experiences organized by Reggio Children and the municipality of Reggio, these leadership groups have developed a unique charac-ter. The city of Reggio inspires people to connect with one another in conversation, in imagination, and in reflection. This state of being together remains elusive within the confines of our ordinary work lives in the United States. Thus, I still have nagging questions about what strategies we can use to keep the interest alive and the learning continuing once we are back home. This is fairly easy to do with teachers, but what should the forum look like for community leaders? My only goal for the first leader-ship delegates was that the positive experience stayed with them the rest of their lives. This might be a reasonable goal for early work but at some future juncture, we have a responsibility to convert the collective experiences into something beneficial for chil-dren. What that will be or how we accomplish it remains a question. This is certainly a work in progress.

Because we have only just begun our project with three schools in Atlanta, we are still talking in theoretical terms to policy makers. We rely heavily on the experiences of Reggio Emilia rather than our own programs in order to discuss key elements such as community investments in children, political systems that can support children's care and education, and the myriad notions encompassed in the "high quality" language. We also rely on early childhood programs in the United States such as Chicago Commons, which is a rare example in the U.S. of a systemic/public approach, rather than a single site/private approach.

Looking back over the last dozen years reminds me that the risk of committing historical accounts to paper is that the linear nature of writing often leaves the reader with a false impression that the events described unfolded in a neat and orderly fashion, and those participating were always aware of the choices being made and the consequences of those choices. Thus, it is worth noting that much of what has evolved was the result of trial and error. Meeting people has been a strong value that we have pursued. As both Karen and Jeanne have already described, the salient aspects of this work have been the slow evolution of ideas, an ever-widening network of people, and a continual resistance to feeling comfortable in a cozy nest where everything is working well or, at least, predictably.

The strongest realization I have had in the last two or three years is that the work cannot be linear. It has to involve as many complexities as can be conceived. Therefore, there is always a place for extending oneself into communities of people that might not be familiar, whether they are political, business, sporting, financial, literary, arts, or service communities. If our notion of a more perfect community includes the idea that we can create better care and education for young children, then we need a diversity of people to encounter this idea with us. Like Karen and Jeanne, I have also witnessed the strength that others bring to the work. The more we reach out, the more of us there are to reach out and, thus, our reach is extended beyond anything one person can do alone. While many U.S. educators describe themselves as not particularly political, teaching remains a political act. The experience of Reggio Emilia reminds us of what can be accomplished when such a notion is fully embraced.

THE CHALLENGE IS OURS

The heightened emphasis on leadership and advocacy among American early childhood professionals reflects a heightened need—not for resources, but for resolve. The contrast between our nation's ability and its will to care for its youngest citizens has never been so clear. (New, 1997, p. 232)

Karen, Jeanne, Margie, and their colleagues have accepted their responsibility as educators and citizens to advocate for the rights of children, teachers, and parents in their diverse communities. Each has approached this challenge in a completely different way, but what is common to their experience is a willingness to take risks, to continually reevaluate their actions and motivations, and to experiment with new strategies to achieve their goals. Each of these educators has emphasized the slow and gradual nature of the process of growth and change. They have accepted the role of time in the evolution of their own learning, and that of their colleagues and community members. At the same time, they have resisted being satisfied with the status quo and are determined to reach out to a diverse group of professionals to encounter the issue of better care and education for young children.

Together with their colleagues and community members, these three educators have discovered the power of collaboration and shared experience. They have sought to develop a broader sense of community, to strengthen and sustain relationships, to facilitate understanding, and to move forward together. Karen, Jeanne, and Margie have challenged themselves and their colleagues to think about how to generate the interest of policy makers and community leaders in early care and education, and how to connect with the reality and experiences of those who may be interested in supporting their work and their values about childhood. They have discovered the fundamental importance of making their work visible to an ever-widening range of people through the documentation of the learning experiences of the children, teachers, and families in their communities as well as those in Reggio Emilia. In this way, they are offering their community members the possibility to think about children in new and different ways, to be more aware of the capabilities of young children. This is one of the most fundamental "next steps" for those of us who are inspired by the Reggio educational philosophy. If we believe in the value of the work we are doing and in the future of our society, this step is essential. We have the ability, and with the collaboration of our colleagues, we have the power and the energy to make a difference for children in our own corner of the world.

References

Addams, J. (1960). *Twenty years at Hull House*. New York: New American Library.

Agee, J., & Evans, W. (1941). *Let us now praise famous men*. Boston: Houghton Mifflin.

Bandura, A. (1971). *Social learning theory*. Morristown, NJ: General Learning Press.

Bentley, W. A. (1931). *Snow crystals*. Mineola, NY: Dover.

Bondioli, A., & Mantovani, S. (1987). *Manuale critico dell'asilo nido* [Critical Manual for Infant-toddler centers]. Milan: Franco Angeli.

Bove, C. (2001). Inserimento: A strategy for delicately beginning relationships and communications. In L. Gandini & C. Edwards (Eds.), *Bambini* (pp. 109–123). New York: Teachers College Press.

Bowlby, J. (1969). *Attachment and loss. Vol. 1. Attachment*. New York: Basic Books.

Bray, J. N., Lee, J., Smith, L. L., & Yorks, L. (2000). *Collaborative inquiry in practice: Action, reflection and making meaning*. Thousand Oaks, CA: Sage.

Bredekamp, S. (1987). *Developmentally appropriate practice in early childhood programs serving children form birth through age eight*. Washington, DC: National Association for the Education of Young Children.

Bredekamp, S. (1993). Reflections on Reggio Emilia. *Young Children, 49*(1), 13–15.

Bredekamp, S., & Copple, C. (1997). *Developmentally appropriate practice in early childhood programs: Revised edition*. Washington, DC: National Association for the Education of Young Children.

Brown, J. L., & Moffit, C. A. (1999). *The hero's journey*. Alexandria, VA: Association for Supervision and Curriculum Development.

Burrington, B., & Hobbins-McGrath, W. (1995). *Common ground: Understanding, developing & working together, the role of documentation and collaboration in teacher development*. Unpublished manuscript. Burlington, VT: The University of Vermont, Department of Early Childhood Education.

Cadwell, L. B. (2002). *Bringing learning to life: The Reggio Emilia approach to early childhood education*. New York: Teachers College Press.

Catalogue of the exhibit, "The Hundred Languages of Children." Reggio Children: Reggio Emilia, Italy. http://www.info@reggiochildren.it

Ceppi, G., & Zini, M. (1998). *Children, spaces, relations: Metaproject for an environment for young children*. Modena, Italy: Grafiche Rebecchi Ceccarelli.

City of Reggio Emilia. (1987). The Hundred Languages of Children: Catalog of the Exhibits. Reggio Emilia: Assessorato Schole Infazia e Asili Nido.

Cole, M., & Wertsch, J. (2001). Beyond the individual-social antimony (sic) in discussions of Piaget and Vygotsky. *The Virtual Faculty.* Retrieved June 18, 2002 from the World Wide Web: http://www.massey.ac.nz/~alock/virtual/colevyg.htm.

Coles, R. (1997). *Doing documentary work.* New York: Oxford University Press.

Dewey, J. (1934). *Art as experience.* New York: Perigee Books, The Berkley Publishing Group, Penguin Putnam.

Dewey, J. (1959a). My pedagogic creed. In M. S. Dworkin (Ed.), *Dewey on education* (pp. 19–32). New York: Teachers College Press. (Original work published 1897).

Dewey, J. (1959b). The school and society. In M. S. Dworkin (Ed.), *Dewey on education* (pp. 33–90). New York: Teachers College Press. (Original work published 1897).

Dewey, J. (1966). *Democracy and education.* New York: The Free Press. (Original work published 1916).

Dewey, J. (1969). *Education and experience.* Toronto, Ontario: The Macmillan Company. (Original work published 1938).

Doyle, W., & Ponder, G. (1977–78) The practicality ethic in teacher decision-making. *Interchange, 8*(3), 1–12.

Dunn, J. (1993). *Young children's close relationships: Beyond attachment.* Newbury Park, CA: Sage Publications.

Dunn, M.A. (1993). The peek-a-boo game. *Psychoanalytic Review, 80*(3), 331–339.

Edwards, C., Gandini, L., & Forman, G. (Eds.). (1993). *The hundred languages of children: The Reggio Emilia approach to early childhood education.* Greenwich, CT: Ablex.

Edwards, C., Gandini, L., & Forman, G. (Eds.). (1998). *The hundred languages of children: The Reggio Emilia approach—Advanced reflections.* Second Edition. Greenwich, CT: Ablex.

Edwards, C. P., & Raikes, H. (2002). Extending the dance: Relationship-based approaches to infant/toddler care and education. *Young Children, 57*(4), 10–17.

Erikson, E. (1985). *Childhood and society.* New York: Norton.

Ewald, W. (1985). *Portraits and dreams, photographs and stories by children of the Appalachians.* New York: Writer's and Reader's Publishing, Inc.

Ferrari, M. (2001, May). In graphic form. Presentation to delegates. Reggio Emilia, Italy.

Fogel, A. (1993). *Developing through relationships: Origins of communication, self, and culture.* Chicago: University of Chicago Press.

Forman, G. (1992). The constructivist perspective to early education. In J. Roopnarine & J. Johnson (Eds.), *Approaches to early childhood education* (2nd ed.). Upper Saddle River, NJ: Merrill/Prentice Hall.

Forman, G. (1995). The amusement park for birds and the fountains. In G. Piazza (Ed.), *The fountains.* Reggio Emilia, Italy: Reggio Children S.rl.

Forman, G., & Fyfe, B., (1998). Negotiated learning through design, documentation, and discourse. In C. Edwards, L. Gandini, & G. Forman, *The Hundred Languages of Children: The Reggio Emilia approach—Advanced reflections.* Greenwich: CT: Ablex.

Forman, G., & Gandini, L. (1994). *An amusement park for birds.* [Video]. Amherst, MA: Performanetics.

Freud, S. (1969). *An outline of psycho-analysis: The James Strachley translation.* New York: W. W. Norton.

Fullan, M. G., & Miles, M. B. (1992, June). Getting reform right: What works and what doesn't. *Phi Delta Kappan,* 745–752.

Fullan, M., & Hargreaves, A. (1991). *What's worth fighting for in your school?* New York: Teachers College Press.

Fyfe, B. (1994). Images from the United States: Using ideas from the Reggio Emilia experience with American educators. In L. G. Katz & B. Cesarone (Eds.), *Reflections on the Reggio Emilia approach.* Urbana, IL: ERIC Clearinghouse on Elementary & Early Childhood Education.

Fyfe, B., & Cadwell, L. (1993). Bringing Reggio Emilia home. *Growing Times, 10*(3).

Fyfe, B., Geismar-Ryan, L., & Strange, J. (2000). The potential of collaborative inquiry. *Innovations in Early Education: The International Reggio Exchange, 7*(4).

Gandini, L. (1984, Summer). Not just anywhere: Making child care centers into "particular" places. *Beginnings,* pp. 17–20.

Gandini, L. (1991). Not just anywhere: Making child care centers into "particular" places. *Child Care Information Exchange, 78,* 5–9.

Gandini, L. (1993a). Educational and caring spaces. In D. Edwards, L. Gandini, & G. Forman (Eds.), *The hundred languages of children: The Reggio Emilia approach to early childhood education.* Greenwich, CT: Ablex.

Gandini, L. (1993b). Fundamentals of the Reggio Emilia approach to early childhood education. *Young Children, 49*(1), 4–8.

Gandini, L. (1994a). Not just anywhere: Making child care centers into "particular" places. *Child Care Information Exchange, 96,* 50.

Gandini, L. (1994b). What we can learn from Reggio Emilia: An Italian-American collaboration. *Child Care Information Exchange, 96,* 62–66.

Gandini, L. (1998). Educational and caring spaces. In D. Edwards, L. Gandini, & G. Forman (Eds.), *The hundred languages of children: The Reggio Emilia approach to early childhood education* (2nd ed.). Greenwich, CT: Ablex.

Gandini, L. (2001). Reggio Emilia: Experiencing life in an infant-toddler center, an interview with Cristina Bondavalli. In L. Gandini & C. P. Edwards (Eds.), *Bambini: The Italian Approach to Infant/Toddler Care.* New York: Teachers College Press.

Gandini, L., & Goldhaber, J. (2001). Two reflections about documentation. In L. Gandini & C. Edwards (Eds.), *Bambini: The Italian approach to infant/toddler care.* New York: Teachers College Press.

Gandini, L., & Edwards, C. (Eds.). *Bambini: The Italian approach to infant/toddler care.* New York: Teachers College Press.

Gatto, J. T. (2000). *A different kind of teacher: Solving the crisis of American schooling.* Berkeley, CA: Berkeley Hills Books.

Glassman, M., & Whaley, K. (2000). Dynamic arms: The use of long-term projects in early childhood classrooms in light of Dewey's educational philosophy. *Early Childhood Research and Practice, 2*(1).

Glesne, C., & Peshkin, A. (1992). *Becoming qualitative researchers: An introduction.* White Plains, NY: Longman.

Goldhaber, J., Smith, D., & Sortino, S. (1997). Observing, recording and understanding: The role of documentation in early childhood teacher education. In J. Hendrick (Ed.), *First steps toward teaching the Reggio way.* Upper Saddle River, NJ: Merrill/Prentice Hall.

Goldman-Segall, R. (1998). *Points of viewing children's thinking: A digital ethnographer's journey.* Hillsdale, NJ: Lawrence Erlbaum Associates.

Haigh, K. (1999). Building collegiality: Reflections on organizational structure and the impact of role definition, motivation and leadership on collegiality. *Innovations in Early Education: The International Exchange, 7*(2).

Hendrick, J. (Ed.). (1997). *First steps toward teaching the Reggio way.* Upper Saddle River, NJ: Merrill/Prentice Hall.

Holloway, S., & Valentine, G. (Eds.). (2000). *Children's geographies: Playing, living, learning.* London: Routledge.

Isaacs, S. (1930). *Intellectual growth in young children.* London: Routledge & Sons.

Josselson, R. (1996). *The space between us: Exploring the dimensions of human relationships.* Newbury Park, CA: SAGE Publications, Inc.

Kantor, R., & Whaley, K. (1998). Existing frameworks and new ideas from our Reggio Emilia experience: Learning at a lab school with 2- to 4-year-old children. In C. Edwards, L. Gandini, & G. Forman (Eds.), *The hundred languages of children: The Reggio Emilia approach—Advanced reflections* (2nd ed.). Greenwich, CT: Ablex.

Katz, L. G., & Chard, S. C. (2000). (2nd ed.) *Engaging children's minds. The project approach.* Greenwich, CT: Ablex.

Katz, L. G., Evangelou, D., & Hartman, J. (1990). *The case for mixed-age grouping in the early years.* Washington, DC: National Association for the Education of Young Children.

Krechevsky, M., & Mardell, B. (2001). Form, function and understanding in learning groups: Propositions from Reggio classrooms. In Project Zero/Reggio Children (Eds.), *Making learning visible.* Reggio Emilia, Italy: Reggio Children. pp. 284–295.

Lane-Garon, P. (1998). *Professional problem-solving process.* Unpublished paper.

Lawson, L. (2000). Personal communication. Burlington, VT: University of Vermont.

Mahn, H. (in press) Critical periods in child development: Vygotsky's contribution. In V. Agee, B. Gindis, A. Kozulin, & S. Miller (Eds.), *Vygotsky and culture in education: Sociocultural theory and practice in the 21st century.* Cambridge, MA: Harvard University Press.

Malaguzzi, L. (1992, May). Introduction to the educational philosophy of Reggio Emilia. Presentation to a U.S. delegation visiting the schools in Reggio Emilia, Italy.

Malaguzzi, L. (1993, November). For an education based on relationships. *Young Children, 49*(1), pp. 9–12.

Malaguzzi, L. (1993b). History, ideas, and basic philosophy. In C. Edwards, L. Gandini, & G. Forman (Eds.), *The hundred languages of children: The Reggio Emilia approach to early childhood education.* Greenwich, CT: Ablex.

Malaguzzi, L. (1993c). A bill of three rights. *Innovations in Early Education: The International Reggio Exchange, 2*(1), 9.

Malaguzzi, L. (1998). History ideas, and basic philosophy: An interview with Lella Gandini. In C. Edwards, L. Gandini, & G. Forman (Eds.), *The hundred languages of children: The Reggio Emilia approach—Advanced reflections* (2nd ed.). Greenwich, CT: Ablex.

Malaguzzi, L. (1998). In L. Artioli (1984, May). Che io infilassi la strada dell' insegnare [My taking the road toward teaching]. In *Ricerche Storiche*, Reggio Emilia, pp. 40–54.

Mayhew, K. C., & Edwards, A. C. (1936). *The Dewey School.* New York: D. Appleton-Century Company.

McLaughlin, M. (1995, May). Will Reggio Emilia change your child's preschool? *Working Mother*, 62–68.

Meier, D. (1995). *The power of their ideas: Lessons for America from a small school in Harlem.* Boston: Beacon.

Missouri Department of Elementary and Secondary Education. (1992). *Project Construct: A framework for curriculum and assessment.* Jefferson City: Author.

Municipality of Reggio Emilia. (1994). *Historical notes and general information.* Reggio Emilia, Italy: Department of Education, Municipal Infant-Toddler Centers and Preschools, the Municipality.

Municipality of Reggio Emilia. (1996). The Hundred Languages of Children: Catalog of the Exhibit. Reggio Emilia, Italy: Reggio Children S.rl.

Nabhan, G. P., & Trimble, S. (1994). *The geography of childhood: Why children need wild places.* Boston: Beacon Press.

New, R. (1990). Excellent early education: A city in Italy has it! *Young Children, 45*(6), 4–10.

New, R. (1997). Next steps in teaching "the Reggio way": Advocating for a new image of children. In J. Hendrick (Ed.), *First steps toward teaching the Reggio way.* Upper Saddle River, NJ: Merrill/Prentice Hall.

Noddings, N. (1984). *Caring.* Berkeley: University of California Press.

Olds, A. R. (2001). *Child care design guide.* New York: McGraw-Hill.

Palmer, P. (1993). *To know as we are known.* San Francisco: Harper San Francisco.

Palmer, P. (1998). *The courage to teach.* San Francisco: Jossey-Bass, Inc.

Piaget, J. (1973). *To understand is to invent: The future of education.* New York: Grossman.

Piazza, G. (Ed.). (1995). *The fountains.* Reggio Emilia, Italy: Reggio Children S.rl.

Rankin, B. (in press). The importance of intentional socialization and interaction among children in small groups: A conversation with Loris Malaguzzi. *Early Childhood Education Journal.*

Rawcliffe, F. W. (1924). *Practical problem projects.* Chicago: Compton.

Reggio Children, Italy. (Various dates). Publications available from Learning Materials Workshop, Burlington, VT. [Online] www.learningmaterialswork.com.
Tenderness (1995)
A Journey into the rights of children (1995)

The little ones of silent movies (1996)

Reggio Tutta: A guide to the city by the children themselves (2000)

Theater curtain: The ring of transformations (2002)

Rinaldi, C. (1992, May). *Social constructivism in Reggio Emilia, Italy.* Paper presented at the Summer Institute, "Images of the Child: An International Exchange with Leading Educators from Reggio Emilia, Italy," Newton, MA.

Rinaldi, C. (1993). The emergent curriculum and social constructivism. In C. Edwards, L. Gandini, & G. Forman (Eds.), *The hundred languages of children: The Reggio Emilia approach to early childhood education.* Greenwich, NJ: Ablex.

Rinaldi, C. (1994, June). *The philosophy of Reggio Emilia.* Paper presented at the Study Seminar on the Experience of the Municipal Infant-Toddler Centers and Pre-primary Schools of Reggio Emilia. Reggio Emilia, Italy.

Rinaldi, C. (1998). Projected curriculum constructed through documentation: *Progettazione.* In C. Edwards, L. Gandini, & G. Forman (Eds.), *The hundred languages of children: The Reggio Emilia approach—advanced reflections* (2nd ed.). Greenwich, CT: Ablex.

Rinaldi, C. (2001a). Infant-toddler centers and preschools as places of culture. In Project Zero/Reggio Children (Eds.), *Making learning visible.* Reggio Emilia, Italy: Reggio Children, pp. 38–46.

Rinaldi, C. (2001b). Introductions. In Project Zero/Reggio Children (Eds.), *Making learning visible.* Reggio Emilia, Italy: Reggio Children, pp. 28–31.

Rinaldi, C. (2001c). Reggio Emilia: The image of the child and the child's environment as a fundamental principle. In L. Gandini & C. P. Edwards (Eds.), *Bambini: The Italian approach to infant-toddler care* (pp. 49–54). New York: Teachers College Press.

Rinaldi, C. (2002). The pedagogy of listening: The listening perspective from Reggio Emilia. *Innovations in Early Education: The International Reggio Exchange, 8*(4), pp. 1–4.

Rodari, G., translated by J. Zipes. (2000). *The grammar of fantasy: An introduction to the art of inventing stories.* New York: Teachers & Writers Collaborative.

Rogoff, B. (1990). *Apprenticeship in thinking: Cognitive development in social context.* New York: Oxford University Press.

Sanderson, M. (1999). Reaping the rewards of project work with infants and toddlers. *Innovations in Early Education: The International Reggio Exchange, 7*(1), 5–8.

Schlechty, P. (1997). *Inventing better schools.* San Francisco: Jossey-Bass, Inc.

Sheldon-Harsh, L., with Gandini, L. (1995a). The model early learning center: An interview with teachers inspired by the Reggio approach. *Innovations in Early Education: The International Reggio Exchange, 2*(4), 3.

Sheldon-Harsh, L., with Gandini, L. (1995b). The model early learning center: An interview with teachers inspired by the Reggio approach. *Innovations in Early Education: The International Reggio Exchange, 3*(1), 3.

Shonkoff, J. P., & Meisels, S. (2000). *Handbook of early childhood intervention* (2nd ed.). Cambridge, England: Cambridge University Press.

Smith, S. C., & Scott, J. J. (1990). *The collaborative school.* (ERIC/CEM School Management Digest Series, No. 33). Eugene, OR: ERIC Clearinghouse on Educational Management.

Taylor, G. (1936). *Chicago Commons through forty years.* Chicago: John F. Cuneo Company.

Thoman, E. (1987). *Born dancing: How intuitive parents understand their baby's unspoken language.* New York: Harper & Row.

Thompson, R. A. (1998). Early sociopersonality development. In W. Damon (Series Ed.) & N. Eisenberg (Ed.), *Handbook of child psychology* (5th ed.), *Vol. 3: Social, emotional, and personality development* (pp. 25–104). New York: John Wiley.

Trevarthen, C. (1995). The child's need to learn a culture. *Children and Society, 9*(1), 5–19.

University of Vermont. (2000). Preschool vision statement. Burlington, VT: Author.

Vecchi, V. (1998). The role of atelierista, an interview with Lella Gandini. In C. Edwards, L. Gandini, & G. Forman (Eds.), *The hundred languages of children: The Reggio Emilia approach—Advanced reflections* (2nd ed.). Greenwich, CT: Ablex.

Venolia, C. (1988, 1993). *Healing environments.* Berkeley, CA: Celestial Arts.

Vygotsky, L. S. (1978). *Mind in society: The development of higher psychological processes.* Cambridge, MA: Harvard University Press.

Vygotsky, L. S. (1998). *Child psychology. The collected works of L. S. Vygotsky: Vol. 5. Problems of the theory and history of psychology.* New York: Plenum.

Wenger, E. (1998). *Communities of practice.* Cambridge: University Press.

Whiting, B. B., & Edwards, C. P. (1988). *Children of different worlds: The formation of social behavior.* Cambridge, MA: Harvard University Press.

Williams, D. C., & Kantor, R. (1997). The challenge of Reggio Emilia's research: One teacher's reflections. In J. Hendrick (Ed.), *First steps toward teaching the Reggio way.* Upper Saddle River, NJ: Merrill/Prentice Hall.

Winnicott, D. (1965). *The maturational process and the facilitating environment.* New York: Basic Books.

Index